Post-Pop Cinema

Post-Pop
Cinema

*The Search for Meaning in
New American Film*

Jesse Fox Mayshark

PRAEGER

**Westport, Connecticut
London**

Library of Congress Cataloging-in-Publication Data

Mayshark, Jesse Fox.
    Post-pop cinema : the search for meaning in new American film / Jesse Fox
    Mayshark.
      p. cm.
    Includes bibliographical references and index.
    ISBN-13: 978–0–275–99080–0 (alk. paper)
    ISBN-10: 0–275–99080–X (alk. paper)
    1. Motion pictures—United States.   2. Motion picture producers and
    directors—United States.   I. Title.
  PN1993.5.U6M3135   2007
  791.430973—dc22   2007003043

British Library Cataloguing in Publication Data is available.

Library of Congress Catalog Card Number: 2007003043
ISBN-13: 978–0–275–99080–0
ISBN-10: 0–275–99080–X

First published in 2007

Praeger Publishers, 88 Post Road West, Westport, CT 06881
An imprint of Greenwood Publishing Group, Inc.
www.praeger.com

Printed in the United States of America

∞™

The paper used in this book complies with the
Permanent Paper Standard issued by the National
Information Standards Organization (Z39.48–1984).

10 9 8 7 6 5 4 3 2 1

CONTENTS

1
INTRODUCTION

At one point in his gigantic, punch-drunk 1997 novel *Infinite Jest*, David Foster Wallace takes some time out from his rickety narrative to survey the popular culture around him. "It's of some interest," he writes, "that the lively arts of the millennial U.S.A. treat anhedonia and internal emptiness as hip and cool . . . We are shown how to fashion masks of ennui and jaded irony at a young age where the face is fictile enough to assume the shape of whatever it wears. And then it's stuck there, the weary cynicism that saves us from gooey sentiment and unsophisticated naiveté. Sentiment equals naiveté on this continent."[1]

Wallace had elaborated on this theme in an essay published a few years earlier, "E Unibus Pluram," in which he lamented the way television had made irony the default setting for a generation of writers. "And make no mistake," he wrote,

> irony tyrannizes us. The reason why our pervasive cultural irony is at once so powerful and so unsatisfying is that an ironist is *impossible to pin down*. All U.S. irony is based on an implicit "I don't really mean what I'm saying." So what *does* irony as a cultural norm mean to say? That it's impossible to mean what you say? That maybe it's too bad it's impossible, but wake up and smell the coffee already? Most likely, I think, today's irony ends up saying: "How totally *banal* of you to ask what I really mean."[2]

These observations came in the midst of a cultural tide of pop postmodernism that reached a peak in the music, film, literature, and fashion of the

1990s. Knowing pastiche and choreographed irony were the standards of the day, from the anthemic indifference of Nirvana to Quentin Tarantino's recombinant crime movies to the acrid genre-tweaking of the *Scream* horror films. Reflexive self-awareness was the favored fin de siècle pose, one that coincided neatly with the rise of the Internet and digital media. As technology made the archives of art and culture both more accessible and easier to replicate, it became ever more tempting to mix and match the aesthetics of the past, from the cool-eyed perspective of the present. What was striking about Tarantino's first two movies, *Reservoir Dogs* and *Pulp Fiction*, was the winking familiarity that allowed him to play on and subvert the audience's expectations. Tarantino was relying on his viewers' shared assimilation of pop culture as a starting point for riffs that were not really about story or characters so much as they were about pop culture itself. To paraphrase Marshall McLuhan, the form became the content. This was evident in *Pulp Fiction*'s antichronological plot sequencing, which was a joke built on the audience's awareness of the movie as a movie, and the movie's awareness of that awareness, etc. Telling the story out of order did not serve any particular narrative function, but the narrative wasn't the point; the disruptive sequencing repeatedly interfered with the suspension of disbelief, reminding the audience that it *was* an audience, watching a movie, and calling attention to Tarantino's cut-and-paste, grab-bag plundering of cinematic conventions.

Inevitably, the detachment inherent in those appropriations created an ironic distancing of the material from the audience, and from itself. The films essentially became their own spectators, providing a layer of commentary on themselves as they unspooled. The audience, watching a movie that was watching itself, was relegated to somewhere in the back of the theater. (It is hardly surprising that the 1990s saw the flourishing of the cult-hit TV series *Mystery Science Theater 3000*, which featured a regular cast of characters watching and ridiculing old B-movies.) The result of all this formal razzmatazz could be entertaining, as in Tarantino's movies, or aggressively irritating, as in Oliver Stone's busy, bruising *Natural Born Killers* (based on a screenplay by Tarantino, who disowned the final product). It proved a good fit for a series of films of the 1990s based on old TV shows—confections like *The Brady Bunch Movie* and *Charlie's Angels*, which revisited and revamped their source material with a kind of ironic nostalgia. But it presented some conundrums, too.

As Wallace noted, ironic self-consciousness can be a Venus flytrap, paralyzing and enervating the forms it devours. Once you know so much—about how stories are constructed or movies are made, about genre conventions and their social and political ramifications, about the complex relationships between the author, the characters, and the audience—how then do you do the thing you set out to do in the first place: How do you create and convey meaning? The philosopher Jean Baudrillard considered these questions in a 1987 lecture on the legacy of Andy Warhol and the Pop movement. He suggested that Pop represented a sort of simultaneous culmination and negation of the artistic instinct:

> If I had to characterize this new state of affairs, I would call it "after the orgy." The orgy is in a way the whole explosive movement of modernity, with its various kinds of liberation—political liberation, sexual liberation, the liberation of productive and destructive forces, women's liberation, children's liberation, the liberation of unconscious drives, the liberation of art—the assumption of all models of representation, of all models of anti-representation. . . . If you want my opinion, today everything is liberated. The game is over, and we collectively confront the crucial question, "What are you doing after the orgy?"[3]

Baudrillard's notion was that art would be stuck in a kind of constant recycling, sifting back through the forms and innovations of the past in search of new combinations that would inevitably be secondhand references to the original sources. He identified this thread in postmodern art of the 1980s, which he described as "manufacturing images, a profusion of images, *in which there is nothing to see.*"

These diagnoses of aesthetic stultification coincided not insignificantly with the end of the cold war, which produced a more triumphalist strain of game-over pronouncements. Most memorably, the political philosopher Francis Fukuyama decreed that the fall of the Soviet Union marked "the end of history," in an article (and then a book) of the same title:

> What we may be witnessing is not just the end of the Cold War, or the passing of a particular period of post-war history, but the end of history as such: that is, the end point of mankind's ideological evolution and the universalization of Western liberal democracy as the final form of human government.[4]

The end of history, the end of art, the end of the century and millennium—in the United States, the 1990s were permeated by this kind of talk, a great sense of summing-up, with either apocalypse or utopia just around the corner.

At least for a while, it was tempting to believe that some kind of conclusion had been reached, that the essential patterns had been set—in politics and economics as well as art—and all that was left was to retrace them. "A state of simulation," as Baudrillard said, "in which we can only replay all the scenarios, because they have already taken place, either really or virtually."[5] He was as uncertain as Wallace about whether there was a path to somehow getting beyond this suffocating self-awareness. After Warhol's soup cans, and long after Duchamp's urinal, how could there be any art that wasn't also "art," that wasn't self-conscious of its position and the arbitrariness of its status *as* art?

One answer, of course, was just to retreat to tradition and cliché, do things the way they had always been done. In the case of movies this meant characters, plot, story arc, some sense of resolution or moral or meaning at the end of it all. In fact, this is what most American filmmakers (and fiction writers, and television producers) did straight through the postmodern era, and continue to do today. The Oscar-winning films of the past few decades have mostly been earnest movies about earnest subjects, told in conventional forms. If there was a fear of sentiment or self-importance at large in America, you wouldn't know it from Hollywood. (Not all of these have been bad films; the old formulas can still work.)

But ignoring the challenge outlined by Wallace and Baudrillard is not the same as meeting it. A way forward may not have been obvious in the postmodern haze of the late 1980s and early 1990s. But even Baudrillard acknowledged that art had evolved before—from the world of religious representation to that of secular expression—and asked, "Why shouldn't we assume that another mutation of the same kind could happen?"[6] A better question might be, how could anyone assume that it *wouldn't* happen? Baudrillard's "orgy" and Fukuyama's "history" were not, of course, really the end of anything; they were just demarcations on a timeline that would continue on long past them. As Wallace admitted in "E Unibus Pluram," "It's entirely possible that my plangent noises about the impossibility of rebelling against an aura that promotes and vitiates all rebellion say more about my residency inside that aura, my own lack of vision, than they do about any exhaustion of U.S. fiction's possibilities." He continued:

> The new rebels might be artists willing to risk the yawn, the rolled eyes, the cool smile, the nudged ribs, the parody of gifted ironists, the "Oh, how *banal*." To risk accusations of sentimentality, melodrama. Of overcredulity. Of softness.[7]

Wallace was specifically writing about his own field, literature. (The essay originally appeared in *The Review of Contemporary Fiction*.) So maybe he can be excused for not noting that the thing he was predicting was to some degree already happening in American films.

Starting in the early 1990s, a new group of American directors emerged, bubbling up through the independent art house and festival circuit, defying easy categorization, and taking aim in a variety of ways at the tyranny of irony. They were an odd bunch, and not even obviously identifiable *as* a bunch. They appeared as a string of individual, stylistically distinct talents. They shared some things with Sundance contemporaries like Tarantino and Kevin Smith—a love of pop culture, an immersion in film history, a freewheeling approach to plot structure—but their films were for the most part free of chic cynicism and glib self-mockery. For all of their hip references and technological and narrative trickery, their movies were deeply concerned with ethics and morality, the obligations of the individual, the effects of family breakdown, and social alienation. Where *Pulp Fiction* was ultimately a movie about movies (and about TV shows, and pop music, and pop culture), films like Wes Anderson's *Bottle Rocket* (1996) and Paul Thomas Anderson's *Boogie Nights* (1997) were ultimately about their characters. Using some of the same tricks as the postmodern pranksters, they found ways to reveal something more than the workings of their own clever construction. They were generous toward both characters and audience in a way that set them apart. If that meant treading the edge of the pits of gooey sentiment, they were willing to risk it.

Among the others who broke through in the early to mid-1990s were Richard Linklater (*Slacker, Dazed and Confused*), Todd Haynes (*Poison, Safe*), and David O. Russell (*Spanking the Monkey, Flirting with Disaster*). Toward the end of the decade, the screenwriter Charlie Kaufman arrived, with his collaborator/directors Spike Jonze (*Being John Malkovich, Adaptation*) and Michel Gondry (*Human Nature, Eternal Sunshine of the Spotless Mind*). Then there are a handful of contemporaries who have made at least one film that fits comfortably on the list: David Fincher (*Fight Club*), Sofia Coppola (*Lost in Translation*) and Richard Kelly (*Donnie Darko*).

Although they represent a range of styles and subject matter, their works all revolve in different ways around questions of identity, empathy, and the difficulty of establishing and maintaining emotional connections between family members, lovers, friends, strangers, and cultures. Some of them are very funny, but their aims are serious. They represent a step forward from Wallace's stand-off between irony and sentiment, toward a sort of self-conscious *meaningfulness*. Having grown up on the wink-and-nod knowingness of postmodernism,

Oscar time: The real Charlie Kaufman (left) shared an Academy Award with Michel Gondry (center) and Pierre Bismuth for the *Eternal Sunshine* screenplay. (Courtesy of Photofest)

they use it as a starting point rather than a conclusion. They take deconstructionism as a given, and redirect its analytical toolkit toward something more holistic; reconstructionism, maybe.

Because of the idiosyncrasy of their work, this group has largely escaped labeling. The most serious effort so far came from Armond White, film critic for the weekly *New York Press*. In a review of Russell's 2004 film *I Heart Huckabees*, he dubbed them the "American Eccentrics" (a phrase he said he borrowed from a friend). He distinguished them from their 1970s forebears, who he said were "drawn to exploring American experience and pop tradition in order to understand their place in the world." In contrast, he wrote, the Eccentrics, "don't connect to life outside their own world, but view it as absurd and different. . . . [T]here is an insistence on braininess rather than connection with popular sentiment."[8] This is arguably an unfair reading; the films certainly express the difficulty of making interpersonal and extrapersonal connections, but they are more apt to lament it than celebrate it. But White at least seems interested in their efforts; in the review, he admires *Huckabees's* "philosophical rigor." A review of the same film in another weekly, the *New York Observer*, showed a lot more antipathy. Under a headline that excoriated "Film's New Hacks," the veteran critic Rex Reed started off in high dudgeon and didn't let up: "Kneeling at the trough of psycho-gibberish that has come to symbolize contemporary movies," he wrote, "a piece of crap called *I Heart Huckabees* sinks to new depths of incoherent pretentiousness."[9] The jeremiad went on to indict Russell as "a member of the new group of anarchists that includes Wes Anderson, Paul Thomas Anderson, Spike Jonze, freaky Todd Solondz and the dismally overrated non-writer Charlie Kaufman."

Reed's personal taste aside, anarchic seems a better word than eccentric, which suggests neighborhood cranks pottering about in the woodshed. But neither quite comes to grips with the styles and substance of the movies in question. They are not revolutionary films in any political sense; there is more chin stroking in them than bomb throwing. Nor are they just fanciful personal digressions. They represent, in their own ways and on their own terms, a generation's efforts to make sense of itself and the world it inhabits.

Any grouping of artists into schools or movements is inevitably somewhat arbitrary in terms of who gets included and who doesn't. In Armond White's quick roundup, he mentions Alexander Payne but excludes Todd Haynes; Reed, meanwhile, excludes Payne (because he likes him), and throws in Todd Solondz. So it seems necessary to address a few exclusions from my own list, whose absence from this book might raise questions. Solondz, Payne, Neil LaBute, and Noah Baumbach are obvious contemporaries of the filmmakers under discussion, and in some cases have collaborated with them or used some of the same actors. For example, Philip Seymour Hoffman—a mainstay of Paul Thomas Anderson's films—figured prominently in Solondz's *Happiness*, and Ben Stiller, who has worked with both Wes Anderson and David O. Russell, had a major part in LaBute's *Your Friends and Neighbors*. But Solondz and LaBute seem qualitatively different in their perspective. While they have both made movies I admire, there is a moralizing bitterness in their work (and in LaBute's plays) that is colder and more scabrous than most of the films considered in this book. (For example, while Todd Haynes's *Safe* is certainly a meditation on alienation, it is more existential and less judgmental than the films of Solondz and LaBute. And Haynes's work as a whole has strains of humanist sympathy that those two filmmakers lack.) The universal themes running through Solondz and LaBute's films are misery, selfishness, and moral perversity. Their characters are made to suffer. They are less akin to their American peers than to the current wave of sadistic European moralists, which includes Lars von Trier, Michael Haneke and Catherine Breillat.

Noah Baumbach, on the other hand, has some similarities in both subject matter and approach to, say, Linklater and both Andersons. He cowrote Wes Anderson's *The Life Aquatic with Steve Zissou*, and Anderson in turn produced Baumbach's intelligent 2005 family drama *The Squid and The Whale*. But Baumbach is a more conventional filmmaker than the aforementioned directors, lacking their distinctive visual, technological, and narrative innovations. Baumbach seems not to have absorbed the postmodern influences of his compatriots so much as bypassed them altogether. The same is true of the much-lauded Payne. His initial pair of Midwestern black comedies—*Citizen Ruth* and *Election*—had a bracingly low tolerance for fools and foolishness, and a willingness to shock (*Citizen Ruth* is a comedy about abortion) that set them apart. His next two, *About Schmidt* and *Sideways*, were more traditional comedies about lonely men on metaphorically significant road trips. Payne's films are well written and smart, but not particularly anarchic *or* eccentric.

So then, to those included here. What ties them together? There are, first of all, obvious if superficial connections: Except for Michel Gondry, they are all American; they are all white, and mostly from middle-class or upper-middle-class backgrounds. Except for Haynes, they are all heterosexual. Except for Coppola, they are all male. And they were mostly born in the 1960s, with a few outliers on either side (Russell was born in 1958, Coppola in 1971 and Kelly in 1975). They share actors (Mark Wahlberg, Bill Murray, Ben Stiller, Julianne Moore, Jason Schwartzman), collaborators (the musician Jon Brion), and sometimes more (Jonze costarred in Russell's *Three Kings*, and was married to Coppola).

More significantly, their works are variations on many of the same basic themes. Their overriding concern is a sort of yearning for connection, but one that is colored by an awareness of all the things that get in its way—the misunderstandings and deliberate or indeliberate injuries that mark human relationships; the barriers of sex, race, class, and culture; and, most of all, the simple and ceaseless inability to transcend the boundaries of body and consciousness. In Linklater's romantic drama *Before Sunrise*, Jesse (Ethan Hawke) says, "I have never been anywhere that I haven't been. I've never had a kiss that I wasn't one of the kissers. I've never gone to the movies that I wasn't there in the audience. I've never been out bowling that I wasn't there, making some stupid joke. I think that's why so many people hate themselves, seriously—they are sick to death of being around themselves." That sense of self-imprisonment is dramatized most literally in *Being John Malkovich*—in which long lines of people eagerly pay hundreds of dollars to spend just

15 minutes as someone else—but it surfaces in characters like Carol in *Safe*, whose unidentifiable illness seems to stem from some deep, unacknowledged part of herself; Albert Markovski in *I Heart Huckabees*, who hires existential detectives to investigate his inner recesses; and the nameless narrator in *Fight Club*, who is so desperate to escape himself that he constructs an entirely separate identity.

Notably, the films do not seek transcendence via spirituality. Although they are shadowed by an awareness of religion, they are firmly rooted in the secular world. Even supernatural flourishes like the conversations with the dead in Linklater's *Waking Life* and Charlie Kaufman's *Human Nature* suggest an afterlife of, at best, contemplation and regret. In these movies, redemption—if possible at all—can come only in life, through connections with other people.

But those connections don't come easily, even, or especially, on the home-front. The view of the modern American family that emerges from these films ranges from darkly comic to simply dark. Parents tend to be either absent or suffocating—sometimes both, like the father of Stanley Spector in Paul Thomas Anderson's *Magnolia*, who neglects his son but also pushes him to win money on game shows; and sometimes worse, like the abusive father in Haynes's *Poison*. The directors themselves, by their own reported accounts, come from a range of family backgrounds—some from happy homes, some less so, some the children of divorce—but their sense of domestic life as a nexus of abandonment, alienation, and frustration is in keeping with their generation's experience. Growing up for the most part in the 1970s and 1980s, they came of age as the postwar ideal of the nuclear family was coming undone. The expansion of professional opportunities for women combined with mounting economic pressures to increase the number of two-career households, while a growing emphasis on individual achievement and self-realization changed expectations of what a happy family or happy marriage should be. A greater imperative to talk about "feelings" and their causes and effects led to a degree of domestic self-consciousness that made even children increasingly aware of and articulate about the dynamics of their own house-holds: parental tensions, sibling rivalries, the manipulation of children by parents and vice versa. Children on TV and in the movies were portrayed as emotionally complex and savvy about everything from pop culture to sexuality. Even in the wholesome *Cosby Show*, the 1980s' most popular manifestation of the old-fashioned family sitcom, the competing, often selfish agendas of parents and offspring were detailed in ways that would have been shocking a generation earlier.

So it is no surprise that the current generation of American filmmakers leans toward a jaundiced view of family life. But that view takes a variety of forms, and the bitterness is often underscored by a longing for something better. In the films of Todd Haynes and Paul Thomas Anderson, characters tend to find some kind of self-confidence and acceptance only by leaving stifling homes: Eddie Adams flees his mother's clutches and reinvents himself as Dirk Diggler in Anderson's *Boogie Nights*; in Haynes's *Velvet Goldmine* and *Far From Heaven*, family life is marked by suppressed homosexuality, and liberation comes only from walking out the door. Wes Anderson's family dramas, on the other hand, give some greater hope of reconciliation; in *The Royal Tenenbaums* and *The Life Aquatic with Steve Zissou*, problematic fathers reach difficult accord with estranged children. (Whether Ned Plimpton is actually Steve Zissou's son is never completely clear, but building a relationship with him allows Steve to come to terms with himself.) David O. Russell's first two films also revolved around parent–child relations, in both painful and funny ways.

The portrayal of romantic love is just as fraught and complicated. These are, for the most part, postfeminist films. The sexual-equality face-offs of preceding generations, which revolved around the confusion of shifting gender roles, has given way to an era of films in which equality of certain kinds—intellectual, professional—is assumed. But new complications have replaced the old: how are women (and men) supposed to think about sex now? Or marriage, for that matter? Both *Being John Malkovich* and *Eternal Sunshine of the Spotless Mind* present female characters who want to have children butting up against male partners who resist. In *Flirting with Disaster*, the arrival of a baby sends Mel, the neurotic young husband played by Ben Stiller, caroming around the country in search of his biological parents, while his wife, Nancy, tags along trying to sort out her own new role as a mother.

With the obvious exception of Haynes, the filmmakers are generally heterocentric. There are gay characters in a few of Paul Thomas Anderson's films, but they tend to be sad types. Russell pays more sympathetic attention to the gay federal agents in *Flirting with Disaster*, whose relationship woes mirror those of Mel and Nancy. Haynes, of course, deals at length with sexual orientation, from a number of perspectives. Crucially, he is rarely didactic; *Far from Heaven*, his homage to the melodramas of Douglas Sirk, tells the story of a closeted 1950s family man from the perspective of his wife. Her sense of hurt and bewilderment is granted at least as much consideration as her husband's emotional turmoil. And in *Velvet Goldmine*, Haynes reimagines the glam-rock era of the 1970s as an ephemeral utopia of affirmation for everyone, gay, straight, and many shades in between.

Race is even less prevalent as a subject in these films, and when it is present, it carries mixed messages. In *The Royal Tenenbaums*, Wes Anderson portrays the family patriarch, Royal, as a racist; but the film also lets Royal off the hook a little, suggesting that his racist comments are mostly a cover for jealousy of a black man who is marrying his ex-wife. Anderson also uses the Indian actor Kumar Pallana repeatedly in comic roles as a comic ethnic type; Pallana is funny, and Anderson has obvious affection for him, but the roles still feel condescending. Paul Thomas Anderson has a somewhat similar affiliation with Luis Guzman, although his roles have more range than Pallana's. And Coppola's approach to Japan and the Japanese in *Lost in Translation* is intended to dramatize the alienation of her two American protagonists, but she falls prey too easily to racial gags (the Japanese are short, can't pronounce the letter R, and so forth).

Which is to say, these are films made by middle- and upper-class white Americans, and they sometimes reflect—consciously or not—a sensibility that still views other races and cultures as "Other" races and cultures: a little alien, maybe intriguing and "exotic," and too often good for a quick laugh. Some of the directors are more prone to this than others, but it is hard not to notice that only one of the films considered here—*Far from Heaven*—has a nonwhite character in anything but a supporting role.

Of course, white American culture itself comes in for a good bit of skepticism and ridicule. The more politically astute of the filmmakers, notably Linklater, Haynes, and Russell, tackle questions of power and privilege head on. Linklater's *Dazed and Confused* is partly a treatise on social power structures, in the form of a high school frolic; Russell's portrayal of not-so-innocent Americans abroad in *Three Kings* indicts Yankee ignorance and arrogance (even if it ultimately affirms a basic American decency); and Haynes, as a minority voice himself, is reflexively but imaginatively hostile to moral and political authority, seeing it as rotten with hypocrisy and meanness.

The films also span the pre- and post-9/11 years. As such, they represent American liberalism in a state of some confusion. ("Liberal" is a fair label for their collective outlook, although they are political to different degrees.) The dominant politics of their generation was inward-looking—concerned with issues of identity, race and gender, sexual orientation—and that is reflected in these movies, with their emphasis on individual struggles and existential crises. If there is a defining dialectic, it is between the self and the world. But that tension is conditioned by larger social and economic forces, which determine the place of the individual *within* the world. So a shared class consciousness, for example, shapes the relationship of Max Fishcher and Herman Blume in Wes Anderson's *Rushmore*, just as class differences mark the boundaries between the New Yorker writer Susan Orlean and the redneck philosopher John Laroche in Kaufman's *Adaptation*.

The events of the Bush years have refocused liberal attention back outward again, but this group of directors has for the most part avoided easy polemicism. *Far from Heaven*, for example, implicitly links gay rights with the civil rights movement, but it doesn't preach about it; the politics are embedded in the relationships of the characters. Even more subtly, Linklater marks the shift in U.S./European relations in the post-Iraq war era in the complex relationship of the trans-Atlantic lovers Jesse and Celine in *Before Sunset*—but again, the geopolitics serve as a metaphor for the characters' relationship, rather than vice versa.

Much more than serving as commentary on any particular issue or policy, the films considered here represent a certain restlessness and insecurity that seem like apt expressions of American uncertainty on the cusp of what will almost certainly not be an exclusively American century. The perks and prerogatives of American power are eroding everywhere in these films: in the vibrant Latino culture that the well-meaning Anthony stumbles into in *Bottle Rocket*; in the seductively numbing Tokyo of *Lost in Translation*; in the emasculation anxieties of *Fight Club* and *Human Nature*. They are expressions of a culture mired in self-doubt—the flipside of the authoritarian bluster that has served as America's face to the world in recent years.

But maybe paradoxically, these are not on the whole bleak or cynical movies. For all of the unhappiness and thwarted aspirations they chronicle, they rarely succumb to hopelessness. *Before Sunrise* and *Before Sunset* are fundamentally romantic, despite their reservations about romanticism. *Flirting with Disaster* ends up affirming nuclear family values, just as *Three Kings* affirms the good intentions of the American fighting man. *Magnolia* gives all of its damaged characters a chance at redemption. Even *Velvet Goldmine*, with its vision of a sexual revolution betrayed, is more a celebration of the revolution than a lament for its betrayal. There is a lightness about many of these films, a dry comic tone and a nimbleness that has sometimes been mistaken for lack of purpose or seriousness. On the contrary, the movies are deeply serious, and that is part of their point: This is what seriousness looks like in the era that David Foster Wallace has described. The films are self-conscious and self-referential, but also funny and knowing and, most importantly, honest about their own limitations. Characters in these movies are forever confronting the inadequacies of their attempts to connect with others, to find meaning or significance in their lives.

The filmmakers take formal liberties that mirror their narrative convolutions, from the stylized storybook design of *The Royal Tenenbaums* and *The Life Aquatic* to the trippy digital effects that illustrate Russell's philosophical concepts in *I Heart Huckabees*. The plastic dolls Haynes uses to tell the story of *Superstar* are echoed by the arresting puppet sequences in *Being John Malkovich*. Characters in *Velvet Goldmine* and *Magnolia* break into song, in sequences that update classic movie musicals by way of MTV. Meanwhile, the actual MTV veterans Spike Jonze and Michel Gondry bring a fluid surrealism to Kaufman's spiraling screenplays (there are two separate chase sequences that take place entirely within someone's subconscious). There are flashes of science fiction in *Poison*, *Velvet Goldmine* and *Eternal Sunshine of the Spotless Mind*. Wes Anderson re-creates the feel of the 1970s' documentaries and action shows in *The Life Aquatic*. Haynes faithfully replicates the entire visual vocabulary of Douglas Sirk's melodramas of the 1950s in *Far from Heaven*. Linklater, meanwhile, has made two animated features, using a new form of digital rotoscoping.

Some of this is textbook postmodernism, in the limited postmodern sense of freely sampling from the whole historical range of styles, genres, and schools of art and philosophy. But it is more than postmodern. Knowledge of style and genre is assumed in these films, as is the complicated relationship between artist and audience, all of the references that each brings to the work at hand, and the ways they relate to each other. These movies do not need to spend a lot of time obsessing over the obvious—"This is a movie that is being watched by you, the viewer, and to which you bring a set of expectations and understandings that this movie may or may not meet"—because all of that is taken for granted. What these filmmakers try to do, over and over, is reach beyond that basic self-awareness to some kind of transcendent connection.

In 1963, the art critic Jasia Reinhardt remarked of the Pop artists then emerging, "What is interesting about these young artists, who lack neither courage nor eloquence, is that they say neither No nor Yes to the world. They don't accept things as they are, they make fun of them, they make use of them out of context, but they don't rebel against anything. They have made use of every scrap of information, news, emotion, publicity, bad luck, etc., that comes their way. Like hungry animals they have swallowed the world wholesale, and quickly forgetting its meaning they continue to lead their own lives and to play their own games."[10]

In trying to restore some sense of that meaning—rebuilding Humpty Dumpty out of deconstructed parts—the filmmakers considered here have moved through and beyond the distancing mechanisms of Pop. Instead of saying "neither No nor Yes to the world," they tend toward a provisional Maybe. "Making fun" of the way things are isn't enough (although it never completely loses its appeal); these movies strive in their various ways for a sense of how to actually live in the world. They are emphatically not nostalgic for some simpler "past." They are at home in the complicated present. But that does not mean they are comfortable here, exactly; they are not products of comfortable times.

In a profile of Charlie Kaufman, the cultural journalist Lynn Hirschberg offered a description of *Adaptation* that could equally serve for many of these films. She wrote that the movie "is wildly self-conscious while at the same time inching toward some postironic point of observation. Both sincere and achingly aware of the limitations of sincerity, knowing yet engaged, the script, and its hyperaware author, could not be more out of the Hollywood mainstream, nor more of the moment."[11]

2
RICHARD LINKLATER

Richard Linklater did not invent the idea of movies about people sitting around talking. (Or standing around talking, walking around talking, driving around talking, etc.) There are obvious precedents, from Godard to Woody Allen to *My Dinner with Andre*. But Linklater has been uniquely single-minded in his dedication to conversation. He established the template with his first major release, *Slacker*, in 1991, which is literally a collection of snippets of dozens of characters talking (and talking, and talking). But even the more conventional films that have followed—in particular, the ones he has written himself—have tended to revolve around long monologues and dialogues. When he makes a romance, it's about two people talking. When he makes a high school movie, it's about high school kids talking. When he makes an animated film, it's about animated characters talking. And in his adaptation of Philip K. Dick's sci-fi drug film *A Scanner Darkly*, the convoluted plot partly serves as a pretext for extended scenes of paranoid, chemically addled banter.

In Linklater's films, words are action. They express personality, identity, conflict, attraction, rejection, sympathy, alienation, affection, evasion, disclosure, and concealment. Mostly, they represent attempts to make sense of the world, to understand people and places and events, and an individual's relationship to all of those things. Many of the riffs are funny, some are disturbing and some are just nuts—Linklater shows an uncondescending interest in the things that genuinely crazy people say, the possible insights they enfold and the range of discomforts they provoke. His movies are full of conspiracy theories, which seem to appeal to him not so much for their content as their impulse, the effort they make to look beyond accepted versions of reality. Like stoner Socratic dialogues, his characters' conversations bounce from topic to topic, circling back over and over to a few major existential questions: Why are we here? *Are* we actually here? Where is here? Who are we, anyway? And given the uncertainty about all of the above, what is the best way to conduct our lives from day to day?

For such a verbal filmmaker, Linklater has a surprisingly fluid visual style. He likes characters in motion, and even when they sit still, his camera rarely does. He is playfully experimental, as in *Slacker*'s casual shifts from third-person to first-person point of view. He loves handheld camerawork, and was an early adopter of high-definition video. He also helped pioneer the digital animation method used in *Waking Life* and *A Scanner Darkly* (it is a form of rotoscoping, in which animation is overlaid on filmed footage). Narratively, or at least when he has narratives, he likes condensed time frames; several of his movies take place in a single day or night, and two of them—*Before Sunset* and the play adaptation *Tape*—take place in real time. All of these techniques seem designed to give Linklater maximum access to the small moments of daily life, the way people relate to each other when they meet on the sidewalk or get together for a beer, and the things that occupy their thoughts when they are not otherwise occupied.

Although he grew up in Huntsville, Texas, a small town outside Houston, Linklater as an artist is a product of the Texas bohemian subculture of Austin. He moved there after dropping out of college and spending a few years working on an oil rig, a job that let him save up enough money to buy a Super-8 camera. In his early twenties, he set about teaching himself to make movies, beginning with several shorts and technical experiments. He also cofounded the Austin Film Society in 1985 (he is still a board member), screening foreign, classic, and independent films to crowds of cinephiles. He completed his first feature, *It's Impossible to Learn to Plow by Reading Books*, in 1988. It is a subdued, largely plotless movie about an aimless young man, played by Linklater himself. From there, he started work on what became *Slacker*, scraping together about $25,000 in cash, $40,000 in deferred payments and a lot of donated time and services, and filming it in the streets, homes, bookstores, coffee shops, and bars of Austin in the summer of 1989. Ironically, given its status as a hallmark of 1990s indie cinema, it was rejected by the Sundance Film Festival the next year. It was only after receiving positive notices elsewhere that it was accepted upon resubmission in 1991. (These stories are all well told in the booklet that accompanies the expansive Criterion Collection DVD release of *Slacker*.)

Linklater's next film, *Dazed and Confused*, showed he was capable of more conventional storytelling and—after developing a strong cult following on video— burnished his commercial credentials. Although he has directed only a couple of genuine box-office hits, Linklater has been unusual in his ability to move between the realms of independent film and the Hollywood mainstream. His more commercial movies (not all of which have actually been commercially successful) show him to be an affable craftsman, able to adapt his amiable looseness to the demands of formula. And the commercial films feel to some degree connected to his more personal work: He was attracted by the Texas setting of the period gangster film *The Newton Boys*; Jack Black's fraudulent grade-school teacher in *School of Rock* is a clownish variation on the underemployed misfits of *Slacker*; even Linklater's remake of *The Bad News Bears* makes sense as a revisitation of a movie that 1970s teens of *Dazed and Confused* might have snuck into.

He has also proven himself an adept collaborator, turning *Tape* (by playwright Stephen Belber) into a tautly effective film despite its claustrophobic motel-room setting, and finding plenty of common ground with the parking-lot slackers of Eric Bogosian's *SubUrbia*. (His adaptation of Eric Schlosser's book *Fast Food Nation*, which he and Schlosser wrote together, premiered at Cannes in May 2006 to mixed reviews.)

Still, the movies he has written and directed himself stand apart as thematically and artistically coherent, which is why they are the focus of this chapter. (I'm including *A Scanner Darkly* in the group, because the adaptation—while largely faithful to Dick's novel—is shaped in ways that mark it as very much a Linklater film.) Taken together, they are an episodic diary of Linklater's generation, or at least his own subset of it—following them from rock 'n' roll high school to unmoored young adulthood, through early romance to some kind of conditional maturity, all the while asking the same questions and getting not particularly closer to satisfying answers. He will be interesting to grow old with.

One particular aspect of Linklater's movies that is worth singling out is his interest in women as fully functioning human beings. Unlike many of his male peers, he does not present his female characters as primarily objects of either awe, fear, or scorn. The women in his films are just as talkative, peculiar, self-confident, self-deprecating, insightful, delusional, and imaginative as the men.

This is partly thanks, no doubt, to Linklater's willingness to let his actors shape their characters—to the extent that Ethan Hawke and Julie Delpy share screenwriting credit on *Before Sunset*. In an interview with *MovieMaker* magazine, Linklater said that both in auditions and in working with actors on set, his primary approach is the same as his approach to storytelling: sitting around talking. "Yeah, we do a lot of talking," he said. "The characters do a lot of talking. I think the best thing you can do is talk. We just talk about everything."[1]

Slacker (1991)
WRITTEN BY: RICHARD LINKLATER
CAST: TOO MANY TO MENTION

The year 1991 was in a lot of respects not a great time to be a young adult American. It kicked off with the Persian Gulf War, which was mercifully brief, and a deepening recession, which was not. A front-page headline in *The New York Times* that spring informed college graduates that they were facing the worst job market in 20 years. They would be joining the ranks of an underemployed group that *Time* magazine had singled out the previous summer with a cover story, under the headline "Twentysomething" and the subtitle, "Laid Back, Late Blooming or Just Lost?" The article's opening paragraph began, "They have trouble making decisions. They would rather hike in the Himalayas than climb a corporate ladder. They have few heroes, no anthems, no style to call their own."[2] That last sentence, at least, would not survive 1991 unchallenged.

The year saw the release of three works that would quickly come to seem, individually and collectively, like generational demarcations: Nirvana's album *Never-mind*, which came out in September; Douglas Coupland's discursive novel *Generation X: Tales for an Accelerated Culture*, released in March; and the even more discursive *Slacker*, which premiered at Sundance in January and opened in national release in July. Suddenly there were words to describe the people *Time* was talking about—slackers, members of Generation X. And they had an anthem too, albeit one that ended with the mumbled line, "Oh well, whatever, never mind."

Of the three, *Slacker* was the most modest in both concept and execution. Nirvana might have been virtually unknown, but they were on a major label and there was nothing obscure about the roar of Butch Vig's production. Kurt Cobain's use of the first-person plural ("Here we are now, entertain us") certainly made him sound like an aspiring generational spokesman, whatever his protests to the contrary. Coupland's book was self-conscious about its sociological ambitions, from its portentous title to the definitions of invented words that littered the text. It was trying to capture a zeitgeist. (Coupland did not invent the phrase "Generation X"—it was, among other things, the name of Billy Idol's old punk band—but he gets deserved credit for applying it astutely.) *Slacker* had no such agenda. Inspired by things Linklater had seen, been told about, or overheard in casual conversation, it aimed to capture the quotidian oddness and ramshackle structure of ordinary lives. But in its riffs on politics, the media, celebrities, conspiracies, art, physics, romance, and the meaning of life—and also in the free-floating status of its characters, few of whom seem to have jobs and some of whom don't even have homes—it captured a zeitgeist of its own.

The first voice in the movie is Linklater's. In a role identified in the credits as "Should have stayed at bus station," Linklater appears as a young traveler arriving in Austin by bus, carrying only a backpack. In a taxi on the way into town, he recounts a dream to the driver, who shows no interest whatsoever. In his dream, Linklater says, he read a book, the premise of which was that "every thought you have creates its own reality." To the extent the movie has a theme or a method, that's it: separate realities in the same city, all jostling up against each other, crossing paths, and spinning off in unpredictable directions.

Few of the characters have names, and they are identified primarily by what they talk about, making the credit roll a de facto sketchpad of the movie: "Walking to coffeeshop," "Dostoyevsky wannabe," "Paranoid paper reader," "Old man recording thoughts." They are mostly young, mostly white, mostly liberal, intellectual, and countercultural. And mostly a little weird, too, or at least unfazed by weirdness. They are the kind of people who tend to populate college towns, whether or not they actually go to college. The cast seems to have been plucked right off the street, but in fact Linklater held auditions for all of the roles. (Many of the performers he chose were members of Austin rock bands.)

If you didn't know the film was made in the midst of a recession, it wouldn't be hard to guess. Almost nobody in it has any money, and the bumming and bartering of cigarettes, beer, spare change, and places to stay gives the movie a steady undercurrent of economic marginalization. Political disaffection also simmers throughout, from conspiracy theories about NASA and the Kennedy assassination to dissections of the elder George Bush's electoral mandate and the pros and cons of voting. Some of these are earnest and some are delivered with the cockeyed enthusiasm of the delusional, but Linklater is not passing judgment on any of them. In the director's commentary included on the Criterion release, he says, "I liked the idea of unaccredited information. This, to me, was the real stuff. You can't believe the news, you can't believe official media outlets. I think the actual buzz of life is coming from the conspiracy theorists, the schizophrenics." (The movie is a reminder, if anyone needs one, that "unaccredited information" was in wide and constant circulation long before the World Wide Web. If it were set 15 years later, a lot of the characters would probably have blogs.)

There are also more intimate conversations in the film, early displays of Linklater's ear for the give-and-take of flirtation and relationships (which would reach its full potential in *Before Sunrise* and *Before Sunset*). In a scene where an unemployed musician encounters a woman he hasn't seen in a while—she's been in Dallas, she says, in a hospital—his offer to put her on the guest list for his band's show that Friday is made and received with the awkward hesitancy of courtship. Similarly, a negotiation between a boyfriend and girlfriend about what to do with the rest of day—she wants to do something outside, he wants to stay in, read the newspaper and have sex—suggests in a quick snippet the outline of their relationship, and its slim chances for longevity. The candid girl-talk between three women in a bar, and the way it changes when they are approached by a flirtatious young man, presents a convincing snapshot of female friendship.

But perhaps inevitably, many of the movie's most-quoted lines revolve around pop culture. Its signature scene—the one featured in trailers for the film and referenced on the cover of the DVD—features a hyperactive woman (played by Teresa Taylor, who was then the drummer for the Butthole Surfers) bounding up to a man and woman on the street and interrupting their conversation with a story about Madonna's pap smear, of which she claims to have procured a sample. She fishes a small bottle out of her pocket and removes a glass slide from it reverentially. "I know it's kind of disgusting," she says, "but it's sort of like getting down to the real Madonna." Then she offers to sell it to them. It is a smart routine that reflects cheekily on the canonization and commodification of celebrities. The pap smear bottle is like a relic from a shrine.

In another scene, two male friends at a bar gravely analyze the social-conformist messages embedded in *Scooby-Doo* and *The Smurfs*. Both cartoons encourage cooperation with authority and maintenance of the status quo, they observe. The dialogue is funny both because it has some legitimate insights—What is Papa Smurf but the patriarchy writ small?—and because it is a deadpan send-up of the trendy deconstructionism that mushroomed in the 1980s and 1990s. The *Slacker* generation came of age in a time when no corner of the culture went unscoured for political, social and sexual agendas.

There is also a disquieting thrum of violence in the film, beginning with a scene in which a disturbed young man runs over his mother with a station wagon. In another scene, one character says "Terrorism is the surgical strike capability of the oppressed" (a line that sounds different in a lot of ways after the September 11 attacks). Later, a gun-wielding burglar surprises a gray-haired man and his daughter. But the older man talks the younger one into giving up his weapon, and then treats him to a long diatribe on the importance of anarchy and the need for violent action, pausing to praise both Leon Czolgosz (who assassinated William McKinley) and Charles Wittman, who shot and killed 15 people from the top of the University of Texas clock tower in 1966.

The most surreal and haunting scene of the film comes when one young man visits a friend in a room cluttered with television sets, videotapes, and VCRs. The friend even has a TV strapped to his back, turned on and playing. He says he doesn't leave the house anymore, explaining, "To me, a video image is much more powerful and useful than an actual event." He recounts a stabbing he witnessed in person outside a bar, and says, "I have no reference to it now. I can't refer back to it. I can't press rewind. I can't put it on pause, I can't put it on slo-mo and see all the little details." Then he offers to show his visitor a new video he's acquired, which purports to be the final message from a grad student recently killed by a SWAT team after taking his thesis committee hostage. On the tape, a young man in a T-shirt and owlish glasses talks about the frustrations of trying to achieve some ideal of human potential. Eventually, he picks up a rifle. Pointing it at the camera, he says, "Every action is a positive action. Even if it has a negative result."

These scenes suggest a fascination with nihilism. But Linklater pulls back from wholly endorsing it. Near the end of the film, the camera follows a car with a mounted P.A. system. The driver, a stern young man with long hair identified in the credits as "Post-modern Paul Revere," is announcing over the loudspeaker a "free weapons giveaway program." "I wanna see knife-cuttin', slice-cuttin', choppin', blowin' up," he says, with a sneer. "Gonna solve all these goddamn problems." Just then, a car with the top down and seats full of laughing young men and women pulls up. As they pass "Paul Revere" at a stop sign, *Slacker* goes into its final, giddy scene. It slips into first-person point of view as the group in the convertible passes around small Super-8 cameras and the movie becomes, essentially, a movie of itself.

The soundtrack—for the only time in the film—bursts into nonambient music, full of jaunty guitars and horns. Reaching the top of a hill overlooking a reservoir, the group alights from the car, dancing and drinking beer. Finally one of them takes a camera, winds up like a baseball pitcher, and hurls it off the cliff. The closing shot is the spiraling, spectrographic record of its descent, a burst of exuberant impressionism that ends the movie on an unexpectedly celebratory note. For all of the uncertainty, paranoia and alienation contained within it, *Slacker* is ultimately affirmative.

On the director's commentary, Linklater says, "It was kind of sad to see 'slacker,' the word, as it broke into the national mainstream, become kind of a negative. Because I always felt very positive. I thought to be a slacker would be a badge of honor." The title itself started as an in-joke, a word Linklater and his crew used to cajole each other into working still harder on a movie that none of them were getting paid for. Like Linklater and his friends, the characters in *Slacker* are not idle. They're not making money, but they're making music, constructing art, concocting theories, writing, reading and—especially—talking. They are engaging with life on their own terms.

In a deleted section of the movie's opening scene, included on the Criterion DVD, Linklater's talkative taxi passenger mentions that he's been reading *The Autobiography of Malcolm X*. "He's always saying, 'The squeaky wheel gets oiled,'" Linklater says to the impassive cabbie. "That's pretty cool. But you know, I don't think I even want any oil. I'm pretty shy, I guess. I just wanted to be a squeaky wheel for a while." In an equivocal review of *Slacker* in *The New York Times*, critic Vincent Canby called it "a 14-course meal, composed entirely of desserts." But that's not quite right; there's nothing exactly sweet about it. *Slacker* is a movie of squeaky wheels. And Linklater is more interested in listening to them than oiling them.

Dazed and Confused (1993)
WRITTEN BY: RICHARD LINKLATER
WITH: JASON LONDON (RANDALL "PINK" FLOYD), WILEY
   WIGGINS (MITCH KRAMER), RORY COCHRANE (RON
   SLATER), MICHELLE BURKE (JODI KRAMER), PARKER PO-
   SEY (DARLA MARKS), BEN AFFLECK (FRED O'BANNION),
   MATTHEW MCCONAUGHEY (DAVID WOODERSON), ADAM
   GOLDBERG (MIKE NEWHOUSE)

It says a lot about Linklater that while his Sundance peers were trying to remake *Mean Streets*, he remade *American Graffiti*. Like George Lucas's kids-cars-and-rock 'n' roll mosaic, *Dazed and Confused* uses a day and night in the life of a group of teenagers to illuminate a whole era. Or the end of an era, more specifically. But where Lucas's film was an elegy for lost innocence, a lingering look back at the Kennedy years, Linklater's is a paean to jadedness. Like Paul Thomas Anderson's *Boogie Nights* and Todd Haynes's *Velvet Goldmine*,

Dazed and Confused recalls the 1970s as a brief blossoming of freedom, emphasizing the point by setting its story in the bicentennial year of 1976. Post-Vietnam, post-Watts, post-Woodstock and Altamont, post-Watergate, there is no innocence left for the kids in Linklater's small-town Texas high school to lose. What they have instead is knowledge. If *American Graffiti* is nostalgic for an adolescent Eden, *Dazed and Confused* looks back longingly at that first burst of liberty out of the garden.

Based loosely on his own adolescent experience in Huntsville, it might be Linklater's best movie, and is certainly his most charming. It has a sparkling young cast (including Matthew McConaughey and Ben Affleck in their first major roles) and a script full of quotable exchanges. It was early in the wave of 1970s revivalist films that continued through the 1990s, and it gets the period details right without making a big deal about them. The wardrobes, hairstyles, cars and slang are casually accurate, but they are not milked for easy laughs or used as shorthand for setting or character. (The film was too close to life for some of Linklater's former schoolmates; in 2004, three of them sued him for appropriating their names—Wooderson, Slater and Floyd—and damaging their reputations.)

Like most high school films, *Dazed and Confused* is populated with a mixture of jocks, geeks, cheerleaders, smart kids, dumb kids, and a range of misfits. But it doesn't play favorites; the script shows some sympathy for everyone, even Affleck's blustery, pathetic Fred O'Bannion, who enjoys the ritual hazing of underclassmen a little too much. Still, the obvious hero is Randall "Pink" Floyd, the movie's brainy pothead quarterback, who moves easily between social cliques. He finds a protégé in Mitch Kramer, an incoming freshmen and star athlete. The two share an instinctive distaste for bullying and the abuse of power.

Power and its means of transmission is a running theme in the movie, which begins on the last day of school in May 1976 and ends shortly after sunrise the next morning. It takes the form of hazing, in which rising senior boys and girls round up members of the next year's freshman class and subject them to assorted punishments (vicious paddling for the boys; group humiliation for the girls). All of this takes place in public, with the apparent acquiescence of parents and teachers. "What's fascinating," observes Mike Newhouse, the movie's misanthropic intellectual geek, "is the way not only the school, but the entire community seems to be supporting this, or at least turning their heads." It also takes the form of a pledge that the school's tough-talking football coach asks his players to sign, promising to not do drugs or engage in any other unlawful activity. Most of the players sign it without a second thought, but Pink sees it for what it is: an assertion of institutional authority over his life. Both the hazing and the pledge are part of the same system, one that sanctions aggression of the stronger against the weaker, and rewards those who conform. (In a not-so-subtle indicator of the community's attachment to reactionary values, the school itself is named for Robert E. Lee.)

But that traditional structure is up against the political and cultural landscape of the times. An eighth-grade teacher uses stories from his Vietnam service to keep his class in line. A high school history teacher tells her students, "This summer, when you're being inundated with all this American bicentennial Fourth of July brouhaha, don't forget what you're celebrating—and that's the fact that a bunch of slave-owning, aristocratic white males didn't want to pay their taxes." During a smoke break in the bathroom, a girl berates two friends for not recognizing the "male pornographic fantasy" inherent to *Gilligan's Island*. Ideas and events from far beyond Texas have found their way into these students' lives.

There is little didactic about any of this. One of Linklater's strengths as a writer is the ability to put big ideas, shaggy-dog philosophizing, and rambling speculation in the mouths of fully believable characters. The kids in *Dazed and Confused* talk about things that concern them directly and personally; but Linklater remembers that what concerns kids directly and personally, besides girls and boys and beer and music and drugs and football, is power—that adolescence is a long tug-of-war between dependence and independence. And what the movie captures in its most electric moments is the intoxicating jubilance of nascent self-determination, stolen in a few hours or a night away from parents, teachers, coaches, and cops.

Nor is it lost on Linklater that, as a 1970s teenager himself, he experienced that freedom at its peak. The movie depicts an era that seems unthinkably licentious by contemporary standards, when the drinking age was 18 and rarely enforced (as in a scene where Mitch, a freshman, buys a six-pack of beer from a blasé clerk), drug use was in a post-1960s free-for-all and the rock music on the movie's soundtrack—Aerosmith, Foghat, Rick Derringer—was still a decade away from earning the marketing designation "classic." More importantly, the establishment was in disarray, and the authority of everyone from the president to parents to classroom teachers was suddenly called into open question. It couldn't last, and it didn't. When Pink balks at signing the football team's antidrug pledge, a sympathetic classmate says, "God, what are they gonna do next, give you guys urine tests or something?" Two years after *Dazed and Confused* was released, the Supreme Court upheld the constitutionality of random urine testing of high school athletes.

But the film is also aware that even under the best of circumstances, teen liberation has a short shelf life. The point is driven home by the character of Wooderson, a likable cheeseball who hangs around the high school social scene despite having graduated several years before. He has some kind of municipal job, and although he talks about going to junior college, he obviously is having trouble letting go of his adolescence. Likewise, it is suggested that the sadistic meathead O'Bannion has deliberately flunked his senior year so he can stay for another one.

Linklater's handle on the rhythms and rituals of adolescent males is admirable if not surprising, and the movie has an obviously male perspective. But it pays close attention to the world of girls, too—the dynamics of female bonding and rivalry, and the era's newfound sense of feminist confidence. The girls exist in their own orbits, separate from but intersecting with the boys. (Crucially, they have their own cars.) The alpha female, Darla, who supervises the hazing of the freshmen girls, is never shown with a boy at all. She is pretty and popular, but what little we see of her suggests some deep reserves of anger. The last glimpse of her is at a party, drunk, yelling to no one in particular, "Lick me! All of you!"

The movie is also deceptively insightful about drug culture. Although it is enveloped in a haze of pot smoke, and has its share of reefer jokes, it recognizes the way marijuana functions as a social determinant. Like sex, it creates a dividing line between those who do it and those who don't. Alcohol is at least tacitly accepted by the power structure, but cannabis sets its users apart—as losers in the eyes of authority figures (and those who follow their lead, like some of Pink's football teammates), and as rebels in their own bloodshot eyes. Linklater doesn't exactly bring anything new to the gallery of cinematic stoners, but the character of Slater, played with shambling grace by Rory Cochrane, is at least a worthy addition. His long disquisition on the probable pot-smoking habits of George and Martha Washington plays like a tribute to Cheech and Chong, but a good one—it's funny.

More than any of Linklater's other movies, except maybe *School of Rock*, *Dazed and Confused* uses music as a narrative device. The film opens to the shimmering, bleary drone of Aerosmith's "Sweet Emotion," with a slow-motion shot of an orange GTO easing into the school parking lot. The tension and release of the chorus and verse mirrors the burbling excitement of summer vacation about to burst out—and when the release comes, with the final bell, it is accompanied by Alice Cooper's declamatory "School's Out!" The biggest accomplishment of the soundtrack is to make these songs exciting again after decades of rock-radio regurgitation, by putting them back in their original context. Incorporated without a trace of nostalgia or irony, chestnuts like "Slow Ride" and "Never Been Any Reason" sound liberating and sexy. And when Lynyrd Skynyrd's elegiac "Tuesday's Gone" plays as the movie's late-night beer bust fades toward morning, Linklater achieves something close to a perfect unison of song and story. (Despite all of its songs being widely available elsewhere, the soundtrack album sold so well that it spawned a sequel, *Even More Dazed and Confused*.)

Unlike *American Grafitti*, which ended with thumbnail portraits detailing each character's fate, *Dazed and Confused* gives no clear sense of where any of its protagonists are headed. One slow-motion shot of Wooderson walking into a pool hall with Pink and Mitch trailing behind him suggests that they might all be following the same arc to Wooderson's post–high school limbo. But maybe not. Pink, at least, seems to have bigger plans; toward the end of the movie, he says to his friends, "If I ever start referring to these as the best years of my life, remind me to kill myself." The last shot shows the sun rising over an open road. As Wooderson's Chevelle cruises down the highway with its passengers bound for Houston, it's not even clear if they'll make it in time to buy their Aerosmith tickets. But it's hard not to hope so.

Before Sunrise (1995)
WRITTEN BY: RICHARD LINKLATER AND KIM KRIZAN
WITH: JULIE DELPY (CELINE), ETHAN HAWKE (JESSE)

Before Sunset (2004)
WRITTEN BY: RICHARD LINKLATER, KIM KRIZAN, JULIE DE-
    LPY AND ETHAN HAWKE
WITH: JULIE DELPY (CELINE), ETHAN HAWKE (JESSE)

In its own small-scale, low-key way, Linklater's two-part romantic duet is an audacious work. There is nothing else quite like it. Following a night in the life of a young man and woman who meet on a European train, and then an afternoon in the life of the same characters nine years later, it is a beguiling story that works both because and in spite of its narrative gimmickry. The movies are of a piece, but they are also distinct and self-contained, with different methods and moods. Where *Before Sunrise* covers 20 hours or so and buzzes with youthful impetuosity, *Before Sunset* takes place in real time, about 80 minutes of one day, and is convincingly sadder and wiser. The first can obviously stand alone, as it did for nine years before the sequel appeared, and the second movie also works as a one-act. But together, they add up to a generational portrait in miniature.

They are as densely verbal as any of Linklater's movies—apart from a discreet love scene in *Before Sunrise*, talking is pretty much all the two central characters do, with occasional interjections from people they meet on the streets of Vienna and Paris, where the respective films take place. The dialogue is loose-limbed and naturalistic, full of stammers and nervous laughs and digressions. Movies this wordy tend to get called theatrical, especially movies with just two characters. But these films wouldn't work as plays; the small-scale spontaneity of the conversations would not survive a stage. To convey what Linklater wants to convey, he needs the intimacy of the close-cropped frame, every glance or smile or half-frown and every bit of body language the camera can register. He also needs the cities, with their classical architecture and weathered grandeur. The movies are cinematic idylls, romantically old-fashioned in their American embrace of Old Europe, even as they reflect sociocultural tensions in the sometimes prickly trans-Atlantic relations of the two principals.

Those tensions show up early, when Jesse, a young American traveler, first meets Celine, a young French woman, on a train from Budapest to Paris. Jesse asks her why her English is so good; she says she has spent time in Los Angeles and London. Then she teasingly says, "And of course you don't speak any other language, right?" "Yeah yeah, I get it," he replies. "So I'm the crude, vulgar, dumb American who doesn't speak any other languages, who has no culture." Even as they get to know each other intimately over the next day, that gap is never completely bridged. He is the brash American, she is the cool Continental; he says he feels like a 13-year-old boy, preparing for his eventual adulthood; she says she feels already like an old woman. The New World/Old World contrast is a little diagrammatic, but Jesse and Celine are never reduced to the sum of the various things they represent.

That is partly because they also have a lot in common with each other—and with any number of Linklater's other articulate, intelligent characters. Some of their riffs, like Celine's complaints about the corporate media ("It's a new form of fascism, really") or Jesse's speculation about how new souls are created, could have been vignettes in *Slacker*. But that is not because Linklater's characters all sound alike so much as that he specializes in creating a certain *kind* of character—young, skeptical, well-read, bohemian—that can inhabit different corners of the world.

Celine, a daughter of May 1968 radicals, sums up her conflicted feelings about her parents: "They love me more than anything in the world, and I've been raised with all the freedom they fought for," she says. "And yet for me now, it's another type of fight. We still have to deal with the same old shit, but we can't really know who or what the enemy is." Jesse is a different generational archetype, having grown up in the wake of a bitter divorce. "Everybody's parents fuck them up," he says. Their problems are specific to their characters, but they are also products of their era and cultures. The personal is always political in Linklater's movies, and vice versa.

The romance that unfolds between the two of them is sweetly predictable in its general outlines, but consistently surprising in its details. In the intelligence of their interchanges, Linklater and his cowriters (who, on the second movie, included Hawke and Delpy) put Jesse and Celine through all the different things a conversation between two people can be: a ritual of introduction, a mutual interrogation, a fencing match, a tennis game, a round of hide-and-seek, a pas de deux, a debate, a harmony. They talk about themselves, their families, their ambitions and fears, first loves and breakups, about politics and religion, men and women, philosophy and sex. "I have this awful, paranoid thought that feminism was mostly invented by men so they could fool around a little more," Celine says in a typical exchange in *Before Sunrise*. "You know, 'Woman, free your mind, free your body, sleep with me!'"

But what all the talk is really about is love—falling in it, in *Before Sunrise*, and dealing with its disappointments in *Before Sunset*—and what the word actually means. "If there's any kind of magic in this world," Celine says about halfway through the first film, "it must be in the attempt of understanding someone, sharing something. I know, it's almost impossible to succeed. But who cares, really? The answer must be in the attempt." The two films together chart the complex course of that attempt.

On the surface, it is easy to call *Before Sunrise* a fantasy of love and *Before Sunset* its hard-nosed reality. The first movie floats on Viennese air, drifting through dusky cobblestone streets to the strains of Strauss and Bach, following Jesse and Celine through bars and restaurants and a riverboat to a grassy moonlit park. (Linklater shoots the city like he's working for the chamber of commerce; it glows.) It ends suspended, still floating, with the future left open. Maybe they will meet again, maybe they won't. But the tantalizing possibility is what sustains the movie's romantic effervescence right through the closing credits.

Before Sunset seems at first to bring all that crashing down. They didn't meet again. He showed up at the designated train station, she didn't. And it has haunted them both, him enough that he has written a book about their night together. Jesse admits it took him "three or four years" to write, three or four years of reliving that one night. He is married, unhappily. "I feel like I'm running a small nursery with someone I used to date," he says. Celine has been through a series of unsatisfying relationships (including, she eventually admits, the one she is currently in). Even the compressed time of the movie is designed to emphasize that this is real life; rather than the dreamy, elastic nighttime of the first film, they have just over an hour of afternoon daylight before he has to catch a plane.

But for all of the second film's melancholy and disillusionment, there is some sleight of hand going on. As the conversation bores deeper, finally opening up into real candor only at the end, it emerges that both of them still cling to the unfulfilled promises of that night, which has shaped and colored their lives for the past nine years. They have never found happiness with anyone else. The movie ends with them, against all odds, together—and, possibly, intending to stay that way. The conceits underlying all of this affirm every trope in the romantic-narrative playbook: that two people, having met just once, can fall deeply, truly in love; that whatever obstacles arise, they will find each other again; that it is never too late for happily ever after. The real achievement of *Before Sunrise* and *Before Sunset* is not to show "real" life and real love, but to reimagine romantic fantasy for a generation and an era that prides itself on knowing better. The movies constitute a love story every bit as improbable as *Pretty Woman*, but built on a foundation of doubt and self-awareness. Linklater has invented a new genre: fairy-tale *vérité*.

Both films serve as sort of a running commentary on themselves. Early in *Before Sunrise*, Jesse tells Celine about an idea he has for a TV show, which would run for a year and feature 24 full hours in the lives of 365 different people around the world: getting up in the morning, eating, sleeping, etc. "Wait, wait," Celine interrupts him. "All those mundane, boring things everybody has to do every day of their fucking life?" "Well," Jesse says with a laugh, "I was gonna say 'the poetry of day to day life,' but you say it your way and I'll say it mine." Of course, the "poetry of day to day life" is what Linklater himself is aiming for. Throughout the movies, Jesse and Celine display an awareness of being characters within a narrative—not in the literal sense of knowing they are in a movie, but in the sense of having absorbed so many stories from books, movies and TV shows that they have readymade references for every situation. Trying to persuade Celine to get off the train with him in Vienna, Jesse tells her to imagine herself as an old woman looking back on her life, regretting missed opportunities for adventure. Later, when Celine initially resists having sex with him, she tells him, "It's like some male fantasy: meet a French girl on a train, fuck her and never see her again, and have this great story to tell. I don't want to be a great story." But she already is a great story, they are both *in* a great story, and they both know it.

Linklater suggests that in cultures saturated with stories, it is impossible to escape thinking of ourselves as characters, acting out familiar parts. Whether we're falling in love or witnessing a disaster, there is some part of us thinking, "This is like being in a movie."

Before Sunset begins with Jesse at a Parisian bookstore promoting his fictionalized account of his and Celine's night together, answering a question maybe similar to those that Hawke, Delpy, and Linklater had been asked by reporters themselves: "Do you think they get back together in six months, like they promise each other?" Jesse replies, "I think how you answer that is a good test, if you're a romantic or a cynic." It is a meta-question, posed by a character in a movie to his readers, but also to himself, and to the movie's creators and its audience. Are we romantics or cynics? Can we even still *be* romantics, given how readily we recognize and dismiss the clichés of the form? Linklater thinks the answer is, maybe, yes. (Celine gives Jesse her assessment of the book, which sounds a bit like the mostly positive reviews for *Before Sunrise*: "It's very romantic, I usually don't like that. It's very well written.")

The importance of Hawke and Delpy to the films almost goes without saying, although their performances are of a naturalistic, carefully tempered kind that tends to get overlooked in awards ceremonies. The characters are sympathetic not just in spite of their obvious flaws, but because of them; their quirks and anxieties and defensiveness and awkwardness are crucial to believing in and caring about them. And watching the movies back to back gives an honest awareness of aging that no makeup tricks could achieve. Hawke's newly creased forehead and Delpy's thinner, not-so-radiant face register the years between the movies, and suggest they haven't all been easy ones (for either the characters or the actors). Most crucially, both players make the connection between Jesse and Celine seem plausible; it doesn't hurt that they are both attractive, of course, but the personalities of their characters have to make sense together too. Listening to them talk, they sound like people who would be drawn to each other.

The movies also show Linklater's ongoing fascination with time. *Before Sunrise* covers about the same short span as both *Slacker* and *Dazed and Confused*, and *Before Sunset* narrows it even more. The difference in these films is that the characters are aware of the time limitations too. The time onscreen is all the time they have together. The compression encourages an accelerated intimacy and forces big decisions to be made quickly. It also leads the characters themselves to contemplate time, and mortality. "Everything is so finite," Jesse says. "But don't you think that's what makes our time, and specific moments, so important?" The real-time constriction of *Before Sunset* gives the movie a mounting sense of drama, as it counts down toward Jesse's scheduled departure. But the ending turns a neat trick—the deadline comes, and then goes. He will miss his plane. The characters will not be dictated to by the clock; Linklater turns them loose. As Jessica Winter wrote in the *Village Voice*, "The lovers run out of time, into another realm entirely."[3]

The story may or may not be finished. Hawke, Delpy, and Linklater have said they might revisit the characters again. If they do, it won't be because of studio clamoring —the two movies grossed just over $11 million, combined. But they were well reviewed, and *Before Sunset* was named the best film of 2004 in the *Village Voice*'s annual poll of critics.

Having directed two real-time movies in *Tape* and *Before Sunset*, Linklater would seem to have pushed his chronological minimalism as far as it can go. But maybe not. One of the interviewers in *Before Sunset* asks Jesse what his next book will be. Jesse replies that he's always wanted to write an entire novel that took place in the space of just three or four minutes, the duration of one pop song. It's easy to imagine Linklater taking up the same challenge. But he also knows what he's up against, as he makes clear in the W.H. Auden poem Jesse quotes in *Before Sunrise*: "But all the clocks in the city / Began to whirr and chime: / 'O let not Time deceive you, / You cannot conquer Time.'"

Waking Life (2001)

WRITTEN BY: RICHARD LINKLATER
WITH: WILEY WIGGINS, ETHAN HAWKE, JULIE DELPY, ALEX
    JONES, STEVEN SODERBERGH, AND MANY OTHERS

In Linklater's first feature effort, *It's Impossible to Learn to Plow by Reading Books*, his main character at one point watches Carl Dreyer's 1964 film *Gertrud*. "Life is a dream," says Gertrud (played by Nina Pens Rode). "Life?" her male companion asks her. "Yes," she says. "Life is a long chain of dreams, drifting one into the other."

The scene signaled a preoccupation with dreams that has carried through Linklater's work. *Slacker* begins with Linklater's taxi passenger recounting a dream. Early in *Dazed and Confused*, the pensive Tony tells his friend Mike about a dream involving sex with Abraham Lincoln. In *Before Sunset*, Jesse tells Celine about a recurring dream he has of her.

On the commentary track for *It's Impossible to Plow* (included with the Criterion release of *Slacker*) Linklater says of the scene from *Gertrud*, "I guess that was with me early on, as you think about consciousness and what the fuck we're perceiving. Movies are in there somewhere too, you know? So I've always seen that as a big, wonderful jumble. Between life, dreams and movies, in there somewhere is all this."

Waking Life is an attempt to put that "big, wonderful jumble" on screen. On the DVD's commentary track, Linklater calls it his "kitchen sink" movie. "I could include all kinds of weird memories or ideas and not totally understand them," he says. The film throws together characters and ideas from his other work (some scenes reference *Slacker*, one is a bedroom conversation between Celine and Jesse from *Before Sunrise*, and the protagonist is played by Wiley Wiggins from *Dazed and Confused*), along with scattered experiences, obsessions and observations.

What made all of it possible was a new form of digital animation. *Waking Life* is a feature-length cartoon, but it is a particular kind of cartoon: the entire movie was shot and edited on video, with real actors, and then subjected to rotoscoping, in which artists draw or paint on top of existing footage. The technique is nearly as old as animation itself, and was used to varying degrees in classic Disney films. But *Waking Life* was the first full-length feature to use a form of digital rotoscoping invented by Austin animator and programmer Bob Sabiston, who served as the movie's art director. Sabiston animated a few sequences in the film himself and recruited a small stable of artists to do the rest. The shifting visual styles combine with the fluidity of the original handheld video footage to give the whole movie a floating, understated surrealism that matches its ambiguous narrative.

The film begins with a prologue and an overture. First, a young boy standing in his front yard feels himself begin to drift off the ground. Then, after the opening credits and a brief glimpse of Wiley Wiggins's unnamed central character riding a train, comes a scene of the Tosca Tango Orchestra, an Austin ensemble that Linklater hired to score the movie. They are warming up, practicing, and as the music starts to coalesce it becomes the soundtrack to the film, which returns to Wiley's train as it arrives at a station. The glimpse of the orchestra lingers, informing our experience of the music that percolates under the movie. It adds another layer of unreality, the awareness always of a group of people in a room playing what the viewer is hearing.

It is never clear how much of the movie is intended as a dream, although the only real options are "most of it" or "all of it." The whole thing could be taking place in Wiley's head as he sleeps. Or, the movie suggests as it goes along, it could be taking place in his head as he dies. He could be already

Celine (Julie Delpy) and Jesse (Ethan Hawke), the romantic duo from *Before Sunrise* and *Before Sunset*, make an animated cameo in Richard Linklater's *Waking Life*. (Courtesy of Photofest)

dead. He might not have existed in the first place. (Linklater has said that the Wiley character's experience of repeatedly waking within the same dream only to find that he is still dreaming is based on a dream he had himself—as is the prologue with the floating boy.) What the loose narrative structure really provides is a chance for the kinds of disquisitions on philosophy, science, and human relations that Linklater loves.

These disquisitions range over a predictably wide terrain: the coming union of biology and technology; André Bazin's theories of film; the contradictions inherent in the idea of free will. As in *Slacker*, there are also portents of violence, including a barroom anecdote that turns into an accidental shoot-out, and an activist with a loudspeaker who turns deeper shades of red as he drives around town, threatening to bring down the system. (The activist is played by Alex Jones, a former Austin radio host who has become known as a leading proponent of theories that the September 11 attacks were engineered by the U.S. government.) One man, who tells Wiley that "the time has come to project my own inadequacies and dissatisfactions into the socio-political and scientific schemes," sets himself on fire in a public plaza.

Maybe the most unsettling of these scenes shows four young, stern-faced men walking through an alley, fantasizing about mass annihilation. "Society is a fraud so complete and venal that it demands to be destroyed beyond the power of memory to recall its existence," one of them says. Another adds, "Where there is fire, we will carry gasoline." The third one affirms, "Interrupt the continuum of everyday experience and all the normal expectations that go with it." They are given no political or religious affiliation, and the film does not show them doing anything but talking. But their palpable disgust with the world they inhabit, and the implicit violence of their words, would have sounded ominous even if *Waking Life* had not happened to have been released on October 19, 2001. In that context, though, it was hard to hear a character's zeal "to immerse ourselves in the oblivion of action" without a sickening shiver.

Not that Linklater endorses the would-be terrorists, any more than he endorses the barroom gunplay. He seems to be suggesting the dangers of alienation from a culture or political system, or even from a person's own sense of identity. In a long scene that echoes some of the concerns of Wallace and Baudrillard, a philosophy professor explains to Wiley his preference for existentialism over postmodernism: "I've read the postmodernists with some interest, even admiration," he says. "But when I read them I always have this awful nagging feeling that something absolutely essential is getting left out. The more that you talk about a person as a social construction, or as a confluence of forces, or as fragmented or marginalized, what you do is you open up a whole new world of excuses. When Sartre talks about responsibility, he's not talking about something abstract. He's not talking about the kind of self or soul that theologians would argue about. It's something very concrete, it's you and me talking, making decisions, doing things and taking the consequences." He concludes, in one of the movie's obvious thesis statements, "It's always *our* decision who we are."

Crucial to making that decision, the film suggests, is how we relate and connect to the rest of the world. Kim Krizan, who cowrote *Before Sunrise* with Linklater, appears in one scene to discuss the difficulty of communicating abstract ideas to other people, but also the importance of trying. "When we communicate with one another and we feel that we have connected and we think that we're understood," she says, "I think we have a feeling of almost spiritual communion. And that feeling might be transient, but I think it's what we live for." It is an echo of what Celine says about connection in *Before Sunrise*, and it is in turn echoed later in *Waking Life* when Wiley talks with a woman in a restaurant who, it becomes apparent, is dead. She tells him life was "a gift," and says, "I loved all the people, dealing with the contradictory impulses. That's what I miss the most, connecting with the people. Looking back, that's all that really mattered."

Almost inevitably, the film contains commentary on itself. At one point, as Wiley recounts his dreams to another character, he says, "Some of it was kind of absurdist, like from a strange movie." Two men being projected on a movie screen disccuss Bazin's idea of cinema as a collection of "holy moments" that reveal "the face of God." As they talk, they turn into clouds and blow away. A young man in a cafe tells a woman that he is working on a book with no story, "just people, gestures, moments, bits of rapture, fleeting emotions." In a self-deprecating tweak, Wiley catches a bit of a TV interview with the director Steven Soderbergh, who is telling a story about Billy Wilder and Louis Malle meeting in the early 1960s. Malle tells Wilder he just made a movie for $2.5 million. When Wilder asks what it's about, Malle says, "It's sort of a dream within a dream." Wilder replies, "You just lost two and a half million dollars." (*Waking Life* reportedly cost a little under $3 million to make, and grossed just over $3 million worldwide.)

The animation is striking throughout. Linklater's typically mundane shooting locales—sidewalks, restaurants, convenience stores—are transformed into pulsating canvases, filled with unpredictable bursts of color and movement. A few dozen animators worked on the film under Sabiston's direction, trading off scenes or even parts of scenes, but Sabiston encouraged a somewhat minimalist approach that gives the film visual coherence. Although some sections are trippier than others, illustrating dialogue with mini-cartoons inside the frame or rendering backgrounds impressionistically, most of the focus is kept on the more or less naturalistically rendered characters. (Since Wiley is the movie's only continuous character, his changing appearance is the easiest way to gauge the different styles of the artists.)

It was a painstaking process; the rotoscoping took almost a full year, and Sabiston has said that each animator averaged about 15 seconds of completed film a week. But as a formal experiment, it has to be counted as a success. The animation not only complements the movie's themes, it becomes part of them. The film, as written, would not make sense in any other form. Its achievements are also a testament to Linklater's collaborative instincts; after delivering the edited video to Sabiston, he apparently distanced himself from the animation process, consulting regularly but trusting the artists to do their work. It is hard to imagine many directors being so willing to hand over the reins.

In interviews after the film came out, Linklater said he wanted to use the rotoscoping process again, maybe on a science-fiction film. Judging from a scene at the end of *Waking Life*, where a character played by Linklater talks to Wiley about an essay by Philip K. Dick, it seems obvious which science fiction he had in mind.

A Scanner Darkly (2006)

WRITTEN BY: RICHARD LINKLATER, FROM A NOVEL BY PHILIP K. DICK

CAST: KEANU REEVES (BOB ARCTOR), WINONA RYDER (DONNA HAWTHORNE), ROBERT DOWNEY JR. (JIM BARRIS), WOODY HARRELSON (LUCKMAN), RORY COCHRANE (CHARLES FRECK)

Linklater's second full-length venture into rotoscoped animation is in some ways a companion piece to *Waking Life*. Much of the movie is taken up with ambling conversation among a small group of aimless friends. It's no surprise that those scenes come more naturally to Linklater than the film's science-fiction framework, which concerns a corporate-government conspiracy to produce and distribute a brain-destroying narcotic. As a narrative, the movie has some trouble condensing Philip K. Dick's dystopian 1977 novel. But as a series of riffs on drugs, culture, and technology, it has moments of inspiration. Many of those are drawn nearly word-for-word from Dick, but Linklater proves an apt translator, and he's mostly chosen his cast well, with the glaring exception of leading man Keanu Reeves. He also updates Dick—who was already updating Orwell and Aldous Huxley—by giving the story contemporary political echoes.

Dick had been brought to the screen before, of course, by Ridley Scott in *Blade Runner* and Steven Spielberg in *Minority Report*, among others. Linklater can't match Scott and Spielberg as a director of special effects and action sequences, and he does not seem interested in trying. The effects in *A Scanner Darkly* consist entirely of animation, and even that is used naturalistically, for the most part. But Linklater is arguably the most simpatico adapter Dick has had. He is to some degree a chronicler and descendant of the counterculture that Dick belonged to and was a distinct voice of. The undercover agent Bob Arctor and his friends, and the drug haze that surrounds them all, could be plucked from almost any of Linklater's films.

Although the movie retains the novel's near-future setting (it takes place "seven years from now"), it unfolds in a country that looks pretty much like the current one. Partly because of technological advances in the real world since Dick wrote his manuscript, Linklater doesn't need to invent too much to achieve the look and feel of the book's down-at-the-heels quasi-police state.

The level of surveillance imagined by Orwell and adapted for his own purposes by Dick no longer seems fantastical, a fact Linklater plays off sardonically. The film seems all the more sinister for the mundanity of its machinery. The only pieces of Dick's picture that remain in the realm of the fantastic are the "scramble suits" used by undercover agents, which render the wearer unrecognizable except as a "vague blur." The animation works particularly well with these, presenting them as endlessly mutating kaleidoscopes of faces, colors, and patterns.

Like the book, the movie charts the mental deterioration of an undercover drug officer, "Fred," a.k.a. Bob Arctor, who is tracing the distribution of a powerful narcotic called Substance D (for Death). The drug has flooded the streets to the extent that 20 percent of the population is using it. In befriending a small group of addicts, Arctor has become one himself. The exact physical and psychological effects of the drug are never articulated, but in large quantities it produces long-lasting brain damage. In Arctor's case, this takes the form of a dissociative disorder, in which the two halves of his brain begin to work independently, one assuming the identity of Fred and the other of Arctor. In Dick's book, the split happens gradually, with the two voices of Fred and Arctor slowly diverging. But the film, trying to pack in both plot and character development, hurries through the transformation and has trouble illustrating the protagonist's changing mindstates. This is partly because mental collapse is an entirely internal phenomenon, and partly because Keanu Reeves's customary lack of affect makes it hard to tell when he is evincing existential bewilderment and when he is just, well, being Keanu—even at his most engaged, Reeves always seems a little dissociated.

Actually, the most convincing scene of identity crisis comes in a reverie about Arctor's earlier, pre-undercover life. In the flashback, his decrepit tract home reverts to its earlier form as a model suburban rancher, occupied by a model suburban family (Arctor, his wife, and two daughters), and full of gleaming appliances and well-stocked kitchen cabinets. One afternoon, he hits his head on one of those cabinets and is suddenly struck by what seems to him to be the stultifying normalcy of his life, its predictable, unchanging patterns and rhythms. The contrast between Arctor's different worlds—the clean, safe middle-class family life, the hazy, paranoid drug-outlaw life, and the hierarchical, technocratic law enforcement life—provides a typical Linklater riff on the trade-offs and compromises of everyday existence, no matter how you live it.

Reeves aside, the cast works well—it is almost a meta-commentary on the film's subject matter all by itself. Choosing two well-known drug users—the devoted pothead Woody Harrelson and the serial addict Robert Downey, Jr.—to play Arctor's junkie friends Luckman and Barris verges on a stunt, but it pays off. Constantly joking, teasing, and messing with each other's heads, they appear as an older, and therefore more pathetic, version of cinematic stoner duos like Bill and Ted, or Garth and Wayne. The jokes are still funny, but they're painful too, because in the real world refusing to grow up does not protect you from growing old. Where some of Linklater's goofier heroes, like Jack Black's character in *School of Rock*, turn their Peter Pan routines into a livelihood, there's no hope of that for Barris or Luckman. They're not going anywhere, except maybe down. (Barris ends the film in custody of the authorities.) Winona Ryder is also fine as the duplicitous Donna, who uses Arctor as a patsy in the interest of busting the drug cartel. Ryder's still-waifish sex appeal fares well under the rotoscope's dreamy lines, and her own legal history—she was arrested with stolen clothing and an array of prescription narcotics in 2001—only heightens the character's shady verisimilitude.

Along with *Fast-Food Nation*, *A Scanner Darkly* moved the implicit politics of Linklater's movies to the foreground. Dick's paranoid plot lends itself easily to updating; although written before the phrases "war on drugs" and "war on terror" were coined, the book cannily forecasted a conflation of the two. In Linklater's dialogue, drug enforcement agents refer to their adversaries as "drug terrorists." He adds a scene where a man protesting the drug war (played by conspiracy theorist Alex Jones) is swept up into a government van and sped away, as Arctor watches. The film also makes the sinister nature of the New Path corporation—which runs drug treatment centers and, it turns out, manufactures Substance D—more explicit from the start. It emphasizes Dick's vision of a rising fascist state underwritten by big business. Like the book, the film ends on a putatively hopeful note—Arctor is collecting evidence that might yet bring down the drug conspiracy—but, given the level of control over information that seems to be exercised by both the government and New Path, it's not clear how or whether Arctor's revelations will ever be brought to light.

In any case, Dick's primary concern in the book was a mournful (if also sometimes nostalgic) evocation of his own drug days and the people he shared them with. The book's end piece is a heartfelt memoriam to a list of friends who either died or suffered permanent damage from drug use. Linklater repeats the memoriam verbatim in the film's closing credits, but because the film is so divided between developing its characters and building its complicated plot, the gesture feels a little tacked on.

The script is only intermittently successful at capturing the book's mounting sense of loss as the characters disappear more and more inside their addictions.

Still, the film works as a sort of cautionary bookend to *Slacker*, a warning that in the end, doing nothing and being nothing can be uncomfortably hard to tell apart. As Linklater said in an interview with the online publication CulturePulp, he wanted to show "the exuberant, communal upside" to the book's depiction of drug culture, but also its sad dissolution: "[T]he price you pay for that little bit of fun is enormous. It can go from fun to dark paranoid death in one day."[4]

More than 15 years on from *Slacker*, Linklater is still absorbed by the struggle to maintain some sense of self and some sense of purpose in life. The aimless chatterers in *Slacker* tend to fortify the former, at the expense of the latter: better to *be* than to *do*. Bob Arctor in *A Scanner Darkly* is an opposite case study: He loses his identity—his actual knowledge of who he is—but, buried somewhere deep inside, retains a memory of his mission.

Linklater doesn't seem to embrace either end of the be-do dichotomy. He is certainly no slacker in any negative sense—he was the only director to screen two films at Cannes in 2006, *A Scanner Darkly* and *Fast-Food Nation*. And he is not quite an enemy of the establishment. Surely some of his characters would regard his more commercial Hollywood maneuvers as corporate whoredom. But on the other hand, his intelligence and repeated ventures into the philosophical, combined with his modest but carefully conceived formal experimentation, set him consistently apart. He seems to have found a balance in his career that his characters can only struggle to match. (That balance distinguishes him from Philip K. Dick, for example, who was prone to pharmacological excesses and psychological imbalances that shaped his work but complicated—and possibly shortened—his life.)

The filmmakers discussed in this book are not exactly part of a movement or genre, but they are more or less all part of a generation. And to the extent that any of them stands as a generational voice, it is Linklater. His characters verbalize, endlessly, the anxieties, insights, frustrations, and vague but determined search for purpose that permeate the work of the directors discussed in subsequent chapters.

At the end of *Dazed and Confused*, the quarterback Pink finally refuses to sign the football team's no-drugs pledge. But that doesn't necessarily mean he's quitting. "I might play ball," he tells his dour coach, tossing the pledge form away "but I will never sign that." Linklater seems to have set the same standard for himself, in his mingling of personal projects with mainstream multiplex fare. What is most surprising about his quietly remarkable career to date is that he has gotten away with it.

3
TODD HAYNES

odd Haynes emerged as an artist at a time when to call yourself gay was an almost inherently political act. It meant not just asserting an identity but assuming a cause. Haynes was a member in the late 1980s of the AIDS awareness group ACT-UP, whose ubiquitous pink-triangle logo declared "Silence = Death." Homosexuality had come to inhabit a matrix of morality and mortality that gay artists of the 1980s and 1990s found nearly inescapable. Haynes did not shrink from those themes, but neither did he address them in obvious ways. His first film, the 40-minute short *Superstar*, dealt with disease, shame, and secrets, via an imaginary biography of the singer Karen Carpenter, told with disfigured Barbie dolls. His first full feature, *Poison*, which won the Grand Jury Prize at Sundance, wrapped up a bundle of sexual and political themes in a triptych that drew on 1950s science fiction, television journalism, and Jean Genet. Preferring parable to polemic, and reworking pop-culture detritus to his own ends, Haynes has compiled an esoteric filmography full of anxiety, longing, and unexpected flashes of fantasy.

He was a leading figure of what was loosely and maybe recklessly labeled the New Queer Cinema, a group of directors including Gus van Sant and Gregg Araki who came to prominence on the art-house circuit in the early 1990s. None of them really had much in common beyond their sexuality, and their paths in the last decade have gone in very different directions. Van Sant has alternated between multiplex-friendly dramas (*Good Will Hunting*, *Finding Forrester*) and narrative experiments (*Elephant*, *Last Days*), few of them focused on explicitly gay themes. Araki has stuck to tales of polymorphous sexuality and difficult lives on the margins of society. Haynes has done none of the above, telling very different stories with every movie, in very different ways. But there are consistent threads running through his films, most obviously variations on the themes of self-deception and self-loathing. In Haynes's stories, characters are undone by what they hide, whether it's Karen Carpenter starving herself to death in secret or the suburban husband in *Far from Heaven* repressing his homosexuality until it destroys his marriage. It makes sense that his most exuberant movie, *Velvet Goldmine*, celebrates a time when it suddenly, magically became OK for people to be whatever they wanted.

Haynes's own inclinations, both sexual and artistic, seem to have been evident from a young age. Born in 1961, he grew up in Los Angeles, in what he has recalled as a happy family. In interviews, he has said that when he was little he and his sister used to make up elaborate stories with her dolls—an experience clearly reflected in *Superstar*. He was soon drawn to the more expansive narrative possibilities of cinema. "My family had a Super-8 camera and our first big production was *Romeo and Juliet* when I was nine," he told *Interview* magazine in 1997. "I had seen the movie and I was obsessed: I had to do my own version. Of course, I was going to play all the roles, so we experimented with double exposure. My mother and I painted a background on the wall and shot me as Romeo. Then we rewound the film and shot it again with me dressed up as Juliet."[1]

Haynes graduated from Brown University, where he majored in semiotics, and then earned an MFA at Bard. In 1985, he founded a nonprofit independent film company called Apparatus Productions with his friends Christine Vachon and Barry Ellsworth. It produced only seven short films, including *Superstar*, but provided a career launch pad. (Vachon went on to become a notable independent producer, with movies like *Swoon, I Shot Andy Warhol* and *Boys Don't Cry* to her credit, along with all of Haynes's films. She wrote a well-received book about her experiences, *Shooting to Kill*, in 1998, followed by another in 2006.)

There are not many happy endings in Haynes's catalog, which is maybe to be expected of a career that began in the era of AIDS panic and has stretched to the era of gay-marriage panic. But his movies for the most part avoid didacticism; he is a humanist, and for all of the identity politics in his stories he never reduces his characters to abstract representatives of gender, race, or class. He allows them complexity and individuality. Even the

Barbie-doll Carpenters in *Superstar* emerge as surprisingly sympathetic figures. At the same time, Haynes never loses sight of the political and cultural forces that shape his characters' lives and, often, curtail their options. His movies affirm the liberating possibilities of individual action, but have a realistic—and sometimes tragic—awareness of its limitations.

As striking as his themes are the forms he gives them. Borrowing from the movies and TV shows of his childhood, the music of his adolescence and a whole panoply of gay iconography (the plays of Genet, the experimental films of Kenneth Anger, the high camp of glam rock), Haynes creates densely referential films that treat their source materials with notable reverence. On paper, a movie like *Far from Heaven* sounds like an arch bit of postmodernism: a highly stylized 1950s melodrama, featuring a gay suburban dad and a white housewife falling for the black gardener. It could almost be an episode of *Desperate Housewives*. But in Haynes's telling, the story assumes different, more complicated dimensions. His stylistic appropriations are rarely intended with a smirk or a snicker; he plays them straight.

Both *Superstar* and *Poison* generated controversies that put Haynes in the odd position of an artist whose work was more talked about than seen. With *Superstar*, objections were raised first by the Mattel toy company (which was concerned about the use of its dolls) and then, more substantively, by Richard Carpenter, who ultimately forced the film to be withdrawn from distribution and exhibition. The attendant media coverage inevitably elevated Haynes's profile, even as his movie was placed off-limits. *Poison* had the dubious fortune of reaching theaters in the midst of a protracted skirmish over funding of the National Endowment for the Arts. Because the movie included gay sex scenes and had received an N.E.A. grant, it was attacked by conservative religious groups as one more taxpayer-funded outrage. But the N.E.A. stood behind its decision to award the grant, and the ruckus eventually faded from the news cycle.

None of Haynes's subsequent films have generated such vituperative responses, although they have been provocative in their own ways. In fact, almost without meaning to, he has worked his way into something like mainstream acceptance. *Far from Heaven* had his biggest-name cast to date, was nominated for four Oscars (including a Best Original Screenplay nod for Haynes), and grossed over $30 million worldwide. As he said in *Interview*, "It turns out the one thing Hollywood can't handle is someone who doesn't seem to need to be famous. So it's worked in my favor. I've been playing hard to get—and it's worked."[2]

Superstar: The Karen Carpenter Story (1987)
WRITTEN BY: TODD HAYNES AND CYNTHIA SCHNEIDER
WITH: VOICES OF ROB LABELLE, MERRILL GRUVER, MIC-
HAEL EDWARDS, MELISSA BROWN

When Karen Carpenter died in 1983 from the effects of anorexia nervosa, it helped propel the phrase "eating disorder" into the popular lexicon and prompted an onslaught of handwringing essays and reports about why American girls were starving themselves. Feminists saw the promotion of female thinness in advertising, in movies, and on TV as a culprit in fostering unrealistic expectations. They also blamed Barbie. The doll had long drawn fire for presenting an exaggerated and submissive vision of femininity, but now she was charged with the more serious offense of encouraging girls to hate their bodies and hurt themselves.

So Haynes's casting of Barbie (and Barbie-like) dolls in his short, sad telling of Carpenter's life is inspired on several levels. The dolls' blank smiles suit the apple-cheeked image of Karen and her brother Richard, who found a niche in the early to mid-1970s as wholesome purveyors of easygoing pop songs. The Carpenters were touted as a clean-cut, family-friendly act. (In 1973 they performed at the White House for President Richard Nixon, who called them "Young America at its very best.") Barbie, meanwhile, debuted at the American International Toy Fair in 1959, when Karen Carpenter was 9 years old. Karen was a member of the first generation of girls to grow up with the doll.

As puppets, Barbie and Ken would seem to present serious challenges to storytelling. The vapid, changeless cheer of their plastic faces allows for a pretty limited range of expressiveness. But Haynes turns that to his advantage. From the beginning of the film, the dolls' sunny surfaces seem to mask underlying tensions between the Carpenter siblings and their controlling parents. As the story unfolds, and Richard and Karen's lives become increasingly at odds with their public image, those Ken and Barbie smiles seem ever more symbolic of a refusal to acknowledge what's happening underneath.

Haynes molds the dolls to his own ends, coloring their hair and skin and fitting them with period clothes. This takes its most extreme form in the actual whittling away of the Karen doll's body as her anorexia progresses— a gruesome effect that renders the doll nearly skeletal. The casting of the dolls also heightens the sense of the characters' vulnerability, and Karen's in particular; Haynes presents her as constantly pliable to the wishes of her parents, her brother, and music industry executives.

The tone of the film is strange and dark, incorporating a mishmash of narrative strategies that prefigure those Haynes would use in later movies. It begins in black and white, on the day of Karen's death, with a camera moving through the Carpenters' parents' house. An on-screen title informs us this is "A dramatization," and a portentous voice-over asks, "What happened? Why, at the age of 32, was this smooth-voiced girl from Downey, California, who led a raucous nation smoothly into the 1970s, found dead in her parents' home?" But this deadpan TV documentary style quickly gives way to a burst of music—Karen's wistful voice, singing, "Long ago, and oh so far away, I fell in love with you"—and then the introduction of the dolls. Also interspersed through the film are snippets of academic-sounding text and narration, like one that reads, "As we investigate the story of Karen Carpenter's life and death we are presented with an extremely graphic picture of the internal experience of contemporary femininity." These are offered with a straight face and seem to be intended seriously.

In fact, the whole movie is intended more seriously than its mock-stentorian narration lets on. Haynes obviously knows that making "The Karen Carpenter Story" with Barbie dolls is on some levels an inherently funny idea, and there are many moments where the contrast between the human drama and the plastic players produces a certain kind of humor. But it is a humor of nervous laughter and discomfort. There is an expectation that the dolls will allow the audience some distance from the story, but Haynes uses effects—close-ups, montages, a whole raft of horror-film lighting and sound devices—that emphasize the dolls' point of view. There is no mockery in his approach.

It is a low-budget production and looks it, with a graininess to the picture that has only been exacerbated by the duplication of bootleg copies of the film. But Haynes's cinematic instincts are well represented; he uses a variety of camera pans of the detailed miniature sets to compensate for the lack of movement of the dolls, and splices in other material from news programs, old movies, and man-on-the-street interviews to comment on the central story. Some of this feels heavy-handed (e.g., as Karen sings "Close to You," Haynes cuts to soldiers on a Vietnam battlefield). But the montages show his talent for creative editing. The onset of Karen's anorexia is suggested by a simple but ominous juxtaposition of two images: a plate full of food and a box of Ex-Lax pills. A narrator's description of the "high" that can accompany an anorexic's self-denial segues into the opening lines of "Top of the World": "Such a feeling's coming over me . . ."

The movie documents the Carpenters' known struggles: Karen's anorexia and Richard's dependence on quaaludes. But Haynes also suggests an undercurrent of incest in Karen's devotion to her brother, showing her first attracted to the man she eventually married, Tom Burris, when she mistakes him for Richard across a room. And throughout, the Carpenters' parents maintain a looming presence in their lives. When Karen says she wants to move to Century City, an hour away from her parents' home, her mother tries to stop her. Haynes may be suggesting that Karen's anorexia partly arose from a desire to take command of her life in the only way she could from her controlling family, but he doesn't belabor the point. (He also includes flashbacks to childhood spankings by her father, the introduction of a theme that would preoccupy Haynes enough to eventually warrant its own film, the 1993 short *Dottie Gets Spanked*.) He is not seeking simple cause and effect explanations of Karen's condition, so much as suggesting the ways that secrets and shame feed on each other.

In that sense, *Superstar* is very much an AIDS film. Karen's disease is one that was barely recognized at the time, socially or scientifically, and the blame for it tended to be heaped on the victims. There are obvious analogies between the initial response to AIDS and the kind of condescension and hostility Karen encounters from her family and doctors. In an interview after the release of *Safe*, which also concerns a woman with a mysterious ailment, Haynes said, "[T]here's a tradition of illness being projected onto the 'female' that I identify with. I clue into that history. I feel that AIDS as it's associated with homosexuality has a historical connection to illnesses attributed to women."[3]

Superstar is also, of course, about celebrity. The title, taken from a Carpenters song, is more sad than ironic. It suggests the ways that Karen's fame created an image of herself that she died trying to live up to. But Haynes is less interested in fame as a subject than a metaphor, a way of illustrating the tensions between external appearances and interior life—between the image we project to the world and the way we see ourselves from within. Anorexia distorts the way a person perceives herself, and celebrity distorts the way others perceive her, which makes an anorectic celebrity an extreme case of dissonance. But those tensions are to some degree universal, and they recur in different ways throughout Haynes's films.

Finally, *Superstar* is inevitably about music. At the time the movie came out, the Carpenters were beginning to undergo a critical reassessment. Along with other "soft-rock" artists of the early 1970s, they had been broadly reviled and ridiculed by critics and rock audiences of the time. But if Karen's death demolished their carefree public persona, it also made it easier to hear in retrospect how tinged with sadness her singing had always been. Haynes deploys the duo's songs with the artful care of a devotee, using them to color and comment on the story but never condescending to them. He even breaks away at one point for a brief colloquy on the Carpenters' musical legacy, with commentary from three young musicians. Although one of them scorns the duo's "reactionary values," the other two are reverential. "There was just something about Karen Carpenter's voice that you couldn't dismiss," says a DJ identified as Todd Donovan. Joanne Barnett, a singer, adds, "Her vocal range, her phrasing, they were totally unique."

Haynes's respect for the music, however, did not extend to procuring permission for its use in the film. Once *Superstar* started showing at art-house theaters and generating some favorable press, that became a problem. Richard Carpenter sued, and in 1990 the film was taken out of distribution. The Museum of Modern Art reportedly retains a copy, and bootleg versions are screened periodically (and are available online). The attention *Superstar* received both before and during the lawsuit gave Haynes some artistic cachet. But the buzz was nothing compared to what awaited his next movie.

Poison (1991)
WRITTEN BY: TODD HAYNES AND JEAN GENET
WITH: EDITH MEEKS (FELICIA BEACON), LARRY MAXWELL (DR. THOMAS GRAVES), SUSAN NORMAN (NANCY OLSEN), SCOTT RENDERER (JOHN BROOM), JAMES LYONS (JACK BOLTON)

Like a lot of scandals seen in retrospect, particularly those of the culture-war variety, the fuss over *Poison* is a little hard to understand. It is a moody, low-budget and doggedly odd movie, financed and distributed independently and inspired by the writings of a gay French existentialist. Despite the claims of some of its detractors, its sexual content is brief and not very graphic. And, maybe more to the point, almost nobody saw it—it grossed well under $1 million.

But all of those factors, plus a $25,000 postproduction grant Haynes received from the National Endowment for the Arts, made it an attractive target for the American Family Association and Pat Robertson's nascent Christian Coalition. Having successfully stirred up outrage over the photographs of Robert Mapplethorpe and the nude performance art of Karen Finley a few years earlier, the conservative religious groups were on the lookout for further evidence of taxpayer-funded perversity. On paper, at least, *Poison* seemed to fit the bill. It was a film with gay themes by a gay director, and it had already attracted notice at the Sundance festival, winning the Grand Jury Prize. The Rev. Donald Wildmon, head of the American Family Association, denounced the film before it was even released, saying it included "explicit porno scenes of homosexuals involved in anal sex."[4] (Wildmon had apparently not seen the film, and based his tirade on an article in *Daily Variety*.) But John Frohnmayer, who was then the chairman of the N.E.A., responded with a vigor the agency hadn't shown in the earlier clashes. He called a news conference to defend the grant and the film. "The central theme is that violence breeds violence, lust breeds destruction," he said. "It is clearly not a pornographic film." Wildmon's complaint gained little traction in Congress, but it did land Haynes, then 30, on television programs from *Larry King Live* to *Entertainment Tonight*. *Poison* opened shortly afterward, to generally good reviews, if predictably limited distribution.

The brief uproar was an unintentional but apt illustration of the movie's thesis, stated at the start in white letters on a black screen: "The whole world is dying of panicky fright." The foreboding carries over to the three stories that emerge in interwoven narratives, all of them purportedly inspired by the writings of Jean Genet. The first, "Hero," is a fake documentary about a boy who—his mother claims—murdered his father and then fled the house by flying out an open window, never to be seen again. The second, "Horror," is a black and white vamp on the 1950s mad-scientist genre, in which a doctor distills the chemical essence of lust and then accidentally drinks it, turning himself into a carrier of an infectious and fatal disease. The third, "Homo," is the most literal Genet adaptation, about a thief in a 1940s French prison who falls in love with a fellow inmate.

At a remove from its original political and cultural context, and seen in light of Haynes's later, better movies, *Poison* seems neither shocking nor entirely successful. It is a dense and inventive film with maybe too many ideas for its own good. It suggests the variety of influences and stylistic approaches that Haynes would bring to his subsequent work, and further develops some of the themes introduced in *Superstar*, but its three stories fit together awkwardly and some of the thematic connections feel forced. It is in some ways a more interesting film to talk about than to actually watch. Still, it confirmed Haynes as a talented artist whose familiarity with cinematic conventions was matched by his disregard for them.

All of the stories revolve around shame and sex. John Frohnmayer got the gist of it only partly right; certainly violence breeds violence in these stories, but it is not "lust" that breeds destruction so much as ignorance and fear.

The film is not antisexual. If anything, it argues for an end to the secrets, euphemisms, and denial that conspire to conceal sexuality.

There are two secrets at the heart of "Hero." One is domestic violence, which was itself a topic of great "panicky fright" at the time. The 1980s saw an explosion in the public discussion of child and spousal abuse. Farrah Fawcett starred in a widely lauded TV movie, *The Burning Bed*, about a woman who killed her abusive husband. Suzanne Vega and 10,000 Maniacs had hit songs about abused children. But in Haynes's story, the young boy's suffering and eventual vengeance on his father is bound up with his discovery of his mother's infidelity: He walks in on her having sex with a gardener. When the boy later finds his father beating his mother in retaliation for her adultery, he takes a gun out of a drawer and kills his father. Then, he goes to an open window and flies away. Haynes heightens the improbability of this tale by filming most of the segment in flat documentary fashion, with characters identified via on-screen titles and voice-over narration. But he violates this perspective periodically, with flashbacks to key events. This shifting from a mock-objective viewpoint to a subjective one provides some of the film's most striking images—like the boy's vision of his mother in flagrante delicto—but it also muddles the already busy movie, which has trouble juggling its multiple styles to start with.

Haynes gives a more coherent presentation to "Horror," which is a "Twilight Zone" pastiche, complete with portentous narration. Shooting in black and white, he uses the low angles and high-contrast lighting that came down from German expressionism to film noir and horror movies. Those techniques pop up repeatedly in Haynes's films, although usually in more subtle and unexpected ways. There is nothing subtle about "Horror," including the name of its protagonist/monster, Dr. Graves. The parallels to AIDS hysteria are obvious enough, as the diseased doctor is chased through the city by mobs and policemen, until he finally jumps off a building ledge. The jump doesn't kill him immediately, and he is rushed to a hospital where he has a vision of an angel (a stubbled old man) descending to him as he dies.

And then there is "Homo," which uses another jumble of filmmaking approaches. Most of the story is told with a relative realism, in the dark corridors and dirt courtyard of a prison. But it has its own series of flashbacks, to a boys' reform school where the two main characters, John and Jack, first encounter each other. The flashback segments have a deliberately stagey look, with fake trees and a dreamy gold and pink palette. But the events there are in brutal contrast to the idyllic setting: A group of boys torments and humiliates Jack—in the most disturbing scene, they take turns spitting into his open mouth—while John watches from a distance. John is repulsed by the abuse, but aroused by it too. The conflicted feelings form the basis of his violent attraction to Jack, and possibly of his entire sexual identity. Haynes suggests that Jack himself is aroused by humiliation, even as he also resists and resents it. Jack is ultimately killed in a failed prison escape attempt. As a statement on homosexuality, or sexuality in general, the story is fairly grim. But it is not judgmental, in the sense that someone like Frohnmayer would have it. Haynes, unlike audience members who reportedly walked out during the spitting scene, is as intrigued as he is troubled by the power struggles of human relationships and the dark psychic corners of libido. There is a suggestion in the film of unsavory things intertwined deep within the body and spirit.

That uncomfortable frankness is what makes *Poison* a work of personal rather than political art. For all of its topical resonance, Haynes is uninterested in platitudes about tolerance or vague calls for some kind of remedy. He is more concerned with honesty about who and what we are. All three stories present martyrs to sex and violence who die (or disappear) seeking escape of one kind or another from the brutality of biology. But there is no real escape, for anyone. "You think I'm scum," Dr. Graves rants to the crowd gathered to watch him jump from the ledge. "You think I'm dirt, don't you? Well, I'll tell you something. Every one of you down there is exactly the same." The real poison in the movie, and in all of Haynes's films, comes from the constant papering over of actual selves. Things hidden from others, and from ourselves, will fester in the darkness. Haynes developed the theme more narrowly but to greater effect in his next film.

Safe (1995)
WRITTEN BY: TODD HAYNES
WITH: JULIANNE MOORE (CAROL WHITE), XANDER BERKE-
    LEY (GREG WHITE), PETER FRIEDMAN (PETER DUNNING),
    JAMES LEGROS (CHRIS), MARY CARVER (NELL)

Safe is the most understated of Haynes's films, and also the most mysterious. There is some obvious thematic continuity from *Superstar* and *Poison*, in the metaphorical use of illness. The movie aims to evoke a sense of unwellness, a malaise that spreads from its haunting soundtrack through its dusky lighting to infect its characters and, seemingly, the entire world they inhabit.

The story follows the physical and mental deterioration of a suburban housewife, Carol White, who lives in an affluent subdivision outside Los

Julianne Moore (with oxygen tank attached) talks with Todd Haynes on the set of his disquieting disease drama, *Safe*. (Courtesy of Photofest)

Angeles and would not seem, on the surface, to have much cause for anxiety. Her large home is immaculate and cared for by a small household staff; her family (a husband and stepson) is in good health; she is trim and pretty and has nothing to worry her daytime hours except trips to the local beauty salon. But from the opening scene—a long, smooth glide down darkening suburban streets, seen through the windshield of the Whites' Mercedes Benz—there is an air of gathering menace. The scene is accompanied by sustained minor-key synthesizer chords (the score is by Ed Tomney, but is reminiscent of Angelo Badalamenti's spooky work with David Lynch). The Whites' car pauses at a driveway gate, which rumbles open automatically, and then rolls into a garage. The door closes electronically behind them. This is safety: inside a garage, behind a locked door, behind a gate, on a winding San Fernando Valley road lined with expensive houses. And yet the first thing Carol does after getting out of the passenger side of the car is sneeze. Even in here, something has reached her.

The film slowly builds on those themes, Carol's isolation from the world and her vulnerability to it. Julianne Moore, whose luminously pale skin and wide uncertain eyes give Carol the look of animated porcelain, is meticulously superficial in her performance. Carol lives entirely on the surface of her life.

She seems not only in denial about things going on beneath, but ignorant that there is even a beneath to deny. She is, essentially, alienated from herself. But when cracks start to appear in that surface, in increasingly terrifying ways, she is faced with what Haynes, in the notes accompanying the film's DVD release, calls a "sudden catastrophe of identity." In one scene, a woman at Carol's gym, talking about a self-help book she's reading, says, "We don't really own our own lives. We're told what to do, what to think. But emotionally, we're not really in charge." The movie charts Carol's ineffectual efforts to assert herself, to find a self to assert.

The degree of her emotional and spiritual detachment is illustrated early on in a profoundly unerotic sex scene. While her husband humps away, Carol lies stolidly beneath him, inexpressive and mostly unmoving. She doesn't just seem distracted; she seems absent. The first half of the film is full of scenes of Carol gazing blankly at something or someone, responding rotely when she responds at all. Even her smiles feel programmed. (Moore gives a more unnervingly robotic performance than any of the actors in the recent *Stepford Wives* remake.) At the gym, one of her friends notices that she doesn't even sweat. She keeps everything inside.

And then, little by little, things unravel. A two-piece couch is delivered in the wrong color, black instead of teal. It looms in the living room like a pair of beached orcas. Driving in traffic behind a large, exhaust-spewing truck, Carol goes into a severe coughing fit. Her sinuses run. She develops headaches. At the urging of a friend, she starts an all-fruit diet (to "cleanse the toxins" from her system). But that just makes her feel more rundown. She falls asleep at the dinner table. Her doctor tells her she's fine and suggests she see a therapist. The psychiatrist asks her, "What's going on in *you*?" Carol gazes back at him uncomprehendingly.

Looking in the mirror at the hairdresser's, she watches as a trickle of blood runs out of her nose. At a friend's baby shower, she has a panic attack and starts gasping for air. When her husband embraces her one morning after using spray-on deodorant and hair gel, she vomits. After seeing a flier at the gym about environmental illness ("Are you allergic to the 20th century?"), she goes to an informational meeting, and then to an allergist's office, where she goes into shock while being tested. The movie plays all of this like a slow, nauseating revelation, with lingering shots of the smog clouding the California highways, the bottles of hair formula at the beauty parlor, and the dense fog of insect-fumigation chemicals in the air at the dry cleaner's where Carol collapses in a seizure.

Haynes has called *Safe* a horror movie, and his strategy through its first half is to render everyday American life progressively sinister, until Carol seems trapped inside a poisoned world. The movie's design scheme reinforces this, with cool pastels in everything from clothing to interior decoration to the muted tones of the desert. These colors present themselves as soothing, but their repetition becomes something more like deadening. Haynes has said his cinematographer, Alex Nepomniaschy, suggested Antonioni's *Red Desert* as a model for the film's look.[5] *Safe* is deliberately less severe in its expression than Antonioni's fevered landscapes, but it suggests a world just as hostile to human habitation. Visually, Carol herself is kept remote, shown mostly in middle and long shots, emphasizing her isolation and denying the audience easy identification with her. How we are supposed to feel about Carol is ambiguous, all the way through the movie. How sick is she, really? And why? Her husband is presented as something of a dullard, but his incomprehension of her vague condition is understandable.

Carol's arrival at an isolated "wellness center" in rural New Mexico, with the innocuous name Wrenwood, is the point at which the film pivots, slowly and unpredictably. Until then, it seems to be largely an indictment of Carol's lifestyle and—by extension—the literal and emotional toxicity of modern American life. Wrenwood complicates the picture. Carol finds sympathy from its staff and other patients, but there are disquieting signs too. When she arrives in a taxi at the desert campus, she is greeted by a woman flailing and covering her mouth and screaming at the car to turn back. The woman is merely afraid of the taxi's exhaust fumes, but the alarming scene gives an edginess to the ostensibly bucolic setting. Carol meets people at the center with stories of personal healing, including its robust director, Claire. But she is uncertain how to respond to its upbeat, communal vibe. When the residents gather for a regular evening meeting, led by Wrenwood's charismatic founder, Peter Dunning, most of them clap and sing like congregants in an evangelical church. Carol stands still, bewildered. Even among her fellow sufferers, she is an island.

And there is something off-putting about Wrenwood's New Agey focus on personal growth as a strategy for fighting illness. Dunning introduces himself as HIV-positive, but says that he has kept himself healthy through sheer determination. *Safe* is, in its own way, as much an AIDS film as *Superstar* or *Poison*, but it came out at a time when attitudes toward the disease had shifted somewhat. Antiretroviral drugs had improved and life expectancy had lengthened, but all kinds of alternative theories and therapies had also emerged—among them, the kind of power of positive thinking preached by

Dunning. At first, Wrenwood seems like a warm and welcoming place. In a talk when Carol first arrives, Dunning says that people at Wrenwood have "left the judgmental behind." But bit by bit his emphasis on individual attitude starts to seem as judgmental in its own way as the paternalistic condescension of Carol's medical doctor. When one long-term resident dies, Dunning ascribes it to the man's failure to overcome his rage and find "a quiet life." In a lecture to the man's widow, Dunning tells her, "The only person who can make you sick is you. If our immune system is damaged, it's because we have allowed it to be." There is also a quick, telling shot of Dunning's house, an enormous mansion on a hill overlooking the Wrenwood campus. Other people's illnesses have been good to him.

Carol absorbs all of this, unquestioningly. Throughout the movie, she is consistently suggestible. When her friend urges a fruit diet, she does it. When she hears at an informational meeting that some people carry around oxygen tanks, it is only a matter of time before she is doing the same. When she sees an infomercial for Wrenwood, she decides to go there. And when one of the Wrenwood counselors says that some people require total isolation in a sterile environment, it is not hard to imagine that Carol will end up there, too. But all along, no matter what she does, she gets sicker and sicker. (Moore's physical transformation is as quietly remarkable as the rest of her performance. At the beginning of the movie, she looks fit and trim, but she becomes thinner and— almost impossibly—paler as it goes along. Carol develops dark circles under her eyes, and a mysterious blotch on her forehead that seems like a deliberate reference to the Kaposi sarcomas associated with AIDS.)

She does try to get involved in the life of Wrenwood, signing up to help cook dinner one night. And she engages in some chaste flirtation with a handsome young resident, Chris. But her efforts do not quite connect. The dinner goes well, but when Carol is asked to give a little speech at the end of the night, she delivers an awkward jumble that meanders through incoherent clichés about the state of the world. It sounds like a regurgitated mishmash of every awards speech and motivational tape she has ever heard, and it ends in a confused silence. As in so much of her life, Carol is going through motions that she does not really understand.

The movie's final scene finds Carol alone in her room—a small porcelain-lined dome. It is windowless, white and sterile, with greenish fluorescent lighting. Earlier in the movie, Wrenwood's director, Claire, has told Carol that when she first came to Wrenwood she locked herself in a room and looked at herself in a mirror all day, repeating, "Claire, I love you so much." This allowed her to strip everything else away, she says: "All that was left was me." And so the end of *Safe* finds Carol doing the same, facing herself in a mirror and mouthing, quietly, "I love you so much." But she is again just repeating words someone told her to say. Her expression is almost empty of emotion. She looks terrible.

So what, really, is wrong with Carol? *Safe* doesn't offer a single answer. Roger Ebert, in his review of the film, suggested, "maybe it's a tripleheader: Maybe the environment is poisoned, and the group is phony, and Carol is gnawing away at her own psychic health. Now there's a fine mess."[6] Or, Haynes might add, now there's America. Because what ties those three things together is the culture that all of them inhabit. Carol's alienation is not simply a product of personal psychosis. How can she *not* be alienated? She spends her days in large rooms in a large house, shut up behind a driveway gate in an exclusive community that is itself deliberately removed from most of the world. Her whole life is disconnected. (As a narrative strategy, it was smart of Haynes to give her a stepson rather than a son; having her own child would give her an easy external bond.) She treats her Mexican maid with a kind of absentminded arrogance, as if the maid were just more troublesome furniture.

But Carol is not alone in her disconnection; she is just an extreme example of a whole lifestyle built around the individual. It is a lifestyle that is alienated from the world it inhabits, and one that reached a new extreme in 1990s America, with its McMansions and SUVs and dislocated suburban office parks. For people who live from house to car to office to car and back, the "environment" becomes an abstraction. In one early scene, Carol falls asleep on her wrong-colored couch and wakes up to a late-night report on "deep ecology," an environmental movement based on "an understanding of the oneness of all life." These words play over a medium shot of Carol, alone in the dark. It is not hard to imagine her wondering, What oneness?

The flipside of that consumer lifestyle is the self-righteous philosophizing at Wrenwood, where residents are encouraged—and hectored—to turn inward for their answers. At one point, Dunning tells the residents that he has stopped reading newspapers, because he doesn't need their negativity. In its own way, this is a denial of the world as thorough as that of the isolated suburbanite. And both descend from the very American idea of the sovereign individual— the individual who has domain over nature, and can bend it to his or her will, is the same individual who has domain over the body, and can will it to sickness or health. Carol's alienation from the world is not just a symptom of her alienation from herself; both are symptoms of a broader malaise, an inability to connect.

The film's title suggests that the urge behind this drive for individual control is an impulse to render the world "safe" for ourselves. (The movie's anxieties prefigure the post-9/11 obsession with "security"; they suggest underlying insecurities in the culture that were lying in wait for new fears to attach themselves to.) The story traces more or less a straight line of retreat: first into the protective suburbs, behind the gate of the Whites' house, then into the haven of Wrenwood and finally into a single sterile room, all out of Carol's need to shield herself. But her sickness, like Poe's Red Death, follows her everywhere, because in one form or another it has infected everything.

Velvet Goldmine (1998)

WRITTEN BY: TODD HAYNES (FROM A STORY BY JAMES LYONS AND TODD HAYNES)

WITH: EWAN MCGREGOR (CURT WILD), JONATHAN RHYS MEYERS (BRIAN SLADE), CHRISTIAN BALE (ATHUR STUART), TONI COLLETTE (MANDY SLADE), EDDIE IZZARD (JERRY DEVINE), MICKO WESTMORELAND (JACK FAIRY)

What a riotous fantasy this movie is. Haynes' belated valentine to glam rock is a funhouse mirror ball, sparkling and spinning and distorting what it reflects. Part musical, part social history and part coming-out story, it pulls together Oscar Wilde, George Orwell, *Citizen Kane*, and space aliens in an ode to sexual liberation and rock 'n' roll. It is a very gay movie—a fairy tale in all senses of the phrase—but the freedom it celebrates is hardly exclusive to homosexuality. Like Linklater's *Dazed and Confused*, it recalls the years between the fracturing of traditional moral authority in the late 1960s and its reestablishment in the early 1980s, between the cracks in the edifice and the crackdown that followed. Although Haynes's film works very different territory than Linklater's—the world of British glam rockers rather than Texas potheads—both enshrine an era of youthful self-determination, when the kids knew best and all the grown-ups could do was wonder what had happened. And both function partly as time capsules of a cultural revolution, reminders of events that tend to get left out of official accounts.

Velvet Goldmine is, most obviously, a fantasy about David Bowie. The movie's title comes from a Bowie song (a B-side from the early 1970s). The story traces the rise and inevitable decline of a flamboyant, bisexual British pop star, Brian Slade, who tops the charts with a concept album about an alien named Maxwell Demon—a nod to Bowie's Ziggy Stardust. At the heart

Jonathan Rhys Meyers as the Bowie-ish Brian Slade in Todd Haynes's baroque tribute to glam rock, *Velvet Goldmine*. (Courtesy of Photofest)

of it is Slade's tumultuous friendship (which becomes something more) with an American rocker named Curt Wild, modeled loosely on Bowie's friendship with Iggy Pop. Slade also has a glamorous American party-girl wife, Mandy, an analog to Bowie's wife, Angie. Haynes sought permission to use Bowie's music but was refused, which probably works to the movie's benefit. The soundtrack's grab bag of period gems (like Brian Eno's "Baby's on Fire" and T-Rex's "20th Century Boy") combine with neo-glam originals by contemporary bands like Shudder to Think and Pulp to produce a gauzy, impressionistic portrait of the era. Having Bowie's own indelible songs in the mix might have tilted it toward tribute-band literalism, and trapped Jonathan Rhys Meyers, who plays Slade, into simply imitating Bowie rather than riffing on the *idea* of Bowie.

And it is the idea that matters to Haynes. Like *Superstar* (and, probably, like Haynes's forthcoming Bob Dylan movie), *Velvet Goldmine* is not a celebrity biography at all; it is a contemplation of the ways that celebrity and culture interact, the power of images in constructing an understanding of the world, and the relationship of the audience to the artist and vice versa. It is as dense with cultural, political, and historical references as *Poison*, but it integrates them much more successfully. Like an MGM musical, it explodes in periodic bursts of song and surrealism; but unlike a conventional musical, it never returns to any grounded normality. The movie is one long sequence of interwoven fantasies, some of them bright and some nightmarish, but none of them burdened with the responsibilities of realism. A movie like this has two complementary challenges: to sustain the dreamy flow of the story, yet not let it come completely untethered. It is a high-wire act, and Haynes—for the most part—dances right across. The film is airy but never slight, and coherent despite its complexity.

The only real misstep comes with the story's framing device, which is deliberately and a little clumsily lifted from *Citizen Kane*. On the 10th anniversary of a 1974 concert at which Brian Slade faked his own death, a British reporter for a New York newspaper is assigned to do a where-is-he-now story. As in Orson Welles's movie, the reporter tracks down old friends and associates for interviews; the first, Slade's former manager, is hospitalized and wheelchair-bound, just like Charles Foster Kane's old friend Jedediah Leland. And the reporter's conversation with Brian's ex-wife, Mandy, in a deserted nightclub is a ringer for the reporter's interview with Kane's former wife Susan (right down to the sign outside the club announcing "Mandy Slade Appearing Nightly"). But these echoes seem extraneous in a movie already thick with quotations of various kinds. There are some superficial similarities between Charles Foster Kane and Brian Slade—they are both self-invented, enigmatic and megalomaniacal—and both movies are cynical about the motives and methods of the mass media. The major difference here is that the reporter, Arthur Stuart, turns out to have been a peripheral participant in the events he's chronicling. But the problem is that *Citizen Kane* is too familiar and obvious a reference for the movie's purposes. As Bowie's songs might have done if they had been included, the appropriations from Welles bring too much cultural gravity of their own to fit neatly into Haynes's scheme; they weigh the movie down. Fortunately, they become less obtrusive as the film goes along.

At its glittery heart, *Velvet Goldmine* is a story about the liberation of identity (just as *Safe* is about its repression). It begins with a brazen bit of silliness, in which a spaceship swoops down on a city identified as "Dublin 1854 (birthplace of Oscar Wilde)." A maid discovers a swaddled baby abandoned on a doorstep, with a glowing emerald pin affixed to its blanket. A few years later, we see young Oscar in a classroom, declaring to his bewildered teacher, "I want to be a pop idol!" Wilde disappears from the story at that point, but the green gem resurfaces repeatedly—it is discovered by Jack Fairy, a character who seems like a fusion of Roxy Music's Brian Eno and Bryan Ferry, and then passed on to Brian Slade, Curt Wild and, eventually, Arthur.

The script is also littered with quotes from Wilde's writings (as when Brian says of Mandy, in a line from *The Portrait of Dorian Gray*, "Women defend themselves by attacking, just as they attack by sudden and strange surrenders"). The invocation of Wilde as both an otherwordly interloper and the forefather of modern glamour is funny, but it carries a hint of the story's ultimate sadness. What made Wilde alien and exciting—his sexuality, his eagerness to challenge and expose hypocrisy—also generated the backlash that broke him.

The film traces the birth and brief reign of glam rock through the late-adolescent eyes of Arthur Stuart. It is, necessarily, set in the U.K.; glam was a largely British phenomenon, and while its biggest names had some American success, its cultural impact in the States was marginal. The film is not, in that sense, autobiographical; besides being American, Haynes has said in interviews that he only really discovered the glam scene retrospectively, in the 1980s. But he clearly loves the blaring swagger of the music, its theatricality and teasing provocation, and his re-creation of its ebullient milieu in early-1970s London seems faithful in spirit if not in fact. Glam evolved, as the movie playfully documents, from the fashion-conscious Mod subculture of the 1960s. It also reflected the rising visibility and tolerance of homosexuality, which was illegal in Britain until 1967. With its emphasis on makeup, androgyny and Space Age wardrobes, glam presented a vision of a polymorphously perverse future.

Arthur begins the movie as an insecure schoolboy, secretly drawn to the new music, scribbling portraits of Brian Slade in his composition books. He buys the *Maxwell Demon* album at a record store, enduring the hoots and taunts of other boys, and sneaks it home in a brown paper bag like contraband. In his bedroom, he locks the door, puts on the record and avidly pores through music magazines. There is poignance and urgency in these scenes, a sense of the liberating power of art. What Arthur finds in the music, and in images of Brian Slade kissing Curt Wild, is recognition, and validation. In an interview with *The Advocate*, Haynes said, "We felt it was important how this whole thing worked on a young fan: the idea of this kiss being photographed and reproduced and disseminated and then getting to the kid who opens the paper. Desire travels through our little capital system that way."[7]

The film extends that sense of self-discovery to the entire era. In a news conference, Brian Slade gives cavalier answers to reporters' leering questions about his sexuality. "I am married," he says. "Quite happily, in fact. I just happen to like boys as much as I like girls." Recalling the moment 12 years later, Mandy says to Arthur, "Did he realize what he'd actually done? How could he have? I mean, today, there'd be fighting in the streets. But in 1972, it was more like *dancing*." Watching the news conference at home with his oblivious parents, Arthur is transfixed. He imagines jumping up and shouting to his mother and father, "That's me! That's me!" Instead, he sneaks out of the house in tight, sparkly T-shirts and meets up with other glam kids. When his father later discovers him masturbating (as *Maxwell Demon* blares on the stereo) and excoriates him for bringing "shame into this house," Arthur leaves home for good. It is a compact, convincing portrait of a young man's coming out.

In all of this, Haynes is hewing close enough to the record. Bowie famously declared himself bisexual, as did Lou Reed and enough others of the moment for the rock critic Lester Bangs to write an essay saluting the emergence of the queer rock star. The movie takes considerably more liberties in the relationship of Brian Slade and Curt Wild, essentially imagining a love affair between Bowie and Iggy Pop. (Haynes includes a clever scene of schoolgirls acting out the relationship with Brian and Curt dolls—deliberately referencing his own *Superstar*, but also suggesting the ways that fans playact their fantasies through celebrities.) In fact, a scene in which Brian and Curt are found naked in bed is a reference to an anecdote Angela Bowie told in her autobiography, about finding her husband similarly entangled with Mick Jagger. Like the movie's other references to pop lore, the scene works whether or not you know the backstory. Haynes the semiotician has learned to construct multiple layers of meaning and cross-reference without diminishing any of them; the surface is as important as what is beneath it. Really, *Velvet Goldmine* is a swooning testimonial to the power of surfaces—the way lipstick and mascara can bring out something lurking inside—even as it reveals, inevitably, the limited correlation between glitter and gold.

Just as Brian Slade's story slides into a rock-star cliché of drugs and irrelevancy (a cliché Haynes has fun with, showing Slade inhaling mass quantities of cocaine off nude male buttocks), the free-spirited 1970s that Haynes encapsulates in his breathless title sequence—boys and girls in furs, feathers, and stack heels running down London streets—give way to a grim, fascistic 1980s. The latter-day scenes are identified as "New York 1984," but it's an imaginary city that draws more on Orwell (and Terry Gilliam's *Brazil*) than any real place. The buildings are gray, the streets are lined with military police, the people are morose, and giant TV screens pump out cheery messages about the activities of "President Reynolds" and a slick pop singer named Tommy Stone. The contrast between the two decades suggests what the ascendance of Ronald Reagan and the "Moral Majority" felt like to an American—particularly a gay American—who came of age at the height of 1970s libertinism.

The film is full of good performances. Christian Bale is suitably poker-faced as the older Arthur, never letting on his own connection to the story, and palpably excited as the younger glam-era Arthur. Jonathan Rhys Meyers fulfills the most important part of the Brian Slade role, which is to look stunning in a range of ludicrous outfits, from sundresses to spacesuits; his alabaster cheekbones and cold eyes make the character's various turns seem natural. And Toni Collette, as Mandy, gives the movie its most full-bodied (and warm-blooded) character, as a woman more in love with her husband than she can let herself show. Only the top-billed Ewan McGregor, who was on the verge of stardom when the movie came out, has some diffi-culty finding a consistent tone. That's not entirely his fault. Haynes ev-idently decided to turn Curt Wild into not only a reimagined Iggy Pop (McGregor does an enthusiastic imitation of Pop's wild-man live show), but also, with his long blond bangs, a double for Kurt Cobain. Although this suggests some potentially interesting things about the pop-idol continuum and its recurrent tragedies, it also feels like one more idea than the movie needs.

On the other hand, "one more idea" is sort of Haynes's *modus operandi*. And in most of *Velvet Goldmine*, he shows both confidence and skill in his ability to weave together any number of elements—fake TV reports, music videos, newspaper headlines, flashbacks, fast-forwards—to tell a story that is coherent without being linear. The musical sequences show the influence of both movie musicals and music videos, incorporating the offhand surrealism of the latter into the narrative functions of the former. Haynes has noted in interviews that music videos had themselves appropriated montage and narrative techniques from decades of experimental film. So to some degree what Haynes is doing is repatriating those techniques in the service of his story. (He anticipated a lot of what Baz Luhrmann did a few years later in his enjoyably ludicrous *Moulin Rouge!*, which also starred McGregor.) Visually fluid and more artfully arranged than its bedazzled mosaic approach suggests at first glance, *Velvet Goldmine* is a work of bravura filmmaking.

The movie's eventual revelation that Brian Slade has turned himself into the bland pop star Tommy Stone is no surprise—especially considering that Tommy Stone's sleek white suits and coiffed hair are not so subtly remi-niscent of early 1980s David Bowie. This was the Bowie who recanted his earlier sexual identification, declaring himself firmly heterosexual and marry-ing a supermodel, and topped the charts with slick electro-funk. (It was *good* electro-funk, but that might not have mattered too much to anyone person-ally invested in the transgressive stance of his earlier records.) The movie's depiction of Brian Slade as an unabashed opportunist is really just the flipside of Bowie's much-touted abilities as a pop chameleon, able to change with the times and the fashions. It also makes some sense of Bowie's refusal to let Haynes use his music; the portrait might be an affectionate one, but it isn't exactly flattering.

But the betrayals in the film's story can't negate the giddy force of its glam sequences, or its music. A final montage shows the way the music lingers, years after its heyday; beginning with Jack Fairy singing a song onstage, it glides to Arthur and Curt Wild lounging on a London rooftop, then through overhead shots of hypnotized-looking schoolchildren, all entranced by the music, and finally into a dark workingman's bar, where the music is reverberating from a tinny radio. In a voice-over narration at the beginning of the film, a woman's soft British voice says, "Histories, like ancient ruins, are the fictions of empires—while everything forgotten hangs in dark dreams of the past, ever threatening to return." *Velvet Goldmine* is a sumptuous attempt to keep some of those dark dreams alive.

Far from Heaven (2002)
WRITTEN BY: TODD HAYNES
WITH: JULIANNE MOORE (CATHY WHITAKER), DENNIS
    QUAID (FRANK WHITAKER), DENNIS HAYSBERT (RAY-
    MOND DEAGAN), PATRICIA CLARKSON (ELEANOR FINE),
    CELIA WESTON (MONA LAUDER)

Turning from one artistic obsession to another, Haynes followed his musical mash note with this lyrical reinvention of the 1950s melodramas of Douglas Sirk. But like *Velvet Goldmine*, *Far from Heaven* is a lot more than an exercise in stylistic homage. Sirk's best-known films (*All That Heaven Allows*, *Imitation of Life*) revolve around the fault lines where social mores meet private lives. In *Far from Heaven*, those fault lines are race and sexuality, and Haynes navigates them with characteristic intelligence. By placing them within a highly stylized evocation of an earlier era, he simultaneously spins sardonic commentary on that era and gently lays bare conceits about our own.

Reviews of the film understandably focused on its meticulous evocation of Sirk's style, with its hypersaturated colors, dramatic shadows, and vivid, idealized natural settings. But what some critics read as either irony or mere imitation is something both more straightforward and subtle. Haynes adopts the Sirk template not to critique it or merely to pay tribute to it, but mostly to *use* it—to derive from it the same heightened emotional and aesthetic effects that Sirk did. In one interview, he said he thought of the film in some ways as a Sirk movie that Sirk didn't get the chance to make: "Sirk has made reference to wishing he could do a story about a gay man at the time but wasn't able to in that period. So, I suppose I took my lead from that."[8]

The movie tells the story of Frank and Cathy Whitaker, another of Haynes's perfect-on-the-surface families (like the Carpenters in *Superstar*, the Beacons in *Poison* and the Whites in *Safe*). They live on the affluent side of Hartford, Connecticut, where Frank is an executive at a leading local company called Magnatech, and Cathy watches over their two children (with the assistance of a full-time housekeeper) and busies herself in local social circles. The film opens with a lyrical shot of downtown Hartford in autumn, bright yellow and red leaves fluttering in golden sunlight. The dialogue is stilted for effect—the children, picture-perfect bobbins, say things like "Aw, shucks" and unfailingly address their parents as "Mother" and "Father." Cathy and Frank are, literally, a model couple; they pose for Magnatech advertisements and have earned the title "Mr. and Mrs. Magnatech."

But small hints of trouble abound. Frank goes out after work for drinks, without telling his wife. She gets a call one night from the police department, where Frank is stewing after being picked up for public intoxication and "loitering" (he calls it "a big mix-up"). When she tries to comfort him later that night with hugs and kisses, he tenses up and inches away from her, saying he's "so tired." In a giggling discussion with other local wives, Cathy is surprised to hear that some of their husbands want to have sex as often as once a week, or even three times that.

Of course, what Frank is really doing in his late hours is stalking the back rows of the downtown Hartford movie theater, watching flirtations and assignations among discreet men in the shadows. Eventually, he follows a few of them to a gay bar at the end of a long alley, where he begins flirtations of his own. Cathy, meanwhile, has struck up a friendship with her new gardener, Raymond, a college-educated black man with a warm smile. A reporter for a local society paper notes their interaction in a puff-piece profile of Cathy, calling her "a woman as devoted to her family as she is kind to negroes."

These strands collide when Cathy pays a surprise late-night visit to Frank's office and finds him embracing and kissing another man. Even as Frank, in his humiliation, agrees to seek psychiatric help, Cathy finds herself drawn to Raymond—especially after encountering him at an art show in town, where he turns out to know much more about art than she does.

Haynes's two stories have preordained endings: Frank's "treatment" will fail, and so will Cathy's tentative relationship with Raymond. On the one hand, Frank can't conquer or suppress who he really is. On the other, no amount of good will or even the potential of romance can overcome the thorny social barriers between Cathy and Raymond. Their tentative courtship faces hostility from both white and black communities. Turning the clock back from the liberating moment of *Velvet Goldmine*, Haynes details a society in transition. By setting it in the Northeast, he avoids the easy comfort of making American racism a regional problem. In a telling scene at a cocktail party hosted by Frank and Cathy, one woman frets that "what happened in Little Rock could just as easily have happened here in Hartford." "Nonsense," responds another guest, a small balding white man. "For one thing, there's no Governor Faubus in Connecticut. But the main reason? There are no negroes." As his listeners chortle, a black caterer walks by with a tray of canapés.

The black neighborhoods of Hartford are as invisible in their own way as its furtive gay nightlife is. Haynes aims to bring both of them to light, expanding the world of the era. His illumination does not invalidate our existing lily-white stereotypes of the 1950s so much as augment them, adding back things that were left out of the picture. As in *Velvet Goldmine*, he is filling in around the edges of official history. The movie suggests that, somewhere offscreen in all those Sirk films—and all of the other films of that era—these things were going on too. (Maybe literally, considering the prominent role played in several of Sirk's movies by Rock Hudson, who at the time was already widely known in Hollywood to be gay.)

Frank finds his own way into the city's gay life, albeit with the lurking threat of arrest on morals charges. But Cathy needs Raymond to give her entrée to his side of town. "There is a world even here in Hartford where everybody does indeed look like me," he tells her. He takes her to a favorite hangout, a restaurant and bar, where the black staff and patrons react with suspicion to a white woman in their midst. Their hostility gives a sense of the racial danger bubbling underneath the city's surface. By taking Cathy out in public, Raymond is risking not only his own (brown) skin, but that of anyone who might be associated with him.

That risk is most clearly felt in a scene where Cathy tells Raymond they shouldn't pursue their friendship any further. They have become the subject of eyebrow-raising gossip around town, and even Frank has angrily reproached her for causing speculation that could damage his social standing. (While Frank's outrage could seem merely ironic, considering his own compromised position, Haynes positions it a little differently. Frank has been made ashamed in front of his wife by his homosexuality, and now he has an opportunity to return some of the shame to her.) But when Cathy apologetically tells all of this to Raymond on a downtown sidewalk, he is hurt and angry, and reaches a hand out to her wrist as she starts to walk away. Instantly, as if some racial alarm had sounded, a white man in a suit across the street yells out at Raymond, "You, boy! Hands off!" Haynes drops the camera into one of his low-angle horror shots, and turns the entire block suddenly menacing, full of white people turning to glare at a black man with his hand on a white woman. The precariousness of Raymond's position is laid bare. On the street, in public, he has no power. Neither his education nor his physical strength are worth anything. Cathy senses the shift and understands it too.

Haynes ratchets up the sense of peril in the movie's most horrifying scene, in which a group of white boys chases Raymond's daughter. Word of Cathy and Raymond's near-dalliance has reached the schoolyard, and the boys take it on themselves to act as white Hartford's avengers. They pursue the girl into a dead-end alley, and then pelt her with rocks until one stone knocks her unconscious. There are consequences for the boys—one of them is expelled from school—but the incident convinces Raymond he needs to leave town. As he tells Cathy when she comes to visit him, "I've learned my lesson about mixing in other worlds." In a symbolic reversal, Raymond makes Cathy come around to the side entrance of his house to speak to him. It is a precautionary measure—it's not safe for either of them for her to be seen on his porch—but it is also a continuation of Cathy's education in what it is like to be treated as an Other, someone not good enough to come in through the front door. That Raymond takes some slight satisfaction in this, and that Cathy accepts the slight humiliation, is crucial to their understanding of each other as equals.

Meanwhile, Frank's ultimate embrace of his homosexuality is presented as liberating, for all of its difficulties. Despite everything Frank is giving up—his family, his career, his standing in society—Haynes refuses to make him a martyr. In actual films of the 1950s and 1960s, gay characters, when they appeared at all, were almost uniformly made to suffer. Even gay writers, like Tennessee Williams in *Suddenly Last Summer*, tended to portray homosexuality as almost inherently tragic. In contrast, Frank suffers most when he is in the closet. As long as he is trying to suppress his homosexuality, he is alternately weak, angry and morose—and, often, drunk. He starts to seem strong only after a breakdown in which he confesses, sobbing, that he has fallen in love for the first time in his life, and it is with another man.

Throughout, Haynes's command of the Sirkian style is close to masterful. He creates a fantasy world, every bit as much as he did in *Velvet Goldmine*, but a subtly and coherently imagined one. Its dreamy qualities—like the rich autumnal colors in the trees, in Cathy's auburn hair, and in the gold and yellow dresses of her kaffeeklatsch friends—give a sensation of heightened perception, as if the whole film were a little intoxicated. Haynes has great fun with the styles and fashions of the era, from a child's Radio Flyer bicycle to the fresh modernism of the Miami hotel where Frank and Cathy vacation. The newness and sleekness of the designs, like the striking modern art displayed in an exhibit attended by Hartford's high society, suggest the rumbling momentum of liberation gathering beneath the culture's controlled surface. Haynes' characters don't know what's coming a few years down the road, but Haynes does. And just as the exuberance of *Velvet Goldmine* is tempered by hindsight, the depiction of the constricted 1950s is colored with an awareness of the shocks to come. In different ways, Frank, Cathy, and Raymond all prefigure those shocks, and suggest how far back their roots extend.

The fourth major character in the film is the Whitakers' maid, Sybil, a black woman who watches the family's tribulations with a mixture of concern and admiration. She is troubled by Cathy's growing closeness with Raymond, but glad to see her getting involved with the NAACP. In *Safe*, Carol White's icy imperiousness toward her maid was one more symptom of her disconnection; here, Cathy's refusal to condescend to or bully Sybil are marks of her egalitarian instincts. Of all the white characters in the movie, Cathy is the only one who seems to recognize a shared humanity that transcends race.

Haynes's evocation of 1950s films is helped immeasurably by a lush, melancholy score, for which he cannily recruited the Hollywood veteran Elmer Bernstein, who was then nearing 80. Bernstein had composed the music for 1950s dramas like *The Man with the Golden Arm* and *Sweet Smell of Success*, and *Far from Heaven* represented a literal return to form, a period piece free of both nostalgia and pastiche (traits that might have been difficult for a younger composer to avoid). In an interview included with the DVD release, Bernstein says, "The nature of the film allowed me to write the kind of music I haven't been able to write for a long time." It earned him his 14th Oscar nomination (he won only once, for *Thoroughly Modern Mille* in 1967). It was also his last major work; he died in 2004.

For all of its fidelity to an anachronistic style, *Far from Heaven* had plenty of contemporary resonance. Just as *Poison* and *Safe* reflected the emergence of AIDS, *Far from Heaven* arrived on the cusp of a national political fight over gay marriage. Its sympathetic portrait of people both kept apart and forced together by social conventions could hardly seem dated in a country where religious groups were lobbying (with significant success) to restrict the definition of marriage to "a man and a woman."

But beyond politics, the movie succeeds on its own terms: as a drama about three people caught between opposing internal and external forces. In the "making of" feature on the DVD, Dennis Quaid says, "It would have been very easy to parody these people. But there's an emotional integrity to the writing, which I think translates to the screen." Haynes speaks in similar terms: "We all wanted it to be a film that affected us emotionally, affected the viewer emotionally." But he achieves that effect by means of deliberately stilted dialogue and performances, and by drawing on and playing with the audience's collective understanding of the form in which he's working. He is a comfortably postmodern filmmaker, but his postmodernism is never an end in itself; it's just a set of tools and references that he uses to tell the stories that he wants to tell.

Writing in *The New York Times* about the controversy over *Poison*, the critic Caryn James said, "Like Genet, whose release from a lifelong prison sentence was accomplished with the help of Jean-Paul Sartre and Simone de Beauvoir, Mr. Haynes has gone from being the outlaw creator of 'Superstar' to being a praised film maker taken up by the intelligentsia. Soon he will probably be eminently acceptable to the mainstream. Who knows yet whether that is Mr. Haynes's blessing or his curse?"[9] She wasn't completely wrong about his career trajectory, but nobody could have predicted the not-very-traveled paths he would take along the way. There are thematic connections between all of his films—identity and its repression, alienation, an often frustrated urge toward transcendence—but they are very different in subject and style. What is most consistently striking about them is Haynes's ability to pull together personal obsessions, pop cultural riffs and sociopolitical ideas, ransacking genres and forms of the past to create his own dense, deeply felt fantasias.

Because so many of his ideas are lifted from existing sources, it is maybe easy to overlook the fierce originality of his talent. Although *Poison* showed him still experimenting with techniques of storytelling and editing, not always success-fully, his three subsequent movies have been imaginative and accomplished. As much as any contemporary director, he is able to create entire worlds for his stories, using a range of strategies to convey his ideas. Even when his movies look something like "normal" movies—as in *Safe* and *Far from Heaven*—they are engaged in subtle subversions of form and content. *Safe* in particular has acquired stature over the decade since its release. In a *Village Voice* poll of film critics in 1999, it was named the best movie of the 1990s.

Among the least predictable projects Haynes could have turned to after the relatively high-profile success of *Far from Heaven* was a biography of Bob Dylan. Even given the wide range of Haynes's cultural influences, it is not an immediately obvious pairing. But Dylan, like Haynes, is a specialist in the manipulation of surfaces—willfully reinventing himself throughout his career—and his magpie aesthetic, appropriating styles and identities as he sees fit, has some similarities to Haynes's own. Haynes's announced decision to cast seven or eight different actors in the role, playing different aspects of Dylan's persona, sounds like a strategy to exploit that common ground. Haynes's instincts are typically well attuned to the culture; Dylan has had another of his renaissances in the past decade, releasing three well-received albums (the most recent, *Modern Times*, gave him his first number one album in 30 years), writing a best-selling memoir, and working with Martin Scorsese on a popular PBS documentary about his early years. More importantly, Dylan is a pop culture icon of a far greater magnitude than Karen Carpenter or even David Bowie. As one of the leading pop iconoclasts of his generation, Haynes probably could not resist the opportunity.

4
PAUL THOMAS ANDERSON

I t is easy to make too much of the fact that Paul Tomas Anderson was born (on June 26, 1970) in Studio City, California. What is probably more telling is that his father, Ernie, was a television voice actor and former Cleveland TV horror-show host. So Anderson was born into show business, but into the workaday margins of the industry. He himself worked his way in from those margins, shunning film school (he quit New York University's program after two days) in favor of production assistant jobs on TV shows, videos and wherever else he could find work. His first real opportunity as a director came in 1993, when he presented a short film called *Cigarettes and Coffee* at the Sundance festival. The film, an early indication of his interest in intersecting characters and storylines, jumped between three conversations in a diner that are eventually shown to be connected. On the strength of that, he was offered a spot in the Sundance Institute's filmmaker's program, where he fleshed out one of the segments of *Cigarettes and Coffee* into what became his first feature, *Hard Eight.*

Like most American directors of his generation, Anderson has obvious roots in the cinema of the 1970s. His first two films in particular show the imprint of Martin Scorsese, in the restless energy of the camera, the crisp pacing, the smart use of popular music and the low-life seedy settings. Similarly, the large casts and overlapping plotlines of *Boogie Nights* and *Magnolia* show a clear debt to Robert Altman. But Anderson's thematic concerns and perspective on his characters are distinctively his. His movies have their share of violence and emotional rawness, but there is something fundamentally warm about them. Almost every film ends with at least the possibility of redemption for the characters' assorted sins. At the same time, the limits of that redemption are usually clear. Anderson's empathy is joined to what could only be called a traumatized view of human—and especially family—relations.

One of his abiding themes is the search for surrogate love among people who have been cut off for one reason or another from their real parents or children. He presents over and over again the idea of the family home as a kind of poisoned Eden, a place that cannot be returned to but that marks its exiles for life. Sometimes the alienation takes extreme forms, as in *Magnolia*'s molestation plotline. But more often it is the result of less obvious forms of hurt: domineering or absent parents, drug addiction, the suffocating pressures of an overly "close" family. Fleeing all of these things, Anderson's characters seek comfort and connection with other domestic refugees, constructing ad hoc family lives that inevitably bear the scars of past experience. (It seems no accident that Anderson himself has created a sort of loose family of collaborators, with many of his actors and crew carrying over from one film to the next.) The hope that Anderson's films hold out for these imperfect relationships, romantic and otherwise, is always shaded by the knowledge of the damage that they can do. And that sense of danger is heightened by the way the films present even the least likable characters at their most vulnerable and pitiable. In Anderson's view of the world, no amount of scarring is enough to thicken the skin, and everybody can always be hurt again—which makes the way his characters continually reach for love and sympathy seem both brave and foolish.

The same could be said of his films, which have garnered him wide but hardly universal admiration. He takes formal risks that do not always pay off, and he has been tagged by some critics as a sentimentalist. The rain of frogs that intercedes at the end of *Magnolia* is among the most critically divisive plot devices of the past few decades. How you respond to it depends partly on how much you're willing to credit Anderson's insistence that there is hope even for the most damaged. Given the grimness of much of what he presents, it is a sometimes strained and dissonant position. In some ways, Anderson's real antecedent is Frank Capra, whose best-known morality tales (*It's a Wonderful Life, Meet John Doe, Mr. Smith Goes to Washington*) exposed the corruption and dishonesty of social institutions (the capitalist system, the media, politics) only to then assert that they can overcome by sheer force of good will. Similarly, Anderson lays bare the emotional (and sometimes physical) violence of family life and relationships only to reach for some kind of reassurance that love can, in fact, beat back fear and loss. It is a provisional and conditional argument—none of his films end on notes of triumph as transcendent as Capra's—but also a determinedly uncynical one.

Hard Eight (1996)
WRITTEN BY: PAUL THOMAS ANDERSON
WITH: PHILIP BAKER HALL (SYDNEY), JOHN C. REILLY
(JOHN FINNEGAN), GWYNETH PALTROW (CLEMENTINE),
SAMUEL L. JACKSON (JIMMY), PHILIP SEYMOUR HOFFMAN
(YOUNG CRAPS PLAYER)

These abiding themes show up clearly in Anderson's first film, *Hard Eight*. (Anderson had originally titled the film *Sydney*, and was unhappy about the name change forced on him by the studio.) Broadly, it is an almost Dickensian story about an orphan being adopted by the man who killed his father. In the very first scene, which introduces the gruffly paternalistic Sydney and the young naïf John, we learn that John has lost his mother. Sydney, played with inscrutable toughness by Philip Baker Hall, is the first of several deeply flawed father figures in Anderson's films, although exactly how flawed he is takes some time to uncover. From the outset, his affection for John seems genuine if a bit mysterious. Sydney presents himself as a man who keeps clear of emotional attachments—he is traveling alone, and in his early conversations with John he makes no reference to any wife or children. It is not immediately obvious why he reaches out to John, who seems like a hapless loser—literally, since he's just lost his gambling stake trying to win money for his mother's funeral.

Sydney's intentions toward the cocktail waitress/part-time prostitute Clementine are initially just as opaque. He flirts with her—or, at least, is receptive to her flirtation—and takes her to a diner, where he peppers her with questions about her personal life. Clementine notes that John idolizes Sydney—he walks like Sydney walks and even orders the same drinks. She asks if Sydney has any "real kids"; his answer provides the first insight into Sydney's personal history: he has children about the same age as Clementine and John, and he has lost contact with them.

When Sydney takes Clementine back to his hotel room, Anderson initially leaves his motives ambiguous. As she sits on the bed, fidgeting, while he goes to get her a bathrobe and towel, the movie flirts with a kind of surrogate incest—Is Sydney's fatherly interest in Clementine a cover for sexual desire? Anderson's awareness of the sexual undercurrents of family life is Freudian but not didactic. He is troubled by them, but also presents them as inevitable.

When Clementine baldly asks Sydney if he wants to "fuck" her, she is trying to resolve the ambiguity of the situation for herself by taking control of it, treating it as just another sex-for-pay encounter. When Sydney says no, she is confused. But when he tells her that she's sleeping in John's bed (although he promises John won't disturb her), the situation becomes clearer. He has procured her for John. This is made even more explicit the next morning, when John bashfully asks Sydney if he had had sex with Clementine. He is greatly relieved when Sydney says no.

When Sydney suggests that John take Clementine shopping, he is playing matchmaker. He is also, gently but unmistakably, asserting control over their lives. They mostly acquiesce, although John refuses Sydney's offer of spending cash, saying "I've got money, Syd." That night, when John calls from a hotel where he and Clementine have taken a recalcitrant prostitution client of Clementine's hostage, the nascent family relationships become even more obvious. Sydney is angry about the situation, but it's an anger of disappointment, a parent's anger at willful children. He repeatedly threatens to leave and force them to deal with it on their own, but of course he doesn't. After berating them, he finally takes charge and convinces them to do what he tells them—at which point he again becomes affectionate and solicitous, as long as they do what he says. Clementine tearfully apologizes for what was clearly an act of rebellion in soliciting the client in the first place; she has been pulled into Sydney and John's orbit, and the pickup seems like an act of self-assertion. But Sydney's firmness and John's affection pull her back into the family.

John's relationship to Sydney remains fiercely filial throughout. When he brings his friend Jimmy over to Sydney's table early in the movie, it is with the air of a son introducing a friend to his father. And when Sydney shows an obvious dislike for the crude, swaggering Jimmy, John is clearly wounded. He wants Sydney's approval.

Of course, when Jimmy later reveals to Sydney what he knows about Sydney's past, we're able to grasp just how perverse the family scenario is. Sydney killed John's father, then sort of adopted the adult John and now has set him up in a more or less arranged marriage with a prostitute. We can guess that he was driven by guilt to seek out John. But there is more to his motivation—he's lonely. His alienation from his own family (which we can only guess was due to bad behavior on his part) has left him quietly desperate for a substitute. In finding two people with no plans and little resources (in the conversation at the diner, Clementine reveals she has no savings and no particular goals), he is able to make them his surrogate children.

How important the relationships are to him is evident from his reaction to Jimmy's attempt at blackmail. Despite a show of sputtering anger, Sydney caves in quickly. The scene where he pays off Jimmy is one of only two in the film where he appears vulnerable (the other is when he lets a young craps player goad him into a stupid bet). But vulnerability doesn't suit him. He is furious at Jimmy for finding a weak spot and exploiting it, and he also knows that despite Jimmy's assurances, there will be more demands for money to come. And when he murders Jimmy, we finally see the depths of Sydney's brutality. We already know he has killed people in the past, but his calm determination as he waits for hours in Jimmy's house, and his unhesitating execution of Jimmy even when he arrives with a prostitute in tow, suggest the likely dimensions of his past misdeeds.

The final scene, with Sydney back at the diner where he first met John, brings the film full circle. Noticing blood on his cuff, he simply pulls his coat sleeve down to conceal it and continues with his meal. We now know that even in the very first scene, while he was sitting in the same restaurant talking to John, he was already steeped in blood.

How we are meant to respond to all this is left unclear. Anderson is careful to build sympathy for his three central characters, so that we're already invested in them by the time the revelations come. The affection between Sydney and John, and then between both of them and Clementine, is endearing. Its foundation is troubled all the way around, though, and it would be a stretch to call the ending happy. The odds of John and Clementine having a lasting marriage seem slim, as do the odds of Sydney successfully hiding his history from John forever. The film's title itself comes from a long-odds craps roll of double 4's, and suggests that all three of them are making a bad bet. But Anderson finds something hopeful about the gamble—not so much in its chance of success as in the fact that people are willing to make it anyway. If there is hope for his characters, it can only come from a willingness to suspend doubt and believe in each other, however unwisely. Anderson is not a religious filmmaker, but his stories play as secular struggles of faith.

Technically and visually, *Hard Eight* is modest but with hints of more audacious filmmaking to come. A few tracking shots that follow Sydney through casinos have some of the kinetic buzz of the fluid camerawork in Scorsese's and Brian De Palma's movies. The opening scene, framed so that Sydney in the foreground looms darkly over John in the distance, is an obvious bit of foreshadowing that feels a little clumsy. So does the artificial suspense generated when Sydney enters the hotel room where John and Clementine have taken their hostage: although Sydney immediately sees the full room, the camera restricts its—and the audience's—view to him and John, so that for several seconds the audience doesn't know what Sydney is reacting to. It is an easy trick, and it seems cheap. On the other hand, the build-up to Sydney's murder of Jimmy is handled effectively, with shots of Jimmy gambling and carousing interspersed with shots of Sydney waiting calmly at his darkened house.

Among the most satisfying aspects of the movie is its evocation of the gambling life—not as a glitzy world of high-stakes players but as a nocturnal, morally unsteady place populated by lonely people. (There is more than a little Edward Hopper in Anderson's images of wan hotel rooms and late-night diners.) The casinos and hotels are neither glamorous nor foreboding, just banal, predictable, blankly comfortable. For Sydney, gambling is just a job, and these places are where he works. Anderson's subsequent movies are more crowded and varied in their settings, but they show a similar awareness of the mundane worlds of work and home.

Hard Eight is notable for the number of partnerships it initiates between Anderson and his cast and crew. Philip Baker Hall and John C. Reilly reappear in his next two movies, and Philip Seymour Hoffman (who steals a small scene as the gambler who goads Sydney) is in the next three. The score is by Michael Penn and Jon Brion, with a song over the end credits by Penn's wife Aimee Mann. Brion also scored *Magnolia* and *Punch-Drunk Love*, as well as the forthcoming *There Will Be Blood*. And Mann's songs serve as a Greek chorus in *Magnolia*.

One other point of interest: When Jimmy tells Sydney that he knows some of Sydney's old acquaintances back east, the names he drops are Floyd Gondolli and Jimmy Gator. In an Anderson in-joke, those became the names of Philip Baker Hall's characters in *Boogie Nights* and *Magnolia*.

Boogie Nights (1997)

WRITTEN BY: PAUL THOMAS ANDERSON

WITH: MARK WAHLBERG (EDDIE ADAMS/DIRK DIGGLER), BURT REYNOLDS (JACK HORNER), JULIANNE MOORE (AMBER WAVES), JOHN C. REILLY (REED ROTHCHILD), HEATHER GRAHAM (ROLLERGIRL), DON CHEADLE (BUCK SWOPE), WILLIAM H. MACY (LITTLE BILL), ROBERT RIDGELY (THE COLONEL JAMES), PHILIP SEYMOUR HOFFMAN (SCOTTY J.), LUIZ GUZMAN (MAURICE)

Anderson's ode to the pornography industry was his critical and commercial breakthrough. He moved confidently from the small-scale insularity of *Hard*

Eight to a multicharacter tableau with an ambling narrative that stretches to a leisurely 156 minutes. Loosely based on the life of porn star John Holmes, it follows the story of 17-year-old Eddie Adams, who is inducted into sex films by director Jack Horner.

In interviews, Anderson has said that the inspiration for *Boogie Nights* came from his childhood in Studio City, when a neighbor told him a pornographic film was being shot inside a nearby house. "And I clearly remember thinking, 'Wow! I want to see what's going on in there,'" he said.[1]

The world he has imagined behind those blacked-out windows is a strikingly, if perversely, tender one. The life of John Holmes could lend itself to a grim, sordid treatment—he was a porn star/drug addict who died of AIDS and was implicated in a brutal murder, as detailed in the considerably darker 2003 film *Wonderland*. But for all the period details in *Boogie Nights*, and all the bad things that happen in it, Anderson is not primarily interested in the degradation. The film's real story is how people whose lives and families have failed them, or who have failed their lives and families, can find some kind of connection and intimacy.

Boogie Nights begins with elegiac orchestral horns over a black screen, before bursting to life with a blast of light funk and neon signs along a commercial strip that's identified as "San Fernando Valley, 1977." The camera trollies in toward the entrance to a club called Hott Trax. It follows Jack and his star actress Amber into the club and then glides through the crowd, introducing the major characters in a fast-moving, disco-fueled tracking shot that again evokes Scorsese and De Palma.

Boogie Nights tackles the family dynamic from several angles at once. If *Hard Eight* is Anderson's *Great Expectations*, this is his *Oliver Twist*. As in *Hard Eight*, he presents a makeshift clan, cobbled together from the castoffs of other households. And also as before, Anderson presents the surrogate family—however dysfunctional—as preferable to the real family. The only characters whose backgrounds we learn anything about are Eddie and Amber, and both of them are painfully alienated from blood relations. Eddie's family, glimpsed in just a handful of early scenes, is a bed of Freudian antagonism. His mother is shrill and domineering, badgering her meek husband at the breakfast table and harassing Eddie about his jobs and his girlfriends. Eddie is on the verge of leaving home at the beginning of the film, and his mother clearly does not want to let him go. When he stays out late, she waits up for him and yells at him when he comes home. When he tells her he's moving out, she angrily starts ripping posters off the walls of his bedroom, and then cries and begs him not to leave. Once he does, the film makes no further reference to his parents. He is, effectively, alone.

Amber's situation is more difficult. In an early scene, she calls her ex-husband and begs to be allowed to talk to her son. He refuses. A few days later, the phone rings at the house that Jack and Amber share, during a party. It is answered by Maurice, a nightclub owner and family friend, who is confused to find "some kid" calling, looking for his mother, Maggie. Maurice doesn't know Amber's real name, and so he tells the boy there's no Maggie at the house—although she is in the next room, doing lines of cocaine. Later in the film, Amber goes to court to try to convince a judge that visitation rights should be returned to her. But her husband recites her litany of sins—pornography, drug use, an arrest record—and she is denied.

The Fagin figure in all this is Jack Horner, who is, perversely enough, the most sympathetic paterfamilias in any of Anderson's films. He draws the other characters to him for the express purpose of exploiting their bodies for profit, but in the process creates a kind of domestic haven wherein everybody is accepted and no one is judged—as long as they're willing to have sex on film. Anderson stacks the deck in Jack's favor by downplaying his personal sexual interest in his ad hoc brood. Although he lives with Amber, the only affection we see between them is gentle and nearly chaste, and there's no suggestion that he is sexually involved with any of his other actors. His prurient interests in them are mercenary and (he fancies) artistic, not personal.

The movie also depicts all of the porn stars as willing and enthusiastic par-ticipants, minimizing the sleaziness of the enterprise. But there's no escaping the oedipal weirdness of Amber's confused maternal feelings for Eddie/Dirk. In their first scene together for Jack, she coaxes and coaches him through the penetration and ejaculation, part lover and part proud stage mother. Given Amber's alienation from her real son and Eddie's strained relationship with his real mother, the scene takes on an oddly therapeutic dimension, a sort of incest-by-proxy that is made acceptable by its trappings. The presence of the film crew, the pretense of a script, allows the acting out of murky psychological needs. Likewise, when Jack offers up Roller Girl to Eddie early on as a sort of audition, there's an odd sense of a father offering a daughter to his son.

Dirk and his costar Reed initially engage in some quasi-sibling rivalry, but quickly become close friends—surrogate brothers. On the other hand, Dirk's break with Jack comes when the director brings in yet another new young stud. Dirk, by this point a star with a star's ego and a drug habit that makes it increasingly difficult for him to maintain an erection, reacts angrily to the appearance of a newcomer on his turf. He lashes out at Jack—and Jack, who is not accustomed to his authority being challenged, lashes back, firing Dirk and effectively kicking him out of the family. From there, Dirk's spiral into street hustling and an eventual (and disastrously ineffective) attempt at crime is entirely predictable. Tellingly, when he hits bottom and returns home sheepishly to ask forgiveness, the home he returns to is Jack's, not his real family's. He is welcomed back into the fold, a prodigal son returned with some new humility but his prodigious physical gifts intact. As in *Hard Eight*, the happy ending is a shaky one; it's hard to imagine that Eddie or Amber or Jack will be doing too well in five or 10 years. But, the movie suggests, at least they have each other.

A major subtext of the film is the creation and maintenance of identity. Eddie's is, in a lot of ways, a classic Hollywood story, with Eddie in the role of aspiring starlet. His transformation into Dirk Diggler is a Norma-into-Marilyn metamorphosis (he literally sleeps his way to the top). His name is hilariously blunt, in keeping with porn tradition, but his insistence that people call him "Dirk" instead of "Eddie" underscores how much it means to him. Eddie was just a busboy with a hectoring mother; Dirk is practically a superhero. Eddie/Dirk has two scenes in front of mirrors, which recall (intentionally or not) Robert de Niro's mirror scenes with Scorsese. The first, in which Eddie psyches himself up before his first shoot, is reminiscent of Travis Bickle posturing with his gun, willing himself into a new persona. The second, at the end, has Dirk preparing for his porn comeback. His pep talk to himself is similar—"You're a star!" he says—but it sounds different. He's realized the limits of his ambitions, how much of a lie his sense of himself as "Dirk" is. It has an elegiac, pathetic air similar to Jake La Motta's prolonged dressing-room soliloquy in *Raging Bull*. Dirk's final flourish is to unzip his pants and pull out his penis, hitherto the movie's Maltese Falcon, talked about and reacted to but never seen on screen. It is large (a prosthetic, the producers assured the ratings board) and flaccid. It is, Dirk realizes, all he really has. He's not really a Dirk—he's just a dick.

The porn-star identity is similarly complex for Amber Waves and Rollergirl, in different ways. For Amber, it allows her to put aside the problems of Maggie, the drug-addicted mother whose child has been taken from her. But of course the identity of Amber is itself a creation of Maggie's problems. The invented persona is both an escape and an expulsion from her earlier life. Rollergirl, on the other hand, has embraced her porn career out of insecurities about her own intelligence (she flees a high school classroom in the middle of an exam) and confusion about dealing with men. She gets angry when boys at school leer at her; the implication is that in her porn life she is asserting herself, dictating the terms on which she can be ogled and objectified. But that is a somewhat illusory sense of control, and its limits become clear in a scene where Jack unknowingly selects an old classmate of hers for a sex scene in a limousine. The young man recognizes her and calls her by her real name, an assertion of power: he knows her "real" self. She is confronted with the reality that the same guys she escaped are the ones who watch her movies, and that they still feel dominion over her. She reacts angrily, interrupting the coitus and having Jack throw the old classmate out onto the sidewalk, where he is brutally beaten by Jack and his assistants.

Race comes into play in the characters of Maurice and Buck Swope, in arguably problematic ways: The characters serve primarily as comic relief, although Luis Guzman and Don Cheadle are too good as actors to let them become just props. Guzman (who returned in *Magnolia* and *Punch-Drunk Love*) gives some actual pathos to Maurice's porn-star ambitions—which Jack indulges, in exchange for being treated like a king at Maurice's club. What Maurice really wants is to impress his brothers back home in Puerto Rico, show them that he's made good on the mainland. The idea that the peak achievement of Americanness is to have sex with a pretty woman on film is an interesting one, but Anderson largely mines it for laughs, making Maurice something of a mascot for Jack. Buck Swope is a more deliberately race-aware character. His place in Jack Horner's scheme is unspoken but obvious: in the racial reductiveness of pornography, he's the black stud. Discomfort with this registers in the identities he tries on in daily life, all of them in some way tied to racial insecurity. His taste for country music and cowboy outfits baffles his friends and gets him fired from a job selling audio equipment. Whether his Nashville affectations are partly a reaction against being stereotyped seems to be something even Buck doesn't know. When he dons a Rick James-style wig later in the film, he quickly discards it, feeling like a phony in that guise too.

The production assistant Scotty, meanwhile, is the first prominent gay character in an Anderson film. He is also largely a comic figure—his first sighting of Eddie is accompanied on the soundtrack by Hot Chocolate singing "You Sexy Thing"—but like Buck, he has a tragic side. Frumpish and physically uncomfortable with his own pasty body, he idealizes Eddie/Dirk as both a role model and a lust object. His one attempt to kiss Dirk is inevitably disastrous and embarrassing. Like Jack's invisible libido, the treatment of Scotty's gayness feels a little glib; it is all but neutered by the character's soft ineffectuality. It actually feels something like safe-gay types from an earlier era of movies, gentle limpwrists who bordered on asexual. (This is in line with a somewhat reactionary streak in Anderson's movies, an almost pre-1960s moral framework that shows up more explicitly in *Magnolia*.)

At the same time, the film is Anderson's most explicit celebration of pop culture. Its evocation of the disco years and the nihilistic slide into the early 1980s is well observed, even if it feels a little secondhand in the wake of Quentin Tarantino. (Tarantino's movies don't just reference pop culture, they live and breathe it, whereas Anderson uses it largely as ornament.) The period details are right, if a little condensed—the movie squeezes in everything from wide collars to roller skates to shag carpets and Dirk's red 1978 Corvette. The songs are a well-curated assortment that progresses from 1970s good-time funk into 1980s electro-rock. The smartest move is using the pop pomposity of Nightranger's "Sister Christian" to score a long encounter between Dirk and his friends and the cokehead they've come to rob; it seems like exactly the song that a wired Hollywood hedonist would have been listening to in 1983, and its overwrought sense of foreboding amplifies the tension in the scene.

The setting itself, the world of San Fernando Valley porn, is a pop-cultural funhouse. Anderson has said in interviews that he was a porn enthusiast from a young age, and as an adult he has attended industry events like the annual adult film awards in Las Vegas (which is reproduced affectionately in *Boogie Nights*). His interest in porn goes beyond the merely libidinous, into the world of fandom. That partly accounts for the movie's relative lack of prurience. More then making a movie about pornography, per se, Anderson was making a movie about his adolescent pop culture heroes. Anderson doesn't glamorize his porn stars, exactly, but he sands the rough spots a little because he really wants to like his characters and he wants the audience to like them too. (Reaction within the porn industry varied, with some performers appreciating the Hollywood attention and others decrying the emphasis on drugs and dysfunction. Veteran porn star Nina Hartley, who has a small role as Little Bill's pathologically adulterous wife, told an interviewer, "I thought it was very well done and very potent.")[2]

It is hard to miss the parallels between the porn world and the "real" celebrities and Hollywood lifestyles it crudely emulates. All of the characters are stock Hollywood types, from the hack director who dreams of making "art" to the fat, lascivious producer (who, in the character of Jack's patron The Colonel, ends up jailed on pedophilia charges). The story is a backstage drama in the manner of *A Star Is Born* or *All About Eve*. That the central currency is physical reproductive action rather than "talent" or "vision" or "narrative" is just a qualitative difference. Of course, it's a difference that ultimately limits and traps the characters, and renders the whole enterprise a little pathetic. But maybe not *that* much more pathetic than the delusions and self-aggrandizement of Hollywood proper.

Magnolia (1999)
WRITTEN BY: PAUL THOMAS ANDERSON
WITH: JULIANNE MOORE (LINDA PARTRIDGE), WILLIAM H. MACY (QUIZ KID DONNIE SMITH), JOHN C. REILLY (OFFICER JIM KURRING), TOM CRUISE (FRANK T.J. MACKEY), PHILIP BAKER HALL (JIMMY GATOR), PHILIP SEYMOUR HOFFMAN (PHIL PARMA), JASON ROBARDS (EARL PARTRIDGE), ALFRED MOLINA (SOLOMON SOLOMON), MELORA WALTERS (CLAUDIA WILSON GATOR), MELINDA DILLON (ROSE GATOR), RICKY JAY (BURT RAMSEY/NARRATOR), LUIS GUZMAN (LUIS), JEREMY BLACKMAN (STANLEY SPECTOR), MICHAEL BOWEN (RICK SPECTOR), APRIL GRACE (GWENOVIER)

In *Magnolia*, his most ambitious film to date, Anderson goes deeper into the terrain of family bonds. The intersecting plotlines revolve around a series of parent-child relationships: the dying television executive, Earl Partridge, and his bitterly estranged son Frank T. J. Mackey; the dying television game-show host Jimmy Gator, and his cocaine-addicted daughter Claudia; the child prodigy Stanley Spector Gator, and his overbearing father Rick; and the former child prodigy Donnie Smith, who is still angry at the way his parents exploited his intelligence for game-show winnings.

All of these relationships are troubled, poisoned by abandonment, abuse and neglect. Earl walked out on Frank's mother, Lily, his childhood sweetheart, when she was dying of cancer—for which Frank has never forgiven him. Frank has reinvented himself as a foulmouthed huckster who delivers male-empowerment seminars to audiences full of sad-sack men. His approach, which he calls "Seduce and Destroy," encourages men to use lies and manipulation to get women into bed, and then to dump them before they can make any long-term demands. Superficially, he sounds like a vicious misogynist. But Frank's anger is not really at women—it's at his father. His patter is a cartoonish reduction of Earl's behavior, as if Frank has internalized abandonment as a philosophy of life. Meanwhile, the film suggests that Claudia's neuroses and drug problems stem from molestation by her father. She and Frank are echoes of each other, both abrasive and brittle, damaged children driven by barely concealed anger and hurt.

The story's other two damaged children, Stanley Spector and Donnie Smith, are also thematically linked. Stanley is a star on "What Do Kids Know" (hosted by Jimmy Gator), the same game show where Donnie earned his nickname "Quiz Kid" decades ago as a long-running champion. Donnie has never recovered from his early celebrity. Everything from his size-too-small wardrobe to his childish pleasure in carrying a retractable keychain signals arrested development. He's even fantasizing about getting braces to make himself more attractive to the young male bartender upon whom he has developed an unlikely and unrequited crush. Stanley, who appears to be more self-aware than Donnie ever was, functions as the film's Tiny Tim, an endangered child who may yet be saved. But the peril he faces is emotional rather than physical.

Magnolia asks several related questions: How much can be forgiven? Are some injuries too great to be made right? What does it take to drive apart parents and children, and what does it take to bring them back together? Anderson considers these through the kaleidoscope of his varied characters, and arrives at a range of answers. As in *Boogie Nights* and *Hard Eight*, the conclusions are conditional and complex. Emotional connection in *Magnolia* is always perilous, and the potential dangers are real. People are capable of doing terrible things to each other.

But if *Magnolia* is a moral inquest of sorts, it is a strikingly gentle and empathetic one. This is most visible in the way it presents its two potentially least likable characters, the "bad fathers" Earl and Jimmy. Although what we learn about them over the course of the film makes both of them seem deeply flawed at best, Anderson initially builds sympathy for them by presenting them at their most vulnerable. Both are weakened and dying. They want to reconcile with their children, and to apologize to them, but they don't know how. Earl does not even know where Frank is or how to reach him. Jimmy himself searches out Claudia to tell her he's dying, but she throws him out of her apartment.

The film opens with a prologue about three unrelated incidents, each of them a purportedly true story that revolves around unlikely connections and coincidences. (The vignettes are narrated by the magician Ricky Jay—he also had a small part in *Boogie Nights*—who gives them a breezy, carnival-barker's cadence.) On the surface, this sets the stage for the film's maze of overlapping narratives, which all end up connected to each other in various ways. More significantly, the prologue sets up the film's least likely event: the rain of frogs that falls on Los Angeles in the final half-hour, just as all the film's stories are coming to a head. Some critics winced at this *deus ex amphibia*, which in one case actually saves a life: a falling frog knocks a gun from Jimmy Gator's hand just as he's about to kill himself. But it is more than a whimsical plot device or a strained biblical metaphor. Stanley Spector, hiding in his school library, watches the frogs tumble down and says, with a sense of revelation, "This happens. This is something that happens." The frogs represent possibility.

But what is it, exactly, that is possible in *Magnolia*? Kindness, for one thing. The film's scarred and bitter domestic casualties encounter a motley assortment of samaritans, whose interventions save them from their own worst instincts. The best-hearted of these is Phil, the hospice nurse at Earl's bedside who listens with amusement and sympathy to the old man's stories, and takes no offense at his oft-repeated directive to "go fuck yourself." When Phil pieces together Earl's sometimes incoherent and delusional talk about his estranged son, he decides to track down Frank on the off-chance of a deathbed reconciliation. A somewhat more self-interested savior is Officer Jim Curring, an earnest, lonely, and only marginally competent LAPD patrolman. Responding to a neighbor's noise complaint, he finds Claudia alone in her apartment. Oblivious to her nervousness—and to the fact that she's tightly wired on cocaine—he invites himself in for a cup of coffee and begins clumsily flirting with her. But for all the unseemliness of the situation, Claudia responds at least tentatively to Jim's attention. When he asks her on a date, she says yes.

The film's other agent of mercy is Dixon, a young, streetwise inner-city boy who is connected to a murder case that Officer Curring stumbles into. The boy follows Curring back out to his car from the crime scene, offering information to help solve the shooting. He delivers a fast, a capella rap that Curring doesn't understand. Later, Dixon recovers Curring's gun after he loses it while chasing a suspect in the shooting during a rainstorm. This storyline about the murder case is never resolved and feels like a victim of the editing room. But the boy turns up again later, after Linda, Earl's guilt-ridden younger wife, has overdosed on pills in a suicide attempt. Finding her unconscious in her car, Dixon first rifles her purse for cash and then calls 911—saving her life.

In his almost exasperated pity for Curring and Linda, trying to save them despite themselves, Dixon maybe most clearly presents Anderson's perspective on his hurt and hurtful characters. Unfortunately, the vagueness and lack of attention to his thread of the story also makes him the least well-formed of *Magnolia's* players. As in *Boogie Nights*, Anderson seems to be using race largely as a construct to bounce his white characters off of. Curring's patronizing dismissal of Dixon illustrates both his Joe Friday bluster and how little he understands of what happens around him. In his subsequent loss of his gun—a cliché symbol of emasculation—the same black neighborhood serves as his foil and nemesis. But the attention to character and detail that permeate the rest of the film are all but absent in these scenes. As much as anything, this might suggest Anderson's lack of confidence in negotiating a terrain of race and class far removed from his own. It is certainly no coincidence that, as in *Boogie Nights*, many of *Magnolia*'s most convincing characters revolve around the world of entertainment (television this time, rather than pornography). And it is also true that—unlike sprawling liberal fables like *Grand Canyon* and *Crash*—*Magnolia*'s vision of Los Angeles is personal, not political. Still, the film's class and race orientation is unmistakeable.

It also plays out in the character of Gwenovier, the TV reporter who arrives at one of Frank's seminars to interview him. She is a young black woman whose intelligence and poise derails Frank's smugness. Unintimidated by his bluster and posturing—which includes stripping down to his underwear while he's talking to her—she leads him through what starts out as a sympathetic interview into a sort of journalistic trap. She has researched his history (which he had hidden beneath a cover story about a dead father) and knows all about Earl and Lily, and about Frank having to care for his terminally ill mother on his own after Earl left. The revelations infuriate Frank, but they also paralyze him. Instead of lashing out, he sits silently and refuses to answer her questions. Is it significant that he is unmanned by an interviewer of both different gender and race? It seems so. Her status as an outsider to his world gives her a leverage that he doesn't even realize she has until it's too late. She's not just immune to whatever charms he imagines he has, she is in some quiet ways hostile to them. April Grace gives a fine, smart performance, making Gwenovier seem sympathetic in contrast to Frank's bullying cockiness. But she is still more a foil than a character. She has no backstory, and disappears from the movie once the interview is over.

And, again as in *Boogie Nights*, gay characters in *Magnolia* are presented as something a bit sad. During an extended sequence at a bar where Donnie is courting the male bartender, he finds himself vying for the young hunk's attention with a dainty, waspish older gentleman who might have been written into the script as "bitter queen." Their exchanges are well written, and Henry Gibson injects some likable venom into the queen role, but there is still a sense of lilac panic about the scene. The implicit association of Donnie's homosexuality with his childhood trauma feels glib, at best.

All of which seems part of Anderson's oddly retrograde morality. For all of the sex, drugs, and rock 'n' roll in his movies, he at bottom seems like a throwback in some crucial ways. If his view of the world is shaped by a deep awareness of domestic corruption—the toxins that can seep into family life— it also seems inherently to judge that corruption against an almost *Leave It to Beaver*-ish ideal. The parents in his movies are at least a half-generation older than the baby-boomer parents who populate the films of David O. Russell and Wes Anderson (and who come with all of their own complications). They are middle-class and upper-middle-class households with fathers who work and mothers who may or may not (it is not clear whether Eddie's mother in *Boogie Nights* or Claudia's mother in *Magnolia* have jobs). Earl Partridge and Jimmy Gator (and Sydney in *Hard Eight*) are men more suited to the 1950s than the 1960s or 1970s, fathers from a prefeminist era of TV dinners and tract housing. Mothers are either docile (like Jimmy's wife, unable to protect her daughter from molestation or herself from Jimmy's serial adultery), abandoned (like Earl's first wife), or frustrated shrews (Eddie's mother). Even Anderson's critiques of this world seem old-fashioned. The perspective is not just white and middle-class, it's white and middle-class from another era.

It is one reason the period details are more convincing in *Boogie Nights*, which inhabits the world of his childhood, than in the putatively late 1990s world of *Magnolia*. You would never guess from the latter film that California was in the throes of the dot-com gold rush. Cable television seems about the extent of its technological advancement. And the children's show that Jimmy Gator hosts is deliberately archaic, with a jazzy 1950s logo and absurdly highbrow questions. Anderson is not even trying to present a persuasively contemporary setting (which makes the occasional touches like Dixon's impromptu rap seem jarring).

In fact, it is a little hard to tell throughout *Magnolia* how Anderson intends the movie. It is not quite a realist drama, nor—despite some fanciful touches— is it fabulist. The playfulness suggested by the prologue is picked up in periodic intertitles that blithely recount the time, date, and weather forecast. There is a musical interlude when all of the characters sing along to an Aimee Mann song (Anderson has said that Mann's songs—which are mostly about lost love and hurt feelings—inspired the movie). And of course there are those frogs. But set against all of that is the rawness of the writing and performances. There is an awful lot of unadorned emotion in the film (almost every character cries at least once, sometimes violently). Those scenes—like Linda Partridge's near-breakdown at a drugstore where the pharmacist clearly thinks she's a drug addict because of the potent painkillers she's buying for Earl—sit uncomfortably within Anderson's contrived narrative framework, with all its neatly intersecting lines. The result is something of a lurching hodgepodge, and was criticized as such by some reviewers. But it is possible to see even the messiness and inconclusiveness of the film as deliberate, or at least coherent—as an imperfect patchwork attempt to illuminate imperfect patchwork lives. In an interview with Lynn Hirschberg in *The New York Times Magazine* shortly before the film's release, Anderson called *Magnolia* "a beautiful accident," and added that he had put "every embarrassing thing I wanted to say" into the movie.[3]

The film most often invoked in discussions of *Magnolia*—both positively and negatively—is Robert Altman's *Short Cuts*, another collection of intersecting stories set in Los Angeles (adapted from stories by Raymond Carver). The comparison is instructive, but not necessarily to *Magnolia*'s disadvantage. Altman's influence on Anderson is undeniable—that was already apparent in the discursive sprawl of *Boogie Nights*, especially in the large party scenes through which the camera glides, picking up on conversations in midstream, defining characters via small talk and advancing the story in several directions at once. But the parallels between *Magnolia* and *Short Cuts* are largely superficial. Altman's film, drawing on the darkness of Carver's stories, is dour and foreboding—the earthquake that arrives at the end feels judgmental, and coincides with its most repellent act, the murder of two teenage girls. It is not so much about missed connections as *bad* connections. Anderson's film is empathetic where Altman's is misanthropic, and *Magnolia*'s act of nature (or God) is revelatory, where Altman's seems like a condemnation. Whatever Anderson owes to Altman as a storyteller, he is very different as a moralist.

The movie requires performances deeper than those in *Boogie Nights*, to keep the melodramatic material from puddling up the screen. The cast is mostly up to it. Jason Robards and Philip Baker Hall are particularly striking as successful men brought low by disease and looming mortality. Acting almost entirely from the neck up, Robards invests Earl with sometimes comic complexity. His lapses of coherence and flashes of stammering anger effectively convey both his disintegration and his resistance to it. Hall turns his imposing physical presence in on itself. In an excruciating scene where Jimmy Gator, intoxicated and sweating profusely, struggles through a panic attack on live TV, Hall's pitiable confusion makes him seem like an ailing circus bear, defanged and confused. The breakdown of his self-control and confidence is completed later, when his wife finally confronts him about molesting Claudia. Hall presents a mixture of self-pity and self-loathing that suggests Jimmy himself believes he is beyond forgiveness, even as he begs for it.

Tom Cruise's presence in the film at first threatens to be distracting. By far the biggest marquee name in any of Anderson's movies (he reportedly invited

Anderson to write him a part after being impressed by *Boogie Nights*),[4] his first appearance as Frank T.J. Mackey is a little disorienting. As he spouts Frank's profane, macho self-help spiel, it is at first hard not to notice that this is Tom Cruise saying things like "Respect the cock!" But Anderson's writing smartly takes advantage of Cruise's natural ebullience and arrogance, inflating them into Frank's self-constructed public persona. The character deepens, as does Cruise's performance, during the long interview sequence with the TV reporter, who peels back those layers of bravado to the anger and hurt underneath. In Frank's eventual confrontation with his dying father, Cruise finally unwinds the character all the way, leaving him exposed and lost for words. His vulnerability and grief connect with the vulnerability and grief that course through the movie.

As the nurse, Phil, Philip Seymour Hoffman has a nerdy warmth, managing the trick of playing a good-hearted character without reducing him to naifish cliches. There's a good scene where Linda Partridge walks in on Phil as he's on the phone trying to contact Frank. She becomes furious at what she sees as his meddling in a long-buried relationship. The confusion on Hoffman's face as Linda screams at him has multiple levels—surprise and hurt, at first, but then also a dawning comprehension of how wide the chasms are in Earl's family. It is as if Phil has never considered the question of whether all rifts can—or should—be mended. As Linda, Julianne Moore fares somewhat less well. In a movie of mostly well-developed characters, Linda is thinly written. Moore amps up her brittleness, trying to compensate for the sketchy role with overheated emoting. Unfortunately, the character largely comes across as hysterical. Her suicide attempt feels like rote melodrama, and something of an afterthought to the story. It is a much less interesting role than she had in *Boogie Nights*, and her performance suffers accordingly.

The character of Claudia, who spends most of the movie in a cocaine mania, could have lent itself to similar overplaying. But Melora Walters imbues her with an underlying vulnerability that makes her more than a bundle of tics. Her fragility cries out for protection, and Jim Curring's response to it seems natural. And as Curring, John C. Reilly presents a rare thing in an Anderson film (or any Hollywood film, for that matter): a deeply religious character whose faith is depicted without irony or condescension. Curring prays devoutly, without pretense, a well-intentioned but not overly bright guy who admits that he doesn't really understand much about the world. All he wants is to do his job well, and to have someone to love and love him back. Though Anderson's outlook is unabashedly secular, it is a secularism informed by his Catholic upbringing. He depicts the prayers with respect for what they are: the confused pleas of a human being, looking for a little help. And Jim in turn functions as a haphazard, very human angel toward Claudia. When he approaches Claudia at the end of the film, the screen is suffused with light. Anderson's concern is not so much for the specificity of Jim's faith as for what it makes possible: Jim's willingness to reach out to Claudia, and Claudia's possible (secular, corporeal) salvation. The entire film labors under the shadow of death, but Anderson is more worried about what happens in this world than in any to come. The possibility of a sad life made happy is his idea of resurrection.

And that, ultimately, is the hope that *Magnolia* offers. Frank does come to Earl's bedside. Claudia's mother reaches out to her after years of not acknowledging how much she has been hurt. Officer Curring rescues Donnie Smith from the rain of frogs and from Donnie's own worst instincts, convincing him to return money that he has stolen from his former employer. And Stanley walks into his father's bedroom in the middle of the night and tells him, point blank, "You have to be nicer to me." These are all "something that happens," Anderson wants to say, or at least things that *can* happen. Not everything can be forgiven, but wounds can heal. People can learn and grow. Kindness can trump selfishness. Simple enough ideas, but the currents of alienation and anger that course through *Magnolia* suggest how difficult they are to realize.

Punch-Drunk Love (2002)

WRITTEN BY: PAUL THOMAS ANDERSON
WITH: ADAM SANDLER (BARRY EGAN), EMILY WATSON (LENA LEONARD), PHILIP SEYMOUR HOFFMAN (DEAN TRUMBELL), LUIS GUZMAN (LANCE)

The motif of the suffocating family surfaces again in *Punch-Drunk Love*, Anderson's off-kilter attempt at romantic comedy. The film's central character, Barry, a novelty salesman with a temper problem, is the only son in a family of eight children. His seven sisters and his mother are constantly nosing into his life, teasing him, prodding him, criticizing him—and, the film makes clear, they have been doing so all his life. His anger, which he unleashes in comically inappropriate bursts (demolishing a restaurant bathroom, smashing a sliding-glass door during a family dinner), is the pent-up rage of a lifetime of helplessness. His difficulty in finding and sustaining an independent relationship obviously stems from the looming omnipresence of his family.

Lena (Emily Watson) and Barry (Adam Sandler) finally kiss in Paul Thomas Anderson's quirky romance, *Punch-Drunk Love*. (Courtesy of Photofest)

Punch-Drunk Love is Anderson's first full-on consideration of romantic attachment. While there are romances and courtship in his other films, they are subsidiary parts of the action. The relationship between John and Clementine in *Hard Eight* is less important in itself than as an extension of John's surrogate-son relationship with Sydney. Officer Curring's wooing of Claudia in *Magnolia* is well observed, but it is just one piece of the film's mosaic of redemption. In *Punch-Drunk Love*, romantic love is front and center, from the title on. And given Anderson's preoccupation with familial tensions, it is no surprise that he presents romance as, first of all, a vehicle for escape.

But he eases up on the family horror a little, at least relative to his previous films. Barry's sisters are not quite badly intentioned, however cruel they can be. They care about Barry—they criticize him, but they also stick up for him— and their husbands are decent, regular guys. It is more the sheer number of them, their planetary mass, that makes it difficult for Barry to break free, even as they encourage him to. Lena, the woman who becomes the vehicle for his liberation, is actually introduced to him by one of his sisters. Notably absent from the tableau is Barry's father, who is barely mentioned. It may be that after the tortured father figures of *Magnolia*, Anderson was more interested in female family dynamics and the ways they play out for boys and men.

So for Barry, women represent both smothering confinement—even infantilization—and the possibility of transcending it. The paradox is that he cannot establish himself as a fully grown, independent man without the help of a woman. This is a conventional romantic narrative, the man or woman who becomes fully alive and self-determined only through the love of another, and Anderson observes the rules of the genre, up to a point. But since he's neither a romantic nor a comic at heart—he's too pragmatic and too aware of the perils and pain of emotional connection—*Punch-Drunk Love* is a peculiar mix of sensibilities. It has elements of screwball humor, along with touches of surrealism and fantasy, but (like the mishmash of *Magnolia*) it is grounded in visceral human relations. As its title suggests, it might be the angriest romantic comedy ever made.

That anger is embodied by Adam Sandler. It was an interesting casting choice—an obvious one, in that Sandler had already established a screen persona as an unrestrained man-child with a fiery temper; but a risky one too, in that none of his previous roles (largely in juvenile comedies) had required much by way of emotional depth. *Punch-Drunk Love* plays Sandler's outbursts for laughs to some extent, as earlier Sandler movies had, but always with an awareness of their consequences—and, more crucially, of the real underlying personality disturbances they suggest. A grown man whose anxiety on a first date prompts him to kick apart a restaurant bathroom is a grown man with problems.

From a filmmaking standpoint, *Punch-Drunk Love* is a departure. Rather than 1970s realists like Scorsese and Altman, it seems indebted to independent 1980s surrealists, particularly David Lynch and the Coen brothers. The long precredit opening sequence, which finds Barry in a preposterous blueberry-blue suit at his desk in a large warehouse, has a visual and narrative absurdity unlike anything in Anderson's earlier films. The suit, which Barry will wear throughout the movie (with minimal explanation—"I thought it would be nice to wear a suit to work," he says) is the same color as the paint on the warehouse wall, and the color is repeated again in the early morning shadows on the pavement when he steps outside, sipping his coffee. Then, in rapid succession, as Barry stands and watches in anxious bewilderment, three things happen: a car driving down the street blows out a tire and goes into a careening, rolling crash; a taxi van pulls up and deposits a small piano organ at the mouth of the warehouse's driveway; and a white car pulls into the driveway and drives straight up to Barry. Of these three events, only the latter is ever explained. The driver (although she doesn't initially introduce herself) is Lena. In contrast to Barry's blue suit, she is dressed all in pinkish-red, establishing the film's color scheme.

Those colors dominate the abstract, warm-toned credit sequence, with shades of blue and red chasing each other across the screen. The sequence shows a painterly visual confidence that had not been obvious in Anderson's earlier films. Although he has always had a sure command of the camera—the long tracking shots in *Hard Eight* and *Boogie Nights*, the falling-frog's-eye-view in *Magnolia*—*Punch-Drunk Love* effectively conveys character and story through expressionistic color, composition, and lighting. It is skillfully done, but it does not quite rise above its obvious stylistic influences. As a technical filmmaker, Anderson still seems more like an excellent pupil than a fully formed talent. What sets his films apart is still the writing, the emotional range, and empathy of the characters.

On that level, *Punch-Drunk Love* is, if not fully successful, at least unpredictable. As the story progresses and Barry tangles with a growing number of obstacles—a phone-sex operator who tries to blackmail him, a snack-food company offering what seems to be a generous travel-coupon deal, his nagging family—the pursuit of love (in the form of Lena) becomes an obsessive quest. Recognizing an opportunity to change his life in ways he can't quite conceive, Barry pursues Lena to Hawaii, where their embrace dissolves in a delirious fantasia of light and music. There is an edge to the ecstasy, and a woozy dreamlike anxiety to the entire Hawaii sequence. When they are in bed together, their lovers' patter is strange and dangerous-sounding. "I want to bite your cheek and chew on it," Lena says. "I'm looking at your face," Barry whispers back to her, "and I just want to smash it. I just want to fucking smash it with a sledgehammer." (The postcoital scene the next morning is the only one in the movie in which Barry is not wearing his blue suit; he is in a white bathrobe, as if he has been purified or baptized.)

The metaphors of violence make sense within the framework of Anderson's ideas about the conflicts and struggles inherent to intimacy. And they become more than metaphors after Barry and Lena return from Hawaii and encounter thugs sent by the phone-sex company's owner. The thugs cause a car accident in which Lena is lightly injured. This triggers Barry's final freak-out. First, he clubs the thugs into submission. Then he drives to Utah to threaten the small-town crime boss who sent them (Philip Seymour Hoffman, having fun with a blustery role). Still carrying a phone he ripped from its cradle in his office, Barry tells the hoodlum, "I have so much strength in me, you have no idea. I have a love in my life that makes me stronger than anything you can imagine." The hoodlum wisely backs down and apologizes. Barry goes home to Lena, toting the mysterious harmonium, which seems to represent to him the possibilities of a new life.

Like all of Anderson's "happy" endings, this one seems tenuous. On the one hand, Barry has matured over the course of the film. But his impulsiveness and his problematic relations with his family are unlikely to simply disappear. By the end of the movie, he is still in the blue suit—his metamorphosis is not complete. Still, Anderson observes the conventions of the genre enough to allow hope for love to conquer all, even if it is of a battered and bruised variety.

The major weakness in the film is the character of Lena. Having gone to great lengths to establish Barry's situation, and to provide context for his loneliness and anger, Anderson leaves Lena unsatisfyingly vague. She is shy, but not in any unusual way. She mentions past relationships offhandedly, so she is not some romantic-comedy never-been-kissed virgin. She seems kind of normal, actually, which makes her attraction to Barry—who is strange, anxious, and naive—a little hard to figure. The bedroom scene with its flesh-rending dialogue suggests hitherto hidden reserves of either aggression or submission in her, maybe both, but it doesn't connect to her behavior elsewhere in the movie. Lena is appealing because Watson is appealing, and it certainly is not hard to understand Barry's interest in her. But she is more a vehicle for Barry's self-realization than a full-blown narrative presence.

As for the comic bits in the film, some work well. Barry's business, selling novelty items like toilet plungers with little brides and grooms on top, is funny in itself but even more so because of Barry's utter earnestness in conducting it. Sandler is a more sophisticated comedian than he usually allows himself to demonstrate, with most of his movies opting for easy jokes and gross-out gags rather than the dryness he displays in *Punch-Drunk Love*. He shows some classic clown skills in wringing laughs from Barry's mounting frustration.

The movie is maybe most interesting in what it reveals about Anderson's suspicions and reservations about relationships. Given the anger and abuses he seems to associate with family life, it is not surprising that he would be look askance at the two-person unit that forms its core. First comes love, then comes marriage, then come years of resentment and worse, visited on each other and the children. *Punch-Drunk Love* is a romantic film made by someone who has thought through the consequences of romance and still finds it provisionally worth the effort.

Anderson is interesting as a filmmaker partly because he has yet to fully define himself. Although his films are marked by recurring themes and original writing, his style still seems in flux. He is technically gifted—his movies are visually ambitious and inventive, and he confidently pulls off complex, interwoven storylines—but those talents are double-edged. They have allowed him to absorb and replicate an impressive range of influences, without quite evolving into an identifiable aesthetic of his own.

His abiding fascination with the corrosive side of family dynamics marks him as one of the most sour domestic chroniclers among his peers (a group that is itself marked by a fair amount of domestic sourness). At the same time, his sympathy for the things that draw people together—loneliness and, despite considerable obstacles, kindness—offsets the bitterness. None of his characters are so damaged that they are incapable of reaching out.

Anderson's next project is a departure of sorts, although his work to date has been sufficiently varied that it would be hard to call anything entirely atypical. The forthcoming film, tentatively titled *There Will Be Blood*, is a historical drama with topical overtones. It is partly based on Upton Sinclair's 1927 novel *Oil*, a fictionalization of the Teapot Dome Scandal and an exposé of the then-nascent California oil industry. It is easy to imagine contemporary political resonances, as well as classic cinematic ones—California tycoons is a territory well-trod by Hollywood, from *Citizen Kane* to *Chinatown*. It does not sound like an obvious undertaking for Anderson, but his usual preoccupations may well find their way into the story. After all, what is *Citizen Kane* but the story of a bad childhood and its consequences?

5

DAVID O. RUSSELL

I t might not be obvious from a quick survey of his subject matter—incest, war, corporate greed, the meaning of life—but David O. Russell is a comic filmmaker with a flair for farce and slapstick. His movies abound with moments of physical comedy, pratfalls and double takes and wholesale destruction of property (like the post office that gets flattened by a hapless Ben Stiller in *Flirting with Disaster*). But those moments sit uncomfortably close to scenes of actual pathos and pain, like the near-date-rape in *Spanking the Monkey* and the excruciating torture session in *Three Kings*. Russell has a reputation as a "difficult" man to work with, and his films have an emotional rawness that makes that easy to believe. They are funny, but they are also sad and unnerving and unsettled. *I Heart Huckabees* is a movie about an explicit quest for meaning in the universe, but all of Russell's films share a sense of unsatisfied yearning. All of them have heroes who are looking for a way out of their (sometimes self-created) personal binds: the college student in *Spanking the Monkey* desperate to get away from his parents; the young father in *Flirting with Disaster* anxious to *find* his real parents; the soldiers in *Three Kings* hoping to escape their humdrum jobs by finding stolen gold; and the existential searchers of *Huckabees*, looking mostly for something to believe in.

Not surprisingly, Russell was something of a searcher himself even before he settled on film as his medium for inquiry. After graduating from Amherst College in 1981, where he majored in English and political science, he worked as a union organizer in Maine and made a documentary about Panamanian immigrants in Boston. The latter led to a job on the public television series

"Smithsonian World." But his talent for comic absurdity and family dysfunction were evident early on too, in his 1987 short *Bingo Inferno*, about an obsessive bingo-playing mother. Both it and a subsequent short, *Hairway to the Stars*, were shown at the Sundance Film Festival. On the strength of those, Russell received grants worth $20,000 apiece from the National Endowment for the Arts and the New York State Council on the Arts for another short, to be called *Lucky Garden* and set in a Chinese restaurant. Instead, he wrote the script for *Spanking the Monkey*, which he then forwarded to each agency, seeking approval. The state council signed off on it, but the N.E.A. balked— not surprisingly, given the subject matter (incest in a suburban home), the flim's onanistic title and the political pressures on the agency. As Russell later told *The New York Times*, "So I just did it anyway."[1] Even so, he had to round up investors to make up the rest of the $80,000 budget. The film won the Audience Award at the 1994 Sundance Festival and, despite some executives' reservations about its content, was picked up by New Line.[2]

It established a tone that would carry through Russell's subsequent films, a dark humor that never quite turns bitter. His characters can be misguided or cruel, they fight with each other and lie to each other, but they are also always bonded together somehow, by blood or marriage or (in *Three Kings*) military comradeship. There is an underlying empathy in the films that grants a complex humanity even to the abrasive mother in *Spanking the Monkey*, the Iraqi torturer in *Three Kings* and the corporate climber played by Jude Law in *I Heart Huckabees*.

At the same time, the stories are fueled by anxiety and anger, both personal and political. Like Paul Thomas Anderson, Russell returns again and again to themes of family trauma. By his own accounts, these are often autobiographical. Of *Spanking the Monkey*, he said, "I made a movie that said, 'I hate my mother,' which is considered a heresy, certainly at Sundance at that time. A lot of people regarded me as a dirtbag. People in this country are so sanctimonious about the family. . . . But emotionally criminal things happen there, and why lie about them?"[3] The main character of *Huckabees*, Albert Markovski, shares a last name with Russell's father, Bernard Markovski. And in one scene Albert relates a childhood experience of being told his cat has died that is drawn directly from Russell's own life.[4] (In the movie, Albert's existentialist counselor, played by Isabelle Huppert, tells him, "You were orphaned by indifference.")

But the films are also intensely aware of broader cultural and political issues. The family dynamics in the movies partly reflect the conflict between self-absorbed Baby Boomers and their children, the way that the 1960s emphasis on individual self-realization sometimes backfired for those growing up in its wake. At the same time, Russell himself seems shaped by countercultural ideals, which inform both the battlefield cynicism of *Three Kings* and Albert Markovski's anticorporate diatribes in *I Heart Huckabees*. The films are sort of warily idealistic, cautious about the possibility of activism accomplishing anything much but respectful of the impulse to try. And despite, or maybe because of, his affluent suburban background, Russell shows a disdain for the insularity of suburban life that is joined to a thoughtful class-consciousness. More than most of his peers, he is willing to get outside the comfort zones of straight, white middle-class life, presenting characters of different races, classes, nationalities, religions, and sexual orientations with equal amounts of sympathy and skepticism.

He is also a visually creative filmmaker, evolving from the low-budget realism of *Spanking the Monkey* through the color schemes of *Flirting with Disaster* to the arresting, almost surreal washed-out desert brightness of *Three Kings*. The latter movie also makes vivid use of digital effects, depicting the trajectory of a bullet inside a body, that presaged the transcendental moments of *I Heart Huckabees*, in which people's faces and bodies disintegrate into floating shards.

Huckabees, his most intellectually coherent manifesto, opens with a scene of Albert Markovski wandering endlessly down corridors in a commercial building, turning corners and opening doors, looking for the right office. It is a prologue to the philosophical searching to come, but it also stands as an abstract of Russell's work as a whole. His movies are undergirded by a sometimes meandering, sometimes anxious, but unmistakable determination to open closed doors, to find honest answers to difficult questions, and to accept whatever embarrassing consequences ensue.

Spanking the Monkey (1994)

WRITTEN BY: DAVID O. RUSSELL
WITH: JEREMY DAVIES (RAY AIBELLI), ALBERTA WATSON
(SUSAN AIBELLI), CARLA GALLO (TONI PECK), BENJAMIN
HENDRICKSON (TOM AIBELLI), JUDETTE JONES (AUNT
HELEN)

About halfway through Russell's feature debut, the busybody character Aunt Helen tells her nephew Ray, "Family's our greatest asset. You'll find that out as you get older." The line elicits a blank look from Ray and a grim chuckle from the audience. In the claustrophobic world of *Spanking the*

Monkey, family is a lot of things, but an asset isn't one of them. Aunt Helen herself is one of its unpleasant faces, a harebrained, prideful frump whose lack of insight does not in any way restrain her from passing judgment on others. But Helen's transgressions seem minor compared to the gross selfishness of Ray's middle-aged parents, Susan and Tom. Arriving home from college for what he thinks is a brief stay en route to a prestigious scientific summer internship in Washington, D.C., Ray is brusquely informed by his traveling-salesman father that he will have to instead spend several days—and maybe longer—taking care of his incapacitated mother, who has broken her leg. Ray protests to no effect, as his father gives him precise instructions on caring for everything from the car to the lawn to the family dog.

Ray arrives at his home in a semirural suburb to find his mother slumped on her bed, her leg in a cast and her demeanor pointedly resentful. There is a sense of mounting panic in these early scenes, as Ray realizes that he is effectively trapped in his own home—or, more precisely, his parents' home. The independent life he has been building for himself during his first year at college (he attends M.I.T., we're told) vanishes the moment he is pulled back into the orbit of his mother and father. Over the next several days, the family dynamic becomes clear: Ray is intellectually and emotionally closest to his mother, but he also resents her hovering, depressive presence. She, in turn, resents him for having the opportunity to go to college, which she was denied by young motherhood and an unsupportive husband. She is living vicariously through him, up to a point, but she is also hypercritical of his efforts. He copes passive-aggressively, giving her a job-application essay to edit only after he has already mailed it off. His mother's control extends to his romantic life, as she offers suggestions and criticisms about one girl or another. Ray's only outlets for his accumulated frustration are frenzied bouts of masturbation in the bathroom, which are inevitably interrupted by the dog.

Russell has said the film arose from his own experiences (minus the incest) as a college student returning home for the summer to his parents' house in Larchmont, a wealthy suburb of New York City. It's not hard to believe. Everything about the setting feels familiar and lived in (even though the film was actually shot in a town farther upstate). Russell has said in interviews that he had a difficult relationship with his mother, and his father was often away on business. Scenes in which Ray meets up with his old high school friends are well written, quickly sketching the dynamics of his social group. It is obvious Ray doesn't exactly fit in with them, although it is also easy to see why he gravitated toward them—they are brainy slackers, cheerful misfit stoners who like to get high and talk about math. They seem like

Richard Linklater characters, the kind of guys Russell might have hung around with.

But whatever personal dramas drive it, *Spanking the Monkey* also reads more broadly as a bitter parable of the relationship between Baby Boomer parents and their offspring. Ray's parents are not counterculture types (Russell deals with those in *Flirting with Disaster*), but they represent some of the worst of Me Generation excesses. They are a couple caught on the cusp of feminism—Susan is the smarter and more intellectual of the two, but her early pregnancy and marriage forestalled her collegiate ambitions. She is self-pitying and resentful, and she drinks copiously. Her husband, Tom, is a brusque, incurious salesman who is often absent (and, the film reveals, often adulterous). He clearly has little interest in his wife's interior world, seeing her ailments—physical or psychological—solely in terms of how they affect his daily life. He is equally alienated from his brooding, science-whiz son, who he seems to see as primarily his wife's responsibility. The only family member that seems to really arouse Tom's concern and affection is the family dog. (It seems significant that the dog, as Tom's proxy, is constantly interrupting Ray's efforts at self-gratification.)

Ray's relationship with his mother, of course, is the core of the movie. Unlike his father, she is interested, to an exacting degree, in all aspects of his life. But she still sees him largely as an extension of herself. She does not seem especially bothered that he should have to delay a prize internship to care for her. She sees herself as a victim—of Ray's father, of missed opportunities, of Ray himself (whose arrival, after all, was the defining event in limiting her life). She has obviously encouraged Ray's interest in science. But he clearly resents her overbearing supervision of both his educational and romantic pursuits. It is hard to say whether it is actually her goal to turn his sexual attention in her direction, but on at least a subconscious level she seems jealous of anyone else occupying his thoughts.

On that front, Ray is what could be charitably called confused. He has had girlfriends, but given his mother's stifling critiques it seems evident that none of them has lasted long. His romantic interest in the film is Toni, a younger neighbor girl (she's still in high school) whom he meets while walking the dog. She is smart, like him, and admires his scholastic achievements. But her guileless inexperience is overmatched by Ray's barely suppressed neuroses. The first time they kiss, she finds him tentative and distant. Hurt, she asks him if he might be gay. Ray reacts angrily, pulling her clothes off and all but attacking her, and she pushes him off and runs away. There is no suggestion that sexual orientation per se is the source of Ray's angst; Toni's question stings not so much because of its specifics but because of its implication that something is *wrong* with Ray, something he senses himself.

What's wrong, of course, is that he can't find a way out of his parents' clutches and into some clear, separate sense of his own identity. Russell turns that central drama of adolescence into a small-scale horror movie, although the terror is all internalized. (The full-leg cast his mother wears throughout the film turns her partway into an actual monster—the mommy as mummy.) But Ray is not just a victim. In his refusal to break away, he is to some degree a willing participant in his own subjugation. He still wants approval from both of his parents, and, for most of the film at least, he has not reached a point of being able to resist their demands on him.

All of these tensions find a queasy climax in the film's key scene: Ray's sexual encounter with his mother. For any audience after the initial few screenings, it is difficult to gauge what dramatic effect the scene would have with no forewarning. Because word of it spread so quickly and widely, predating its theatrical release by months, almost everybody who saw *Spanking the Monkey* probably had some idea what was in store. Even so, it delivers a woozy, disquieting jolt. The build-up to the consummation feels delirious and dangerous. Incapable of escaping his mother, Ray seems determined to aggressively join her (in her bedroom, where the whole scene unfolds). The two of them get roaringly drunk, and they play a series of escalating games that include an episode of throwing food against the wall. The behavior seems primal, like zoo animals (giving the simian reference in the title another layer). The culminating act represents both Ray's surrender to his mother and his revenge on her: It is a physical manifestation of their tortured relationship, but one that she cannot avoid, ignore, or rationalize.

Very little is actually shown—Ray's hand creeps up Susan's leg, and then the two of them wake up the next morning with shattering hangovers—but the taboo Russell is violating, however metaphorically it is intended, is so potent that it threatens to overwhelm the film's blackly comic tone. This is the material of classic tragedy, not sardonic suburban memoir. And, in fact, the film never recovers its equilibrium. The realization, and indelibility, of the act prompts Ray to attempt suicide in a scene that teeters right on the edge of what the audience can laugh at. His effort seems sincere—miles away from, say, John Cusack's slapstick attempts to kill himself in *Better Off Dead*—and so does his determination to throttle his mother when she thwarts his attempted hanging. What makes the scene work, and what makes a lot of Russell's uncomfortable humor work, is the unvarnished pain inside it.

As filmmaking, *Spanking the Monkey* is necessarily rudimentary. It was shot and edited on the cheap, and Russell, still feeling his way into directing, stuck to the basics. There is little hint of the visual and formal playfulness to come in his subsequent films. The only touch of the fantastical is the bizarre medical news channel that Ray's mother watches constantly, which seems to be always showing one gruesome operation or another. (The macabre effect is undermined a little by the low-budget production, which does not correct for the TV screen's flicker and renders the images murky.)

But Russell elicits fine performances from the cast, no small feat given the squeamishness of the subject matter. He recruited Jeremy Davies for the lead after seeing him in a car commercial, and it was a good choice—he is good looking, but in a sort of nervous, ferret-like way. His sharp features, dark hair and pale skin complement a quiet intensity that recalls the young Anthony Perkins (star of the ultimate mother-son drama, *Psycho*). For Susan, Russell had tried to enlist a high-profile actress—he even flew to Los Angeles to meet with Faye Dunaway—but, not surprisingly, he found no takers. Which is just as well, because a more familiar actress might have made the incest scene seem like a stunt (watch Faye Dunaway pretend to have sex with her son!). Alberta Watson had already appeared in several movies and TV shows, but she was not a particularly familiar face. In her late thirties at the time, she was the right age for the character (14 years younger than Dunaway), and pretty but not overbearingly so. Her brooding gloom throughout the movie—conveyed largely through an unsmiling, fatalistic blankness—effectively suggests chronic depression, with minimal histrionics.

In keeping with the film's naturalism, Carla Gallo (who was making her debut) actually seems like a brainy high school girl—smart but awkward, intellectually confident but physically insecure. Unlike adolescents in so many movies and TV shows, both Ray and Toni seem *young*. They are emotionally immature and unworldly; Ray's cynicism is a pose masking his anxieties.

The film also feels young, and inconclusive. Its quietly symbolic ending gives Ray a rebirth—after leaping into a reservoir and being feared dead, he emerges from the water as if baptized—without any clear sense of what will come next. For Russell, too, it seems like a cathartic film, a way for him to deal with lingering family psychodramas before moving on to broader concerns.

Flirting with Disaster (1996)
WRITTEN BY: DAVID O. RUSSELL
WITH: BEN STILLER (MEL), PATRICIA ARQUETTE (NANCY),
  TEA LEONI (TINA), ALAN ALDA (RICHARD SCHLICHT-
  ING), LILY TOMLIN (MARY SCHLICHTING), MARY TYLER
  MOORE (MRS. COPLIN), GEORGE SEGAL (MR. COPLIN),
  JOSH BROLIN (TONY), RICHARD JENKINS (PAUL), DAVID
  PATRICK KELLY (FRITZ BOUDREAU)

In interviews after *Spanking the Monkey*, Russell said his next film was going
to be an exploration of sexuality in the manner of *Carnal Knowledge*, full of
"the uncomfortable, emotional-sexual honesty and the humor it generates."[5]
Which, to some degree, it is. *Flirting with Disaster* has elements of sex farce:
a troubled marriage beset by temptations, chance encounters in hallways and
bathrooms, risqué dialogue, suspicions and jealousies that may or may not be
well founded. But the movie is both broader and deeper than all that nudging
and winking. In its protagonist's urge to find his birth parents, it presents
the next chapter of Russell's quest for knowledge of the self. It is, basically, a
slapstick roundelay about the search for identity. The theme would resurface
more explicitly and earnestly in *I Heart Huckabees*. But here, Russell is going
for laughs first. *Flirting with Disaster* is his purest piece of comic filmmaking,
even if, as before, his comedy springs from anxiety, alienation, and domestic
dysfunction.

Russell signals all of this in the opening scene, in which the manic Mel
returns home to find his newborn baby son asleep and his wife Nancy lolling
in bed, hoping to begin the kindling of their post-pregnancy sex life. Even
when the baby wakes up, Nancy is determined to continue, telling Mel to hold
the child while she administers a blow job. Mel is uneasy about this mingling
of the carnal and the parental, and the viewer is meant to be too—Russell
has plunged right back into the nexus of family sexual dynamics that Ray
(apparently) escaped at the end of *Spanking the Monkey*.

But if Russell's model was *Carnal Knowledge*, that first scene establishes
how much has changed, how different is the terrain, in the 25 years between
Mike Nichols's bleak 1971 comedy and *Flirting with Disaster*. Nichols's film
(written by Jules Pfeiffer) charted sexual mores from World War II into the
early 1970s, and suggested that sexual liberation per se was no substitute for,
or even much of an aid to, basic human connection. It is a movie about
the failure of sex to bridge the chasms between individuals. By the time of
Russell's film, whose primary characters are the children of the generation

Nichols depicted, sexuality itself is not so much the issue; frank, sometimes comically earnest discussion and depiction of sex pervades the movie, in an unself-conscious manner that was close to impossible a generation earlier. It is interesting how much is by now taken for granted: the assertiveness of women as men's coequals, the expectations for parental involvement in child-rearing, the willingness (and ability) to talk about emotional needs. But it is also undeniable how much continuity there is in the central challenge of romantic relations. Russell's characters are more self-aware than Nichols's and Pfeiffer's, but still capable of self-deception and still susceptible to both doubts and flattery—still human, basically.

The film has two primary female characters, the practical, newly maternal Nancy and the aggressive, high-strung Tina, an adoption agency worker who accompanies the family on Mel's quest. Tina is sexy in a stylized, angular way, where Nancy is all rounded shoulders and plump breasts. They are not a Madonna-whore pair, they represent a dichotomy more in tune with the times: the single career girl, free to pursue jobs and men with equal fervor, and the postfeminist married mother, trying to balance her sense of herself with the traditional demands of domesticity. Each envies the other. Tina has freedom, while Nancy has stability, a husband, and a child. The film's sympathies are most obviously with Nancy, who is supportive of Mel despite his neuroses and who is unfailingly presented as a protective and attentive mother. But Russell isn't really choosing sides. Tina may be self-absorbed, but her problems stem more from anxiety than ill intent. The film could be read to suggest that what she really wants is a good man and a baby, but Russell seems more attuned to her loneliness than her biological clock. There is nothing antifeminist about suggesting that even beautiful, ambitious women get lonely.

Mel, meanwhile, is another in what would become a series of Russell's neurotic male leads, a protagonist mold inherited most obviously from Woody Allen: the insecure, analytical, sensitive but self-absorbed intellectual. Mel's new fatherhood has paralyzed him, bringing to the surface all his suppressed questions about who he really is. He's convinced he can't be a functioning parent, can't even assign a name to his son, until he connects with his biological parents. Of course, this is a fantasy; in an early scene with his adoptive parents—high-strung, affluent New York Jews—it's clear where most of Mel's sense of himself and the world comes from: nurture, not nature. But in engaging the birth-parent quest, Russell allows Mel to play out a common, and very American, fantasy of self-reinvention: What if we are not who we think we are, who we're expected to be? What if we could be someone else entirely?

Mel's angst makes Nancy nervous, and not without reason. His inability to give a name to their child represents a deep uncertainty about their future together. In their relationship, Russell puts a spotlight on the state of American marriage in his generation. In Russell's movies, as in those of many of his contemporaries, old certainties about family, tradition, and career, about an individual's place in society and the world, have crumbled. But they have not yet been replaced by anything solid. Mel's sense of dislocation is endemic of a generation that grew up with, on the one hand, a great sense of individual potential—free to be you and me—but a nagging absence of guidance as to how to fulfill it, or what that fulfillment would look like. Marriage in particular is an institution in the midst of a major evolutionary overhaul. Mel and Nancy's relationship aspires to the modern ideal of a partnership of equals, but that ideal is inevitably compromised by the arrival of a child. Nancy can feel herself being pulled into a more traditional mother role, dominated by caretaking, while Mel continues his breadwinning. Her seduction of him in the opening scene is, among other things, an attempt to reassert herself as an individual and a partner in the marriage, not just a mother.

But as in *Spanking the Monkey*, Russell is really profiling two generations—the Baby Boomers and their children—and the complicated interplay between them. (Russell himself is a late-stage Baby Boomer, born in 1959, and his own parents are older by half a generation than the parents in his first two movies.) Mel's travels allow Russell to paint a mini-tableau of aging, eccentric Boomers, from the tacky California spiritualist Valerie Swaney to the former Hell's Angel Fritz Boudreau to, eventually, Mel's actual parents: the Schlictings, one-time leftist radicals turned New Age desert artists and manufacturers of high-grade LSD. The portraits are drawn in broad, comic strokes, but, combined with the portrayal of Mel's adoptive New York parents, they suggest a generation of well-intentioned, self-absorbed neurotics.

And their children follow in their footsteps. Just as Mel is obviously shaped by the parents who reared him, so are the other offspring in the movie: Valerie's blond, athletic twin daughters, whose sunny West Coast enthusiasm seems completely foreign to the East Coast intellectual Mel; and his actual brother, Connie, whose arty moodiness and deep involvement in the drug trade stem directly from the influence of his parents. In contemplating him, Mel can have some sense of what he might have been like if he hadn't been given up for adoption. He is clearly relieved to have avoided that fate; his fantasy of being someone else runs up against the reality of who that someone else might be. Of course, Connie regards him with the same kind of incomprehension.

Russell is not so much arguing for one set of parents or the other as suggesting how cumulative experiences form identity.

And in finally seeing his fantasy for what it is, Mel is able to come to terms with who he is and the life he has. For all of the anxieties that underlie his movies, Russell has a forgivable proclivity for happy endings. It is arguably his most Hollywood instinct, but it seems honestly earned. To the extent that his template derives from screwball comedy (or, in the case of *Three Kings*, the caper film), he's just being true to his roots. *Flirting with Disaster* needs a happy ending to fulfill its title, which promises chaos, but only from a safe distance.

The film also presents Russell's first (and, so far, only) gay characters, in the form of FBI agents Paul and Tony. What starts out as a simple joke—gay FBI agents, ha ha—turns unexpectedly into two complex characters, whose bantering, bickering, and uncertain motives (Tony, who identifies as bisexual, flirts with Nancy) add interesting angles to the movie's romantic geometry. Some of their dialogue draws on gay stereotypes, but arguably no more than the other characters are built on stereotypes of their own. As self-confident and unself-consciously masculine gay men, they are more sympathetic and believable gay characters than, say, the sad fops in Paul Thomas Anderson's films. In Russell's film, they're just one more couple trying to work things out.

Like most sex farces, *Flirting with Disaster* is only tangentially interested in actual sex. The film's sexual encounters, few of which are brought to conclusion, are important largely in what they represent about the characters' complicated relationships with each other: Nancy's interrupted seduction of Mel in the first scene; Mel's clumsy kiss with Tina in the bed and breakfast, which leaves him scurrying back to Nancy with a sizable erection; Tony's armpit-licking encounter with Nancy, who admits that what she's enjoying is not the armpit licking, but just the plain old attention. In all of these scenes, Russell treats sex not as titillation—his sex scenes aren't really sexy—but as an extension of his characters' awkward, halting, and often frustrating attempts to communicate and connect with each other.

If Russell's real achievement in *Flirting with Disaster* is making a sophisticated, nuanced, slapstick sex comedy, it is matched by a significant maturation of his filmmaking. The movie establishes a zingy lightness in the bold colors and cartoony design of the opening credits, which carries through even its more dramatically fraught moments. Essentially a circular road movie, it uses the geography and climates of its various settings to chart Mel's progress away from and back to what he eventually realizes is his real home. The plastic suburban California of Valerie, the grimy Rust Belt of Fritz Boudreau and the Arizona desert of the Schlichtings are all presented as alien landscapes, places where Mel seems unmoored and incompatible. The New York that he returns to is the only place he's comfortable—where, in fact, he's *from*.

Russell, after the acclaim for *Spanking the Monkey*, had plenty of actors to choose from, and he capitalized on the opportunity. Ben Stiller's performance as Mel is not too different from the put-upon character he has played in lesser films, like the *Meet the Parents* franchise, but it allows him to draw on his intelligence in a way that those movies don't. Tea Leoni manages the difficult trick of being sexy in a funny way, playing against her trim body and long legs by making Tina overbearing, clumsy, and clueless. Conversely, Patricia Arquette (who has been used as eye candy herself in other roles) embraces Nancy's maternal plumpness, using her physical solidity to give the film its most grounded character. And pitting Mary Tyler Moore and George Segal against Lily Tomlin and Alan Alda as Mel's contrasting sets of parents allows all four to play on their own established personas, to good effect.

Taken as a diptych with *Spanking the Monkey*, *Flirting with Disaster* provides what feels like resolution for Russell's familial angst. Having broken free of the parental bonds that nearly strangle Ray, Mel is able to eventually return happily to the fold, as a husband and father himself. (Just as Russell, by that point, was a husband and father.) So it is maybe no surprise that the filmmaker next turned away from purely domestic concerns.

Three Kings (1999)

WRITTEN BY: JOHN RIDLEY (STORY), DAVID O. RUSSELL (SCREENPLAY)

WITH: GEORGE CLOONEY (MAJ. ARCHIE GATES), MARK WAHLBERG (SFC. TROY BARLOW), ICE CUBE (SSGT. CHIEF ELGIN), SPIKE JONZE (PFC. CONRAD VIG), CLIFF CURTIS (AMIR ABDULLAH), NORA DUNN (ADRIANA CRUZ), JAMIE KENNEDY (PV2 WALTER WOGAMAN), SAID TAGHMAOUI (CAPT. SAID), MYKELTI WILLIAMSON (COL. HORN)

"Are we shooting people, or what?"

The opening line to *Three Kings* is a perfect piece of dialogue, encapsulating in six words the lopsided weirdness that was the 1991 Persian Gulf War, in which American forces and their allies suffered almost no casualties while killing upwards of 100,000 Iraqis. It also sets the stage for the moral uncertainties of the story to come. When the film appeared in 1998, seven years after America invaded Iraq, and five years before it did it again, it was unexpected, even unfashionable; in the midst of the Monica Lewinsky scandal and other concerns of the Clinton era, not many people were thinking too much about Iraq. Having fairly well exhausted Vietnam as a subject in the late 1970s and 1980s, Hollywood war films of the 1990s mostly focused on World War II—*Saving Private Ryan, The Thin Red Line, Schindler's List.* That trend arose from several things: a new willingness to revisit the charnel house of that war with clearer eyes and better cinematic effects (like Steven Spielberg's detailed conjuring of D-Day); a sense that an entire generation ("The Greatest Generation," in Tom Brokaw's formulation) was passing on and in need of memoriams to their singular military achievement; and also a longing for the clear sense of purpose embodied by that war, particularly in the post–Cold War drift of Somalia, Bosnia, Rwanda and other places with complicated problems and no easy solutions.

Despite its status as America's most recent military triumph, the Gulf War didn't obviously lend itself to any of the standard war-movie templates. Most of the combat had been conducted from the air, and the conclusion lacked a sense of resolution. Saddam Hussein was still ensconced in his Baghdad palaces, taunting the United States and periodically making himself enough of a nuisance to warrant a burst of aerial bombardment. The brief surge of yellow-ribboning and celebratory parades that followed the declaration of victory wasn't even enough to get the first President Bush reelected, and dissipated quickly in the recession and layoffs of the time. Before *Three Kings*, the only major film about the conflict was Edward Zwick's *Courage Under Fire*, a very 1990s, identity-politics story that essentially affirmed the capability of women to lead troops in combat.

Three Kings is a very 1990s movie too, but in a different way. It reflects the uncertainties of the post–Cold War era, using the surreality of the Gulf War—the virtual war, the CNN war, the war that introduced the words "smart bomb"—as a theater for its moral Punch 'n' Judy show. That surreality is heightened by the movie's striking look, a sunbaked brightness achieved through a process called bleach bypassing, in which a layer of silver that is usually washed off is left on the film. The result is flattened colors and sharp contrasts that make the movie's desert landscapes (actually filmed in the Southwestern U.S. and Mexico) crackle with white light. It is disorienting enough that the DVD release begins with a disclaimer: "The makers of 'Three Kings' used visual distortion and unusual colors in some scenes of this film.

They intentionally used these unconventional techniques to enhance the emotional intensity of the story line."

The selfless, collective heroism of World War II movies is a distant memory here, but so is the hellish blackness of Vietnam movies. *Three Kings* starts from a posture of self-interested cynicism. Everybody with a brain (which, in this movie, is the officers and the media, but not so much the enlisted men) knows that all the patriotic posturing is mostly pantomime for the folks back home. Major Archie Gates sees his military role as primarily a vehicle to further his own interests—in this case, his amorous pursuits as he counts down his days toward retirement. A former commando assigned to do media relations for an army he no longer respects, and a war he respects even less, he gets intimate with the prettier female reporters and trades quips with his cohorts. "I don't know what we did here," he tells his superior. "Just tell me what we did here." "What do you want to do," his superior retorts, "occupy Iraq and do Vietnam all over again?"

The official story line, of course, was that the Gulf War was the un-Vietnam. As Adriana Cruz—a cable TV reporter obviously modeled on CNN's Christiane Amanpour—says while interviewing a group of young soldiers, "They say you exorcised the ghost of Vietnam with a clear moral imperative." One of the soldiers nods and grins and says, "We liberated Kuwait." But the soldiers don't really understand much about where they are or why they're there, as becomes clear in the dialogue between Sgt. 1st Class Troy Barlow and his companions. In a comically offensive consideration of the proper terms to use when referring to Arabs, "sand niggers" and "dune coons" are ruled out as objectionable, but "towelhead" and "camel jockey" are deemed acceptable. Private Conrad Vig, a poorly educated Southern boy from "a group home in Dallas," tells Barlow, "I apologize, it's just a little confusing with all this pro-Saudi, anti-Iraqi type language and all that."

Three Kings initially takes the form of a wartime caper movie, with Barlow and his friends finding a map to nearby stashes of Saddam's gold. (The plot references the 1970 film *Kelly's Heroes*, in which American soldiers conspire to steal Nazi bullion.) But that's just Russell's way into what he is really interested in: that CNN world, the currents of global conflict and confluence, the ways that differences between people and cultures are bridged, and the ways they're not. When Gates, Barlow, and company arrive at the small Iraqi town where the gold is supposed to be hidden, they are forced to confront their ignorance. When Iraqi troops stationed in the town open fire on a truck attempting to deliver milk to the population, the Americans are transfixed, dumbfounded. They have no idea what's going on. And when one of the Iraqi guards shoots a young Iraqi mother in the head to assert his authority and his immunity from American interference, the Americans feel compelled to respond.

That scene, in which the woman crumples to the ground in slow motion, recalls the TV footage of a South Vietnamese officer shooting a prisoner through the head. It also recasts the film's conflict in clearer moral terms. The villagers are good, Saddam's men are bad, and the Americans finally have a side to fight on that they can understand. That they are also fighting for their looted gold keeps the story moored in the self-interest where it started, but in many ways the film becomes a wishful narrative about American altruism. And when, at the end, the Americans sacrifice their gold to save the lives of the Iraqi refugees they have escorted to the Iranian border, the redemption of the characters—and, by proxy, the nation—is complete. For all of its cynicism about American foreign policy in general and the first Bush administration in particular, and for all of its distaste for the shallow patriotism that accompanied the "liberation of Kuwait," *Three Kings* can't help putting a positive gloss on the entire enterprise. While highlighting the administration's broken promise to support Shiites who rose up against Saddam, it nevertheless purveys a fantasy in which at least one small group of those rebels is rescued by Americans—rather than simply being left to be massacred by Saddam's troops, which is what actually happened. In reaching for the happy ending, however provisional it may be, Russell falls prey to the very war-movie conventions that he spends most of the film skewering.

Still, that skewering is effective. In an early scene where Archie Gates explains to his young, inexperienced comrades what exactly happens when a bullet enters a human body, Russell illustrates the lecture with a striking bit of animation that follows a projectile as it ricochets around inside a torso, puncturing assorted organs. It is an ingenious solution to one of the problems of portraying gun violence onscreen, which is that bodily damage happens internally. Russell dramatically reprises the visualization toward the end of the film, when Barlow is shot.

Even more compelling is the prolonged interrogation in which an Iraqi officer tortures Barlow while questioning him. As the officer bitterly recalls an American bomb that killed his wife and child, Russell makes us watch the ceiling crashing in on the baby's crib, and then shows Barlow imagining the same thing happening to his family. It is a simple but emotionally powerful device, forcing empathy from both Barlow and the audience for the Iraqi inquisitor. The moral picture is further clouded when the interrogator tells Barlow he learned his torture techniques from CIA officers. The climax of the scene comes when the torturer asks Barlow if he knows why the U.S. came to the aid of Kuwait:

"You are here for save Kuwaiti people?" he asks. "Really? Lot of people in trouble in this world, my man. And you don't fight no fucking war for them."

"You invaded another country, you can't do that," Barlow says. "It makes the world crazy, you need to keep it stable."

"For what?" the interrogator asks. "Your pickup truck?" He forces Barlow's mouth open and brings forth a bucket dipped from a barrel of oil. Pouring the oil down Barlow's throat he snarls, "This is your fucking stability, my main man."

The scene is uncomfortable both physically and morally. The torturer is a brute, and the audience's sympathy is with Barlow. But the torturer has been wronged too, and his geopolitics is better informed than Barlow's. The barrel of oil, brought forth like damning evidence in a murder trial, provides a nasty jolt. Of all the characters in the movie who ask why the American military is in the Gulf, the torturer is the only one who offers a straightforward answer.

The contrast between the Iraqi's worldly cynicism and the American's blustering naivete is emblematic of the film's view of American power. The American characters are for the most part ignorant, despite their swaggering self-assurance. The Iraqis, on the other hand, are all too aware of America: the torturer begins his session with a question about Michael Jackson; Iraqi soldiers are shown watching the Rodney King beating video on TV; the Iraqis hoard American blue jeans for sale on the black market, and one Iraqi guard is shown munching a Slim Jim. But it's not just American culture that has pervaded the region. The film presents snapshots of globalization, with French hip-hop blaring from a desert boom box and Arab tribal leaders knowledgably discussing different makes of Lexus automobiles. Apart from the taciturn Archie, the American soldiers seem a little in awe amidst these crosscurrents. The world they set out to save turns out to be a very complicated place.

It is in this sense of Americans adrift, in their lack of preparation for or understanding of the forces they encounter, that the film seems most prescient about the second Iraq invasion that would follow it five years later. Although the movie could be read as an indictment of the first President Bush for leaving Saddam Hussein in power, it also raises warnings about the complexities of Iraq and the dubiousness of American motives in its dealings with the country and the entire region. Russell's message seems not to be pro- or antiwar as much as pro-knowledge and anti-ignorance. The Americans' blithe confidence and lack of understanding of the situation they are entering get them in trouble.

Of course, Russell had no idea another Gulf War would come so soon after *Three Kings*. But when it did, he seemed like a natural filmmaker to revisit that terrain. *Soldiers Pay*, a 35-minute documentary about the 2003 invasion and occupation of Iraq, was originally supposed to be included on a DVD release of *Three Kings*. But in the presidential electoral season of 2004, the same year Disney declined to distribute Michael Moore's film *Fahrenheit 9/11*, Warner Brothers decided not to release the film at all. Russell scrambled for distributors and got the movie shown a few places, most notably on the IFC cable channel the night before the election. Unfortunately, for all the fuss, it is an unremarkable little feature, with some interesting reflections from soldiers who had served in Iraq and a lot of warmed-over rhetoric from assorted political talking heads. Russell lets himself get distracted by one not terribly significant incident of looting by American troops—maybe because of its superficial similarity to *Three Kings*—and devotes a lot more time to it than it deserves. Really, even at 35 minutes the film feels padded, and hardly comprehensive. As far as the strangeness and horror of war goes, *Three Kings* is more convincing on every level than *Soldiers Pay*.

I Heart Huckabees (2004)

WRITTEN BY: DAVID O. RUSSELL AND JEFF BAENA

WITH: JASON SCHWARTZMAN (ALBERT MARKOVSKI), IS-
    ABELLE HUPPERT (CATERINE VAUBAN), DUSTIN HOFF-
    MAN (BERNARD JAFFE), LILY TOMLIN (VIVIAN JAFFE), JUDE
    LAW (BRAD STAND), MARK WAHLBERG (TOMMY CORN),
    NAOMI WATTS (DAWN CAMPBELL)

Russell's fourth feature is an attempt to grapple directly with the philosophical anxieties that underpin all of his films. Its protagonist, Albert Markovski, an environmental activist fighting a proposed chain-store development, is Russell's most obvious doppelganger for himself. As noted above, he shares both a family name and a traumatic childhood memory with the director; and his neurotic pursuit of *meaning*—in his life, in the world—is an analog to Russell's own artistic efforts. But for all of its chin stroking, the film has a screwball sensibility that points again to Russell's almost classical bent for comedy. He puts his characters through absurd trials, playing off emotional frazzle, bewilderment and anger. And he has talents for both physical humor (like the deeply silly, mud-splattered sex scene between Albert and the French nihilist Caterine) and sight gags (like the frumpy overalls that Naomi Watts, as a corporate spokesmodel, dons after developing doubts about the value of her work).

The mixture of comedy and philosophy again recalls Woody Allen, and like some of Allen's efforts, *Huckabees* sometimes struggles to balance those impulses. The film is farcical—the conceit of the "existential detectives" played by Dustin Hoffman and Lily Tomlin places it well outside the bounds of realism. But it is also plainly serious in its questions about the nature of consciousness and, especially, connection. It was Russell's first film after the September 11 attacks, and it refers to them directly in the character of Tommy Corn, a firefighter plunged into a personal crisis by the events of that day. Tommy has become almost evangelically convinced of the need for more compassion and caring in the world. Among other things, he has become a fierce environmentalist who pedals a bicycle to fires rather than riding along on the department's truck.

The chain store, called Huckabees, is a stand-in for Wal-Mart, but Russell's concerns are much broader than commercial sprawl. The glib rapacity of the corporation—embodied by Brad, the smiling, duplicitous executive played with gleaming insincerity by Jude Law—represents a nihilistic counterpoint to Albert's yearning idealism. Russell understands that at its core, environmentalism is built on an ideal of connectedness: of humans to the rest of nature, of the individual to the universe. The crisis Albert faces is that, for all his energetic devotion to his causes, he feels disconnected himself. And that Brad, who does not seem to believe in much of anything, is actually able to impose his will on the world in a way that Albert can't. Albert and his environmental group have been talked (by Brad) into accepting a compromise on the store's development that Albert is convinced amounts to a sellout of his principles. What's worse, Brad is moving to take over Albert's group, for corporate public-relations purposes.

Grasping for any sign of higher purpose, Albert latches onto his coincidental encounters with a tall, young African man, Stephen, idealizing him as some kind of otherworldly presence. Russell plays this fixation as a parody of the liberal tendency to look for affirmation from foreign cultures and races, seeing in them a purer manifestation of nature than can be found in the crass, commercial West. Albert's airy ideas run into Chemlawn reality when he and Tommy go to dinner at the home of Stephen's adoptive, white, suburban family. The family represents everything Tommy and Albert have come to see as corrupt about their own culture, but Stephen is completely happy with

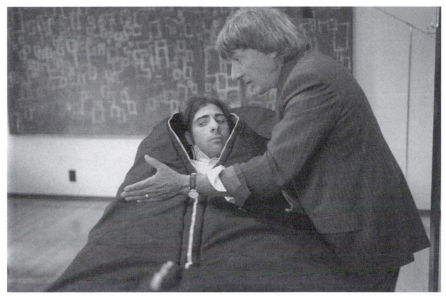

"Existential detective" Bernard Jaffe (Dustin Hoffman) explains the theory of the blanket to Albert (Jason Schwartzman) in David O. Russell's philosophical farce, *I Heart Huckabees*. (Courtesy of Photofest)

them. Tommy's angry hectoring of the family at their own dinner table shows an ugly side to liberal zealotry. Albert and Tommy are driven by their own insecurities and frustrations to lash out, even though lashing out accomplishes the opposite of the interpersonal connection they seek. When both of them find solace in the numb nothingness preached by the nihilist Caterine Vauban, it is as a retreat from the repeated frustration of trying to achieve, or even just believe in, that universal connectedness.

The opposition between Albert and Brad is mirrored by the film's competing philosophers. The existential detectives, Bernard and Vivian Jaffe, believe in connection. Bernard describes the universe to Albert as a blanket, all interwoven, with every person in a distinct spot but all of the spots linked and part of a unified whole. Caterine believes in nothing: no connection, no transcendence, just endless isolation. These are, of course, cartoon distillations of strands of Eastern and Western philosophy—Zen and existentialism, basically—and the level of discourse never really rises above a freshman philosophy seminar. (That may be a good thing, since even as it is, the film left a lot of critics scratching their heads.)

What saves *Huckabees* from ponderous pretension is that Russell, for all of his serious intent, still wants to entertain more than he wants to lecture.

To that end, he cast his battling sages well. Hoffman and Tomlin are smart enough as actors and comedians to ham up the material without simply turning their characters into goofballs; they come across as loopy, but not delusional. They're onto something. So is Isabelle Huppert, who has a grand time spoofing the kind of tormented French intellectual she has played in films like *The Piano Teacher*. Caterine is meant to appear ridiculous, but in a way she is aware of; she is ridiculous because, in her scheme of things, life is ridiculous.

Albert is the third of Russell's neurotic, dark-haired protagonists, and Jason Schwartzman plays him as kind of a triangulation of Ray from *Spanking the Monkey* and his own character Max from Wes Anderson's *Rushmore*: precocious, pretentious, well-intentioned (usually) but boiling over with doubt and resentment. Brad is a good role for Jude Law, whose golden-boy looks and enigmatic grin always give the impression of hiding more than they reveal. (There's something seductively untrustworthy about Law, who is at his best playing ciphers: the "pleasure android" in *A.I.*, the aloof playboy in *The Talented Mr. Ripley*.)

But arguably the two most affecting performances come from Wahlberg and Watts, who play their characters' respective dawning self-awareness with a straight-faced blend of bafflement, anger and wonder. Wahlberg and his directors seem to have figured out that his strength is an ability to maintain an unworldly innocence even after his own corruption, whether that corruption comes via drugs in *Boogie Nights*, combat in *Three Kings* or, here, simply through knowledge. The film, of course, doesn't view him quite as naively as he views himself; in his very first scene, his wife and child are leaving him because of his monomaniacal obsession with philosophical truth. But he remains sympathetic because of his insistent sincerity, which is so often out of kilter with the events that surround him. Watts, meanwhile, pulls another one of her sly reversals, establishing her character as a vapid twinkie just so she can undermine her vapidity. That Dawn and Tommy end up together, hopeful despite their newly sober perspective on the world, is the happiest element of the film's provisionally happy ending.

The movie's kitchen-sink jumble got Russell the most mixed reviews of his career. Apart from inspiring the Rex Reed jeremiad quoted in the introduction—Reed pronounced it "a piece of crap"—*Huckabees* was declared "an authentic disaster" by David Denby in *The New Yorker*,[6] and, for variety, "an unmitigated disaster" by David Edelstein on Slate.com.[7] Some reviewers claimed bewilderment; others merely boredom. But it did have its admirers; writing about it in *The New York Observer* two weeks after Reed had, Andrew Sarris called it "sweet and buoyant" and named it one of the best films of the year,[8] and in *The New York Times*, Manohla Dargis called it "a snort-out-loud-funny master class of controlled chaos."[9] Dargis and Denby both connected the film to the then-imminent presidential election and the country's broader conservative political climate; Dargis said it "captures liberal-left despair with astonishingly good humor," while Denby, more dourly, read it as "virtuous defeatism" in anticipation of George Bush's reelection.

It is certainly easy to see the movie in political terms. Its riffs on current events mark it as at least a politically *aware* movie. But some years removed from its campaign-season release date, its politics seem more clearly personal than electoral. The binary opposition at its heart is not between conservative and liberal or Red States and Blue States; it is, to crib from Sartre, between being and nothingness. And, crucially, the film does not so much take a side as seek to bridge the gap. Russell seems sympathetic to Caterine's existentialist/objectivist cant—he understands alienation —but he is not satisfied with it, because he believes in connection too, or at least the possibility of connection. The film's conclusion reveals that Caterine and the Jaffes are actually working together, intentionally or not, and asserts that, essentially, being alone and being connected are not two different things; they are both true at the same time. It is an affectingly hopeful ending, and one that, like the conclusion of *Spanking the Monkey*, gives a sense of Russell coming to terms (however tentatively) with himself.

Russell represents a particular American type, the manic-depressive white liberal intellectual, and his films in various ways represent the struggles of that genus to make sense of the late twentieth and early twenty-first centuries. There is some acknowledgment in them that liberal intellectualism per se is inadequate to the task.

In *Flirting with Disaster*, he affectionately mocks both hippie idealism and Manhattan yuppieism; in *Huckabees*, neither philosophy nor earnest activism seems up to the job of confronting corporate rapacity; and *Three Kings* presents a political world so complex that it defies both ideology and good intentions. At the same time, Russell's sympathies throughout remain with the liberals, the intellectuals, and activists. He is to some degree sending up his own point of view, but it is still his point of view. The postmodern, post–Cold War, post-everything world might be so riven by uncertainty that all approaches to it require caveats and conditional disclaimers, but Russell still believes in making the effort to connect: across generations, cultures, races, classes, sexes, etc. His movies find hope in the attempt, even if the results are inevitably mixed.

As maybe befits his experience as a labor organizer, Russell is particularly attuned to class and its signifiers, and he doesn't give anyone a free pass. He can present a comic figure like the truck-driving Fritz Boudreau without making him seem either stupid (he's not) or lovable (ditto). The casual bigotry of the working-class soldiers in *Three Kings* is offset by their genuine curiosity about the Arab culture they encounter. Albert in *Huckabees*, the collegiate liberal progressive, is shown to be more condescending toward the young African he befriends than the suburban conservative family that has adopted him. Where there is fault, it is always in making assumptions about other people, and whether those assumptions arise from ignorance or idealism is somewhat beside the point.

6
WES ANDERSON

I t makes sense that the adolescent Wes Anderson resembled to some degree
the adolescent Max Fischer, the hero of *Rushmore* (or, more accurately,
that Max Fischer resembled Wes Anderson). Anderson apparently staged
elaborate drama productions at the private school he attended in Houston,[1]
just as Max orchestrates all manner of extravagant extracurricular activities
(including writing, directing, and starring in a war-is-hell student play about
Vietnam, complete with helicopter and flashpots). As his films have become
progressively more stylized, Anderson has been easy to imagine as Max with
ever bigger budgets, able to spring for ever grander conceits. His movies are
lyrical, sad, funny, and fantastical, in ways that reference literature and theater
as much as cinema. He is an avowed aficionado of J.D. Salinger (Max Fischer
is an obvious descendant of Holden Caufield, and the title family of *The Royal
Tenenbaums* could be cousins of Salinger's Glass family), and his elaborate set
designs are works of self-conscious stagecraft.

But there is a breeziness about his films that keeps oxygen moving through
their sometimes claustrophobic plot and set contrivances. That oxygen is
partly—or maybe largely—thanks to the persistent presence of the unfailingly
breezy Wilson brothers, Owen and Luke, who appeared in and/or cowrote
Anderson's first four films. Owen Wilson in particular, onscreen and off,
seems to act as the obsessive Anderson's puckish foil.

The Wilsons are the most significant of Anderson's partners, but like Paul
Thomas Anderson, he has built an extended family of regular collaborators. His includes the cinematographer Robert Yeoman, the Devo-frontman-
turned-film-composer Mark Mothersbaugh and the editor David Moritz,

along with recurring cast members Bill Murray (who has appeared in three of his films) and the elderly Indian actor Kumar Pallana. And like the other Anderson, Wes Anderson has shown a recurring fascination with family structures and intergenerational bonds and rivalries. After his first film, the sweet-natured crime caper *Bottle Rocket*, his next three movies revolved at least partly around parents (or parent figures) and children. In *Rushmore*, Max Fischer adopts the wealthy Herman Blume as a sort of ad hoc father (while lying to Blume and his schoolmates about his own father, whose scruffy barber-shop embarrasses him). Both *The Royal Tenenbaums* and *The Life Aquatic with Steve Zissou* have problematic fathers at their centers, embodied by Gene Hackman and, again, Murray. (Anderson can take credit for giving Murray roles that helped create and refine the weary, middle-aged male types he went on to play in Sofia Coppola's *Lost in Translation* and Jim Jarmusch's *Broken Flowers*.) Mothers tend to be some combination of supportive and beleaguered, but they are less of a presence, when they are there at all—there are four dead ones among the families of *Rushmore*, *The Royal Tenenbaums*, and *The Life Aquatic*.

It would be too glib to link these themes directly to Anderson's own parents, although they divorced when he was in school and his mother, like Anjelica Huston's character in *The Royal Tenenbaums*, is an archaeologist. More than revisiting his own family, Anderson seems interested in documenting a particular social niche—an eccentric, affluent, precocious slice of America, self-absorbed and often immature, but not, on the whole, badly intentioned. It is a Salinger America, a *New Yorker* America, a Dorothy Parker and Truman Capote America. He likes artists and explorers and scientists, entrepreneurs and oddballs, people whose talents set them apart—he is interested in people who *do* things—but also in some ways hold them back. His characters are misfits whose emotional maturity lags behind their accomplishments, and whose inflated sense of their own importance is consistently challenged by the difficulties of interacting with other human beings. Nevertheless, it is important to Anderson for his flawed heroes to triumph, somehow, over whatever adversities they confront. That those adversities often include their own pride and petulant insecurity just makes the triumphs seem more significant: the greatest achievement for a character in a Wes Anderson movie is simply to grow up.

Anderson had a few pieces of luck in getting his career underway. The first was attending the University of Texas at Austin in the late 1980s, where he ended up in the same writing classes with Owen Wilson. He soon also befriended Wilson's younger brother Luke and older brother Andrew (Luke and Owen became stars, but Andrew also had small parts in Anderson's first three films). It is hard to overstate the importance of the Wilsons to Anderson, and vice versa. They helped create each other. In 1992, Anderson and Owen Wilson produced the first version of *Bottle Rocket*, a black-and-white short that introduced the characters of Dignan and Anthony (played, as in the eventual feature, by Owen and Luke Wilson). The short was well received at film festivals, and attracted the attention—and the financial support—of producers Polly Platt and James L. Brooks, as well as Columbia Pictures. With a $6 million budget, Anderson was able to not only complete the film, but secure the participation of a big-name actor, James Caan.

As a visual stylist, Anderson has gotten progressively more inventive with each film, to the extent that some critics faulted *The Life Aquatic* for neglecting character and plot in favor of elaborately staged set pieces. Although the low-budget naturalism of *Bottle Rocket* showed Anderson's eye for detail and his command of deadpan long shots, the vibrant color schemes, creative editing, and jangling soundtrack of *Rushmore* were a surprise. *The Royal Tenenbaums* and *The Life Aquatic* further developed those attributes, revealing a baroque Pop bent that is not realist, surrealist, or magic realist. If anything, it recalls the fabulism of Terry Gilliam, the former Monty Python animator whose live-action films have retained some of the loopy free associations of his cartoons. But where Gilliam often neglects to populate his ornate soundstages with actual characters, Anderson fills up his movies with complicated, neurotic personalities. (He himself prefers to cite François Truffaut, which makes a certain amount of sense; like Truffaut, he is a comic tragedist, able to suffuse potentially dark material with empathy and humor.) As Owen Wilson says in an interview included on the *Life Aquatic* DVD, "It's a world that Wes creates . . . slightly artificial, but I think within that world the emotions and the feelings are very real."

That world of Anderson's is a distinct and coherent place, a mingling of eras and styles—1950s prep-school literature, 1960s rock 'n' roll, 1970s television, all filtered through an early twentieth-century fondness for the realm of boys' adventure stories. And there are continuities in the details, too: vivid, recurring colors, particularly deep shades of red and yellow; playful character names (some of which are taken from the names of Anderson's friends, including Dignan and Tenenbaum, and some from artists and celebrities, like Robert Mapplethorpe); repeated references to Anderson's own hobbies and interests, like the miniature soldiers that Anthony collects in *Bottle Rocket* (Anderson does too). The photo of Jacques Cousteau on the wall of Mr. Henry's apartment in the same film and a library book Max Fischer reads in *Rushmore* called "Diving for Sunken Treasure" both reflect Anderson's own Cousteau fixation, which came to fruition in *The Life Aquatic*. A design-conscious blog called www.kottke.org has noted that all of Anderson's films make prominent use of the typeface Futura bold, in credit sequences and on signs throughout the movies. (The font was especially popular in the 1950s and 1960s, and was used regularly by Stanley Kubrick.)[2] But despite this whole grab bag of influences, all the baroque affectations, tics and in-jokes, little about the films seems ironic. They are self-aware, but deeply felt. If, say, *The Royal Tenenbaums* is partly a movie about a certain kind of literature, it uses its knowledge of the form not to subvert it, comment on it, or mock it so much as to—as thoroughly as possible—inhabit it.

One of the most interesting commentaries on Anderson came from Pauline Kael, the longtime film critic for *The New Yorker*. She had already retired by the time Anderson started making movies (her last column ran in 1991), but Anderson had grown up reading her reviews and had fantasized about earning one himself. So he tracked her down and called her at home. As he detailed in the introduction to the published screenplay of *Rushmore* (excerpted in *The New York Times*),[3] he arranged for a screening of the movie at a theater near Kael's house in Great Barrington, Massachusetts. He drove her home afterward, and was by his own account disappointed by her response to the movie. "I don't know what you've got here, Wes," she told him. And then, a few minutes later, "I genuinely don't know what to make of this movie."

It is possible, even likely, that Kael's thoughts were less vague and more negative, and she was just being nice. Anderson had gone to a lot of trouble to arrange the screening, and she might have simply wanted to spare his feelings. But it is, really, no surprise that Kael would have been baffled by Wes Anderson. All of the narrative and filmmaking evolution that Kael was around to experience and celebrate as it happened—the brash introductions of explicit sex and violence into the American cinematic vocabulary, the rise of the counterculture and its subsequent absorbtion into the pop mainstream—was part of the received wisdom of Anderson's adolescence. He grew up with Scorsese, Altman, and Coppola as part of the canon. He grew up reading Pauline Kael. He and his peers are the first post-Kael generation of American filmmakers, and so, inevitably, the first to move out ahead and beyond her. The things she spent her career fighting for, aesthetically, were battles Anderson considered already won. No wonder she didn't know what to make of him.

***Bottle Rocket* (1996)**
WRITTEN BY: OWEN WILSON AND WES ANDERSON
WITH: LUKE WILSON (ANTHONY ADAMS), OWEN WIL-
    SON (DIGNAN), LUMI CAVAZOS (INEZ), ROBERT MUS-
    GRAVE (BOB MAPPLETHORPE), JAMES CAAN (MR. HENRY),
    ANDREW WILSON (JOHN "FUTUREMAN" MAPPLETHORPE)

Bottle Rocket did not go unnoticed on its release, but it was not exactly hailed as the arrival of a major talent. At the time, it may have seemed like one more minor variation on the indie crime films that flooded the Sundance circuit in the early- to mid-1990s. (It even sported the requisite cameo by a 1970s icon, with James Caan as the crime boss Mr. Henry.) But with the benefit of hindsight, it seems of a piece with Anderson's subsequent movies. Its protagonists, a trio of would-be thieves, are the first in his string of aspirational dreamers. As with his later heroes, their confidence in their abilities proves comically misplaced. And just as *The Life Aquatic* is a family drama dressed up as a sea adventure, *Bottle Rocket* is not really a crime film. It is a movie about friendship and about learning (or failing to learn) how to live in the real world.

The film opens with a young man, Anthony, leaving a residential mental health clinic. His friend Dignan, who has come to escort him home, thinks Anthony is being held against his will. He has devised an elaborate escape plan, which Anthony goes along with so as not to hurt Dignan's feelings. The sequence encapsulates in miniature the story to come, in which Dignan recruits Anthony for a series of increasingly ill-advised schemes, to which Anthony acquiesces reluctantly. It also represents, in a small way, a significant evolution in the portrayal of mental health treatment. Hollywood had a long history of depicting madhouses and asylums in mostly horrific terms, in movies like *Shock Corridor, Suddenly Last Summer* and, of course, *One Flew Over the Cuckoo's Nest.* Those portrayals, grotesque though they may have been, reflected the unpleasantness of mental health care in America during most of the twentieth century, as well as societal attitudes toward those who required it. But *Bottle Rocket* is a product of the 1990s, the decade that saw an explosion in the use of psychopharmaceuticals and widespread public discussion of depression, anxiety, and other maladies of mood and mind. Psychiatrist Peter Kramer's book *Listening to Prozac* hit the best-seller lists in 1993, followed the next year by Elizabeth Wurtzel's memoir *Prozac Nation.* So the clinic that Anthony has voluntarily entered is shown as a friendly place, with green lawns and picture windows rather than gothic spires and iron gates;

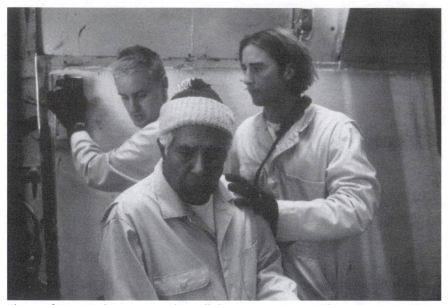

Three of Wes Anderson's regular collaborators—Owen Wilson, Kumar Pallana, and Luke Wilson—prepare for the big heist in *Bottle Rocket*. (Courtesy of Photofest)

the doctor who discharges him with a handshake is avuncular and concerned. And, crucially, Anthony himself is presented as pretty much a regular guy—a little on the sensitive side, but not damaged in any of the ways that movies have traditionally used to signal mental instability. He doesn't twitch, hear voices, or throw fits. The joke in the opening sequence is that Dignan seems much more obviously in need of help than Anthony.

More than any mental problems, what afflicts both of them, and their friend Bob Mapplethorpe, is a lack of purpose. Suspended between adolescence and adulthood, they have not yet found a way to fit into the world. The crime plan that Dignan proposes to Anthony and Bob, at the instigation of his shady employer, Mr. Henry, seems driven more by a need for some kind of accomplishment than a desire for money. Anthony comes from a comfortable background, Bob's family is wealthy and Dignan seems largely oblivious to material concerns. What all three are lacking is any sense of what they are meant to do next. Dignan, the least grounded of the three, is the only one with goals; he has notebooks detailing out his and Anthony's lives for the next 50 years. The plans seem improbable, even to Anthony. But they are, at least, plans.

Bottle Rocket is a riff on the caper film, with a middle section that nods to the conventions of outlaws-on-the-run movies. Anderson and Wilson show a movie buff's fond familiarity with the forms, and the casting of Caan, Sonny Corleone himself, is a nice touch. (In keeping with the film's gentle demeanor, Caan plays Mr. Henry more with amused bluster than malignance.) But the genre trappings never intrude too far on Anderson's bright, wistful tone. Like Anthony and Dignan, the movie is dreamy—and also like them, it sustains its dreaminess even in the face of pain. That is partly thanks to the performances, particularly the Wilsons and Lumi Cavazos, who plays Inez, a motel maid who becomes Anthony's love interest. The three of them enact a kind of emotional ballet. There is a delicacy and grace to the characters, and to the ways they relate to each other.

The romance between Anthony and Inez is the first of several cross-cultural connections in Anderson's films. Where Inez could (and in a lesser film, would) be treated as just an exotic damsel in need, Anderson gives her a full context: the subculture of the motel's Latino employees, the local bars they go to, their specific backgrounds. (Inez is Paraguayan rather than Mexican, which would have been the easy default, especially since Cavazos herself is Mexican.) He plays the language barrier for laughs, most notably in scenes where a dishwasher named Rocky translates for the two lovers. But he does not make Inez or her coworkers into figures of fun themselves. As Rocky says of Inez, "She is a serious person." Compared to Anthony and Dignan, the immigrant workers are all serious people. They don't have the luxury of unseriousness.

Likewise, there's an ambivalent class consciousness in *Bottle Rocket*. Dignan is, apparently, from modest circumstances. (He tells Anthony there would be no point in staging a mock burglary on his mother's house, because there's nothing to steal there.) And he is the one who ends up in jail. Bob is wealthy, and therefore becomes the real target of Mr. Henry's plans. Anthony is of comfortable upper-middle-class stock, and he gets the happy ending.

Anderson doesn't pull back from the sadness in his story, particularly in the character of Dignan, who seems doomed to disappointments of one kind or another. But he resists misanthropy instinctively, as does Anthony, who throughout the film is troubled by instances of callousness and cynicism in the world around him. (As he is leaving the hospital at the beginning, his doctor calls after him, "Don't try to save everybody, Anthony.") So while the closing shot of an incarcerated Dignan walking in a single-file line of prisoners could be heartbreaking, Anderson prefaces it with a scene that allows Dignan his own kind of victory. Sitting on a prison bleacher with Anthony and Bob, who have come to visit him, he suddenly grins and says, "We did it though, didn't we?" Anthony grins back and says, "Yeah, we did it all right." For Dignan, the failure of their heist, and even the knowledge that it was just a diversion so Mr. Henry could burgle Bob's house, is not enough to dispel his sense of accomplishment. He *did* something. And Anthony has accomplished something too. Early on, when Anthony's little sister Grace asks when he's "coming home," Anthony tells her, "I can't come home. I'm an adult now." But there is no conviction in his voice, and she gives him a look of mingled contempt and pity. By the end of the film, that statement seems closer to true.

As modest and light as it is, the film introduces several of Anderson's directorial signatures and quirks. He likes long shots, particularly ones where he can contrast action in the foreground with separate action in the background. (The most obvious example is a bar scene where Anthony and Inez are chatting casually on a bench outside while through the bar's window we can see Dignan being beaten up.) His color palette of distinctive reds and yellows, which assumes more prominence in his subsequent movies, shows up here mostly in the film's wardrobe (including the absurd yellow jumpsuits that the burglary crew wear on their bungled heist). He also uses music well, to juice up the action. Anderson is attuned to specific genres and eras—particularly psychedelic pop and garage rock from the mid- to late-1960s—that dovetail with the romantic exuberance of his characters. In *Bottle Rocket*, he relies mostly on the band Love, using the manic "7 and 7 Is" to pace the fast editing of Dignan and Anthony's practice robbery at Anthony's parents' house, and—to great effect—the erotic build-and-release of "Alone Again Or" to score Anthony and Inez's midday bed romp. The Rolling Stones' "2000 Man" also appears at the end, as a theme for Dignan's stubborn refusal to give in to reality (reality in this case being the police officers who are chasing him). In retrospect, all of these were clues to Anderson's lively imagination and distinct influences. But the range of those attributes would not become fully obvious until his next movie.

Rushmore (1998)

WRITTEN BY: WES ANDERSON AND OWEN WILSON

WITH: JASON SCHWARTZMAN (MAX FISCHER), BILL MURRAY (HERMAN BLUME), OLIVIA WILLIAMS (ROSEMARY CROSS), SEYMOUR CASSEL (BERT FISCHER), BRIAN COX (DR. NELSON GUGGENHEIM), MASON GAMBLE (DIRK CALLOWAY)

Rushmore begins and ends with scenes of Max Fischer triumphant. The scene at the beginning is a daydream, and the one at the end is real and hard-won. The distance between them is the arc of the film's story. But that feel-good ending entails a lot of vitriol, hurt feelings, and property damage along the way. Max Fischer initially appears to be another in a long line of classroom-misfit heros, the nerd who makes good. But his unchecked ego, his sense of entitlement, and his willingness to lash out at anyone who slights him all conspire to confound such pat expectations. It was a coincidence that *Rushmore* came out less than a year before the mass murder at Columbine High School. But the film, as funny as it is, seethes with a barely articulated anger that gets well beneath the skin of conventional schoolyard drama.

That anger is given voice in the opening scene, not by Max but by Herman Blume, the man who will become first Max's role model and patron and then his adversary. Speaking to an assembly at the posh Rushmore academy, Blume—a self-made millionaire and major donor to the school—tells the students, "I never had it like this where I grew up."

"Now for some of you, it doesn't matter," he continues. "You were born rich and you're going to stay rich. But here's my advice to the rest of you: Take dead aim on the rich ones. Get them in the crosshairs, and take them down. Just remember: They can buy anything, but they can't buy backbone."

Blume's speech is a fairly radical bit of class-warmongering, albeit from a clearly capitalist perspective. Blume accepts the prevailing system—he sends his own rich, obnoxious sons to Rushmore—but that doesn't mean he has to like the people who run it. Blume speaks softly, but he carries a big chip on his shoulder; he resents elite privilege, even as he helps sustain it. When he is finished, the only student who stands to applaud is Max.

Although he at first lies to Blume about it, Max is the son of a barber and lives in a modest neighborhood of chain-link fences and carports. His early displays of creativity—writing and staging full-blown theatrical productions while still in second grade—earned him a scholarship to Rushmore, but the scholarship is perennially threatened by his low grades. Near the beginning of the film, the school's headmaster warns Max to curtail his extensive roster of extracurricular activities (which, as detailed in a comical montage, range from president of the calligraphy club to captain of the fencing team). But extracurricular activities are Max's entire *raison d'être*. His academic struggles seem to arise less from a lack of ability than a lack of effort. He is more interested in doing things than learning about them, and his interests themselves are boyishly old-fashioned: stamps and coins, model airplanes, underwater exploration. It is while reading a book on the latter topic that he finds a quote from Jacques Cousteau scribbled in the margin: "When one man, for whatever reason, has the opportunity to lead an extraordinary life, he has no right to keep it to himself." The quote sets Max on a trail that soon leads him to Rosemary Cross, a young British teacher in Rushmore's elementary school. Its resonance with him is unmistakable: as with most of Anderson's flawed heroes, an extraordinary life is his only real goal.

Herman Blume recognizes himself in Max as much as Max sees himself in Blume, and Rosemary Cross finds both of them amusing—at least, for a while. What is most interesting about their romantic triangle is how poignant Anderson and his cast manage to make it, for all of its obvious absurdity. Rosemary, like most of the female objects of desire in Anderson's films, is more sensible than either of her suitors, but she admires their creativity. Anderson tends to present strong women contending with endearing but foolish men. (This is partly because almost all the male characters in Anderson's films are endearingly foolish.) Rosemary's relationship to Herman and Max has something of the sympathy and frustration of a teacher for bright but wayward students. At one point, she tells Max in disgust, "You and Herman deserve each other. You're both little children."

For Herman, both Max and Rosemary represent escapes, or at least diversions, from the status he has achieved but dislikes and distrusts. By the end of the film, the family life he has sacrificed seems not to weigh on him at all. Max, meanwhile, seizes on the courtship of Rosemary with the single-mindedness and confidence in his own abilities that mark all of his other pursuits, which makes the inevitability of its failure that much more painful. It leads not only to the loss of his friendship with Herman, but also to his expulsion from Rushmore, the place around which he has built his entire identity. Within the context of Max's life (and the self-consciously theatrical presentation of the film), it is an almost Shakespearean fall from grace—engineered principally by his own hands, as the tragic-hero form dictates.

But of course, Anderson can't leave it there. As Max's father says, sitting in the audience before the curtain rises on Max's climactic Vietnam play, "I hope it has a happy ending." The line mirrors the anxieties of the film's audience as *Rushmore* enters its final stretch. And as it turns out, the play not only *has* a happy ending, the play *is* the movie's happy ending. It makes Max a success in his new school, solidifies his budding romance with his classmate Margaret Yang, and allows some measure of reconciliation among the core trio of him, Rosemary, and Herman.

The film itself is structured as a play, with curtains rising on the opening credits and then returning to demark each passing month of the story. The months, running from September to January, roughly function as the plot's five acts. Anderson extended this playing with form into his next two films, in different ways. *The Royal Tenenbaums* is presented as a novel, and *The Life Aquatic* as a movie within a movie. The theatrical trappings of *Rushmore* are echoed and heightened by Max's ambitious stage productions, which are in turn primarily inspired by movies, specifically the kind of gritty 1970s American movies that have served as touchstones for other directors of Anderson's generation. One of Max's efforts is an adaptation of *Serpico*, and the other two draw on distinct 1970s genres, blaxploitation gangster movies and Vietnam War epics. In the glimpses of these plays that we see, Anderson both pays affectionate tribute to the original sources and gently satirizes their subsequent adoption and interpretation by his own peers. And by showing Max at his most egomaniacal but also most successful as a director and writer— at the exact school where Anderson himself was a student theater director and writer—he manages the having-cake-and-eating-it trick of making fun of himself and his profession en route to romanticizing both.

In casting the film, Anderson made two crucial choices in Schwartzman and Murray. Schwartzman, who had no acting experience, was supposedly recommended to Anderson's casting director by his cousin, Sofia Coppola (Schwartzman is the son of the actress Talia Shire, Francis Ford Coppola's sister). His thick, dark eyebrows and oversized nose give him a pugnacious air that suits Max's aggressive self-confidence. But Schwartzman is also effective in Max's more vulnerable moments, sobbing as he's being expelled or drunkenly telling Rosemary, "You hurt my feelings!" Anderson wrote Herman Blume specifically for Murray, and the role marked a turning point in the actor's career. In playing a character contending with a midlife crisis, Murray moved fully into his own middle age. Blume has little of the wisecracking petulance that dominated Murray's comic persona through his years on *Saturday Night Live* and in his early hit movies. Instead, the role accentuates the wistful melancholy that Murray would further refine in subsequent movies, with Anderson and other directors.

It seems significant that for the second movie in a row, Anderson and Wilson have their white-American-male protagonist entangled with women of other nationalities or races. Max's crush on Rosemary makes sense as an extension of his identification with Rushmore, which, like all American blazer-and-tie prep schools, has an inevitably Anglo bent. His eventual, if grudging, acceptance of Margaret Yang as his girlfriend seems similarly in line with his integration into an American public school. In some ways, Max's trajectory takes him from a fantasy of transcending his blue-collar American origins—a transcendence promised first (intellectually) by Rushmore and then (carnally) by Rosemary—to accepting his identity as a quintessentially American striver. Even leaving aside his age difference with Rosemary, that identity gives him more in common with Margaret, an upwardly mobile second-generation Korean American.

More problematic on the racial-politics front is Anderson's repeated casting of Kumar Pallana as a bumbling elderly ethnic type. In *Bottle Rocket* he played an incoherent, incompetent safecracker; in *Rushmore*, he is the apparently simpleminded school groundskeeper Mr. LittleJeans; in *The Royal Tenenbaums* he plays the loyal family butler. Pallana is a friend of Anderson and the Wilsons and has by his own account enjoyed the minor celebrity he's gotten from the films, so it seems churlish to suggest that there's something condescendingly buffoonish about his roles. But as with Luis Guzman's comic-relief parts in Paul Thomas Anderson's films, a young white male director consistently casting a nonwhite actor in ethnic-humor roles at least raises some interesting questions.

Rushmore, the movie's fictional school, is obviously a major presence all its own, but not one that Anderson had any difficulty casting. He filmed on the grounds of his own alma mater, the prestigious St. John's School in Houston. Its gabled stone buildings, trees and broad lawns give the film an almost timeless storybook quality—it could be any prep school, any time in the last 50 years. (Well, *almost* any prep school. For 40 years, including during Anderson's time there, St. John's called its teams the Rebels and used the Confederate icon Johnny Reb as a mascot. In what can only be a deliberate jab at that history, Anderson makes Rushmore the home of the Yankees.) Anderson's affection for the place is obvious, even if he, like Max and Herman, has reservations about the privileges it upholds. Its warm, orderly classrooms contrast sharply with the scruffy, fluorescent-lit public school Max is forced to enter after his expulsion. But Max adapts to his new environs, and by the end of the film, Rushmore seems like one more thing he needed to outgrow.

The final scene of the movie is its last theatrical flourish, a virtual curtain call for the entire cast. Max stands at the center, holding a bouquet, as the film speed decelerates into elegiac slow motion. These dreamy bridges to the final credits, always accompanied by swelling rock 'n' roll on the soundtrack, have become a trademark of Anderson's closing shots, a regretful farewell from the filmmaker.

The use of music in *Rushmore* flows almost seamlessly from *Bottle Rocket*, albeit with an aptly British cast to its mid-1960s and early-1970s garage rock and folk pop. The songs show a record collector's taste, spotlighting the relatively obscure Creation alongside the one-hit-wonder Unit 4+2. And even when he opts for outright stars like the Who and Rod Stewart, Anderson does it via songs unfamiliar to classic-rock radio playlists: sections of the mini-rock-opera "A Quick One While He's Away" from the Who, and Stewart singing lead on the Faces track "Ooh La La." The latter closes out the movie, fading in over its final shot, and its chorus sounds both personal and plaintive: "I wish that I knew what I know now/when I was younger." It could be the epitaph of many of Anderson's characters.

The Royal Tenenbaums (2001)

WRITTEN BY: WES ANDERSON AND OWEN WILSON

WITH: GENE HACKMAN (ROYAL TENENBAUM), ANJELICA HUSTON (ETHELINE TENENBAUM), GWYNETH PALTROW (MARGOT TENENBAUM), BEN STILLER (CHAS TENENBAUM), LUKE WILSON (RICHIE TENENBAUM), OWEN WILSON (ELI CASH), DANNY GLOVER (HENRY SHERMAN), BILL MURRAY (RALEIGH ST. CLAIR), ALEC BALDWIN (NARRATOR), SEYMOUR CASSEL (DUSTY), KUMAR PALLANA (PAGODA)

Anderson has called *The Royal Tenenbaums* his New York movie. As he told the BBC, "I am from Texas, but there were so many New York movies and novels which were among my favorites and I didn't have an accurate idea of what New York was like. I wanted to create an exaggerated version of that imaginary New York."[4] More precisely, it is an imaginary Upper East Side, a province of town houses, doormen, and rooftop views of the park, the domain of privilege conjured up by Salinger, E.B. White, and Truman Capote. Anderson has great fun inventing the city, from rattletrap taxis (which all belong to the Gypsy Cab Company) to fictional crosstown bus lines to the improbable 375th Street Y.

The film's title obviously nods to Orson Welles's *The Magnificent Ambersons*, and its tale of a prominent family gone to seed has echoes of Welles' movie (based on a Booth Tarkington novel). Both feature a middle-aged matriarch contemplating a second marriage, to the alarm of family members. The movie's more obvious influence comes from Salinger's interwoven stories of the Glass family. But Anderson's naturally redemptive instincts set him apart, for better and worse, from both Welles and Salinger. For all of the sadness that permeates *The Royal Tenenbaums*, nothing in it resonates with the bitterness of George Amberson Minafer's campaign against his mother's planned marriage—a campaign that essentially wrecks two families—or the numbing tragedy of Seymour Glass's suicide. In Anderson and Wilson's story, the mother's marriage goes ahead, with the eventual blessing even of her ex-husband, and the attempted suicide of Richie Tenenbaum not only fails but leads to familial reconciliation. Like Paul Thomas Anderson and David O. Russell, Anderson and Wilson have an unsentimental view of the damage that can be wrought by nuclear family life. But also like them, the writers of *The Royal Tenenbaums* are ultimately more interested in forgiveness than condemnation.

The narrative conceit this time out is literary. The movie not only begins with a shot of a book called *The Royal Tenenbaums* (and an obligatory hand opening the front cover), it also has an omniscient third-person narrator (the voice of Alec Baldwin). Rather than the five acts of *Rushmore*, it has 10 chapters, plus a prologue and epilogue, each announced with a title page. All of which fits its fiercely literary milieu, a world of people conversant with books and book reviews, newspapers and journals, where even the (relatively) disadvantaged neighbor boy, Eli Cash, grows up to be a successful novelist and a professor of literature. But at the same time, it was Anderson's most imaginatively visual movie yet, with each character, room, building, and prop fretfully designed and arranged to the tiniest detail. Even more than in *Rushmore*, where he relied in part on the readymade gravitas of St. John's School, Anderson in *Tenenbaums* created an entire alternate world, a grown-up storybook setting populated by characters in varying stages of arrested development.

As usual, there is vagueness about the film's time period. The characters seem contemporary, but the wardrobes, hairstyles, and design details are a hodgepodge of 1960s, 1970s, and 1980s references, given coherence by nothing more than Anderson's personal taste. An enlightening short feature on Anderson—directed by Albert Maysles and included in the supplemental DVD with Criterion's *Tenenbaums* package—shows the director obsessing over interior paint colors and carpet patterns for the Tenenbaums' house. His ideas about clothing were so specific that he hired couturiers like Fendi and Lacoste to make exactly what he wanted. Even more than most directors, Anderson uses costumes as an extension of his characters. Like Dignan with his yellow jumpsuit in *Bottle Rocket* and Max with his blue blazer in *Rushmore*, the three Tenenbaum siblings are defined by what they wear: Chas's red adidas tracksuit, Margot's fur coat and black eyeliner, Richie's tennis-pro sweatbands and sunglasses. They don't dress like they grew up in the same decade, much less the same household, but the clashing styles are really an externalization of deeper personal differences, a visual shorthand for the chasms within the family.

The movie's prologue traces the origins of those chasms to the siblings' childhoods, with their parents' separation, the very different relationships all three establish early on with their father, and their early public notoriety as a family of prodigies (or "geniuses," as their mother Etheline calls them in a book she writes about them). Their precocious achievements are detailed in one of the film's several montage sequences, by now established as an Anderson trademark, and set with by-now familiar savvy to an elegiac, orchestral arrangement of "Hey Jude" (a song written for a child, as Anderson certainly knows). But the prologue ends with the narrator reporting that "in fact, virtually all memory of the brilliance of the young Tenenbaums had been erased by two decades of betrayal, failure and disaster." Where both *Bottle Rocket* and *Rushmore* traced arcs of their characters' dreams—from conception through execution to disillusion—*The Royal Tenenbaums* all takes place on the declining side of that arc. The dreams and successes are dispensed with in the first five minutes, leaving the body of the movie as a study in disappointment.

So the Tenenbaums are sad, individually and collectively. They are also, like all of Anderson's protagonists, somewhat ridiculous. Sketched as bundles of talents, hobbies, habits, and neuroses rather than fully articulated characters, they are too vibrant and quirky to be called two-dimensional but still something less than fleshed out. They aren't cartoons; more like slightly elusive figures from a *New Yorker* magazine cover, suggested by flashes of color and angled faces and bodies. They serve the purposes of the movie, because Anderson is as interested in evoking an imaginary place as a particular set of personalities. He compensates for the thinness of these sketchpad characterizations by filling up the frame with them. If you count just Royal and his children, the movie has four main characters to start with. But it adds in Etheline; her suitor, Henry; Eli Cash; Chas's sons, Ari and Uzi; Margot's estranged husband, Raleigh; Raleigh's teenage charge, Dudley; Pagoda, the family's butler and Royal's right-hand man; and assorted other minor but significant characters. The large cast allows Anderson to keep the film in constant narrative motion, skipping around the city and the Tenenbaums' large house from one set of players to another.

At the center of it all is Royal, the most rascally and least defensible of Anderson's ungrown-up men. His infidelities to Etheline are mentioned in passing rather than detailed, but his failings as a father are amply cataloged. He is selfish and self-aggrandizing, defensive and brusque when challenged, and never quick to shoulder responsibility if he can find someone else to do it. His philosophy of life is summed up in one of the scenes in the prologue. During a BB gun war, he shoots Chas from behind. When Chas complains that Royal is supposed to be on his team, Royal crows with a cackle, "There are no teams!" That axiom seems to apply even to his own family: As far as Royal is concerned, it's every man, woman, and child for themselves. Even as he tries to finagle his way back into the affections of Etheline and his children, he can't constrain his own worst impulses, using racial slurs against Henry, interjecting himself into Margot's love life, and lecturing Chas on his parenting.

Longing for the power and security provided by the position of paterfamilias but recoiling from any of its responsibilities, Royal is the embodiment of male prerogative run amok. What makes him interesting, and even appealing, is that Anderson recognizes the freedom promised by male-prerogative-run-amok. Royal is the ultimate expression of the boyish enthusiasm that drives so many of Anderson's characters, and seems, really, to drive Anderson himself. Whatever else he is, Royal is a lot of fun, in ways that nobody else in the family allows themselves to be—except, against their better judgment, when they're with him. He likes adventures, scams, cons, free rides, dogfights, any kind of gamble with a slim chance of a payoff. He is more irresponsible than either Max Fischer or Steve Zissou, but he shares with them a spirited disregard for institutions and conventions. He maintains a boyish confidence in his ability to talk himself out of just about anything, which is as ingratiating as it is immature and irresponsible. Still, when Etheline asks him directly, "Why didn't you give a damn about us, Royal? Why didn't you care?", he can only shrug and say, "I don't know."

His children, meanwhile, seem trapped by their own early successes and failures. The exception is Chas, whose roomy, modernist loft suggests that his investment acumen has continued to pay off. But the loss of his wife in a plane crash has left him fearful and overly protective of his sons, prompting him to move the three of them back into his mother's house. The eventual return of all three siblings to their childhood bedrooms signals their individual unease with adult life and responsibilities, but it also reflects broader trends. At the time *Tenenbaums* came out, at the height of the dot-com bust, the American media was full of stories about adult children returning to the nest. The phenomenon came with its own headline-generating name—"Boomerang Children"—and a host of economic and cultural explanations. The scarcity of well-paid jobs and the rising cost of housing were both usually cited, along with the tendency to delay marriage until the late twenties or early thirties. But it is hard to believe the trend isn't partly related to how comfortable the lives of many American children were in the 1970s and 1980s. The Tenenbaums represent a fantastical extreme, but it can't be a surprise that children who grew up in suburban mini-manses where life revolved around their physical and emotional needs were as loath to move on as Margot and Richie.

Of course, the real source of Margot and Richie's angst is their secret love for each other. Anderson plays the semi-incestuous obsession both for somewhat queasy laughs and for surprisingly affecting pathos. The saddest thing about their mutual infatuation is not its impossibility (even though Margot is adopted, they know they would face moral censure), but what it suggests about the insular, hothouse nature of their childhoods. They sealed themselves off in a private world, and have never been able to fully escape it.

The movie is also Anderson's first to directly consider questions of race, and features his first prominent black character. Henry is a particular kind of black character—highly educated, financially successful, soft-spoken, immaculately dressed—the only kind likely to penetrate the social circles of the Tenenbaums. But none of that shields him from Royal's crude racism. Although Royal's taunts seem intended mostly to needle Henry, there's no mistaking their bitter undertone; he would be angry at any man moving into Etheline's affections, but is even more outraged that it is a black man. The film also reveals that Margot had a brief interracial marriage, to a Jamaican musician, although that is presented largely as evidence of Margot's willfulness and pursuit of the exotic. (The walls of her childhood bedroom are decorated with African animals, and her plays often take place in jungles and other faraway places.) Anderson himself is something of an exoticist; his movies are full of flashes of a nineteenth-century sense of the world outside Anglo-American walls. It is a reactionary sensibility cloaked in nostalgia and boy's-adventure fantasies, and it sits oddly next to the sympathetically drawn multicultural characters who also populate his movies. Compare, for example, the sympathetic subtlety of Inez in *Bottle Rocket* to Margot's wistful remembrance of her Jamaican suitor, who "came out to me in a canoe." The former is a fully seen person, the latter an exotic abstraction.

The Life Aquatic with Steve Zissou (2004)

WRITTEN BY: WES ANDERSON AND NOAH BAUMBACH

WITH: BILL MURRAY (STEVE ZISSOU), OWEN WILSON (NED PLIMPTON), CATE BLANCHETT (JANE WINSLETT-RICHARDSON), ANJELICA HUSTON (ELEANOR ZISSOU), WILLEM DAFOE (KLAUS DAIMLER), JEFF GOLDBLUM (ALISTAIR HENNESSEY), MICHAEL GAMBON (OSEARY DRAKOULIAS), NOAH TAYLOR (VLADIMIR WOLODARSKY), BUD CORT (BILL UBELL), SEU JORGE (PELE DOS SANTOS)

The Life Aquatic is Anderson's first film not to be cowritten by Owen Wilson, and it shows. Although Wilson is in the cast, in his largest role with Anderson since *Bottle Rocket*, the script lacks some of the zonked-out flippancy that he (presumably) contributed to the earlier movies. In its place is a more measured, less leavened melancholy. Although it is Anderson's most obviously absurdist movie—it departs unapologetically from anything like the real world in its very first scene, and never looks back—it is also his most somber. His collaborator this time was Noah Baumbach, a writer-director of comic dramas who shares with Anderson a talent for conveying the difficult dynamics of friend-and-family relationships.

Really, *The Life Aquatic* is three films at once: the seafaring adventure story that Anderson has hinted at throughout his other films, complete with sharks, pirates, and secret island compounds; a midlife-crisis drama about a man adrift on both personal and professional fronts; and a movie about the movie business, which clearly draws on Anderson's experience over the previous decade of dealing with financiers, festivals, critics, rivals, the media, sycophants, and fickle audiences. Almost clairvoyantly, it opens with a scene of its hero, the marine documentary filmmaker Steve Zissou, screening his latest movie for an unappreciative festival crowd. "I think they just didn't get it," a fan tells him afterward. Anderson no doubt needed similar sympathies after *The Life Aquatic* opened. It was his most expensive film to date, and his first certified flop. Disney gave him a budget of $50 million, more than double the cost of *Tenenbaums* and almost 10 times the budget of *Bottle Rocket*. Despite a heavy promotional campaign by the studio, the movie's worldwide gross was about $34 million, less than half what *The Royal Tenenbaums* made. Critical reaction was similarly muted, with the film finding few ardent admirers, numerous detractors, and a general level of ambivalence well summarized by Roger Ebert, who wrote, "I can't recommend it, but I would not for one second discourage you from seeing it."

Critics complained about underdeveloped characters and a general sluggishness of tone, but what seems more likely to have sunk the film's chances at a mass audience is something trickier: for all of its clever contraptions and outsized set pieces, it is arguably Anderson's most personal film. Turned loose with a big budget, he ignored the expectations of the marketplace (if he even understood them to start with, a question his earlier movies perhaps should have caused Disney executives to ask themselves) and built the movie of his dreams. All of its references—to Jacques Cousteau, to David Bowie (whose glam-era songs provide the soundtrack, both in their original forms and as rendered by Brazilian folk singer Seu Jorge), to 1970s TV shows and Tintin and the backbiting world of film glitterati—come from inside his own head, and are connected only by his own fantasies and his sense that they *should* be connected. The prevailing tone is not irony (as some reviewers complained), nor whimsy (or "terminal whimsy," in Ebert's words), but something quirkier and more specific to Anderson. Post-television tragicomedy? Drawing-room postmodernism? You could expend a lot of adjectives circumscribing Anderson's evolving aesthetic. What *The Life Aquatic* made clear was the limit of its appeal, which Anderson seemed to acknowledge in an interview with *Paste* magazine: "I don't think I would know how to deliberately broaden my audience. I mean this movie is a bigger movie than any of the others, for it has the whole adventure element with the gunfights and pirate attacks, but it is definitely a weird movie."[5]

The film is visually arresting in a deliberately retro way. Anderson goes to great pains (and, probably, spent a good chunk of his budget) recreating the 1970s look and technology of Cousteau's underwater explorations. The clips we see of Zissou's films—some of which, we are told, have been big hits—are full of static, expository shots, and decidedly old-fashioned devices. When Zissou wants to show a map, he pulls one down from a classroom-style rollscreen. A long pan of the full-scale cutaway set of the ship (named the *Belafonte*, in a nod to Cousteau's *Calypso*) reveals it to be full of bulky, half-dilapidated machinery. The rickety helicopters and seaplanes used by Zissou and his crew look like relics from *Fantasy Island*, and the deserted island hotel they storm to rescue hostages from pirates also has the feel of a cheesy television set (from *Miami Vice*, perhaps). In all of this, Anderson seems to be trying to recreate not just the TV shows and movies of his youth, but the experience of watching them. His appropriations have a kind of nostalgic yearning, as if by restaging what he remembers, making it new again, he can recapture what it felt like to see it. (This is similar, maybe, to the effect Anderson is seeking with Seu Jorge's dreamy versions of Bowie songs: to take something familiar and make it strange enough for it to seem magical again.)

That yearning sets the tone for the whole film, and dovetails with the weary longing of Steve Zissou himself. He is, ostensibly, hunting the jaguar shark that killed his best friend. But what he's really looking for is a renewal of his own. His career is on a downward slope; he hasn't had a hit film in years, and nattily dressed young men mock him behind his back at the Explorers Club. His relationship with his wife, Eleanor (Anjelica Huston, in another beleaguered-spouse role), has turned frosty. He is having trouble finding money to keep all his projects afloat. The best hope available to him arrives in the form of Ned Plimpton, who might be his son from a long-ago fling. Ned has been a

Team Zissou fan since childhood, and his admiration is undimmed by Steve's declining popularity. Just as importantly, he has $275,000 to invest in Steve's next adventure. But the price Zissou has to pay for accepting Ned is accepting the possibility of paternity. This is no small thing for him. "I hate fathers," he tells Ned, "and I never wanted to be one." (His resistance to the role echoes that of both Herman Blume, who can barely stand to be in the same car with his two insufferable sons, and Royal Tenenbaum.)

Their father-son bonding is tested by their mutual attraction to Jane, the pregnant magazine reporter accompanying the voyage. It is a revisitation of the quasi-oedipal competition between Max Fischer and Herman Blume for Rosemary Cross, but this time both father-figure and son are older, and the advantage goes to the son. Ned also finds himself in competition for Steve's favor with the German crew member Klaus. All of these rivalries and relationships are played straight, with a degree of unabashed sentiment that works improbably well against the corny pastiche of the movie's plot. Anderson and his actors find a surer footing in the freewheeling characters here than they did in the more mannered types of *The Royal Tenenbaums*. Bill Murray, in particular, hits a balance of arrogance, insecurity and, eventually, a kind of scarred serenity that is at least the equal of his more highly praised (and Oscar nominated) performance in *Lost in Translation*. The complex mixture of sadness and satisfaction on his face in the film's closing shot gives unexpected resonance to the oddball tale it concludes.

The death of Ned gives weight to the film's elegiac tone, and makes *The Life Aquatic* the most genuinely tragic of Anderson's movies. It is never clear whether Ned is actually Steve's son—Eleanor's assertion that Steve is infertile throws it into serious doubt—but Steve comes to believe it, or at least to want to believe it. It gives him a chance to pass on his work to another generation, at a time when he is contemplating retirement and worrying about what he will leave behind. When he and the crew finally spot the jaguar shark at the end of the film, shortly after burying Ned at sea, all Steve says as he watches it swim is, "I wonder if he remembers me." It's clear he's not thinking only of the shark.

This obsession with legacy is important to the film's other, meta-strand, its moody contemplation of art, artists, and audiences. The opening scene, at a European film festival, shows Steve contending with fans, reporters, photographers, an ex-girlfriend, a mercenary autograph seeker and, as he's leaving, a sneering heckler outside the velvet rope. It is not a generous portrait of film festivals, but the clashing egos and agendas that permeate film festivals may well not inspire generosity from those who have to deal with them regularly. At the same time, Anderson's portrait of Steve Zissou as a filmmaker does not do much to burnish the mythology of the director. Steve is a preening egomaniac, always thinking about where the camera should be and which scenes will flatter him most. He is insecure about his work, and he reacts angrily when Jane, the reporter, asks him why audiences haven't embraced his recent films. Bromides about art for art's sake aside, he does care what people think of his movies, and he worries constantly about how they—and he—will be received. (There are obvious parallels between the festival scenes in *The Life Aquatic* and Woody Allen's *Stardust Memories*, in which Allen, playing a filmmaker very like himself, encounters fans who tell him they like his "early, funny movies.")

Steve defends his mining of his own life for dramatic material on the grounds of candor, but what he's really concerned with is entertainment value. He initially sees Ned's arrival principally as a good secondary story line. Among other things, this is a reminder that Jacques Cousteau himself was a pioneer of "reality television," constructing narratives in which he and his crew played the leads. At one point, during an argument, Ned angrily says to Steve, "You never wanted to know me. I'm just a character in your film!" Steve snaps back, "It's a documentary! It's all really happening!" But Anderson positions the camera back far enough to reveal the cutaway set of the ship's interior, suggesting the phoniness of the entire enterprise of filmmaking.

Anderson accentuates the phoniness of his own film with an array of playful devices. He includes Jorge as a character, Pelé, a member of the *Belafonte*'s crew who happens to spend most of his time sitting around singing David Bowie songs in Portugese. (Even when he's supposed to be keeping watch, which is what allows pirates to board the ship.) He breaks the film into television-like episodes, with onscreen titles like "Day 27: Rescuing the Bond Company Stooge." And for his underwater sequences, he employs the stop-motion animator Henry Selick to create a menagerie of fanciful, pastel-hued sea creatures, the most striking of which is the enormous, luminous jaguar shark. The animals seem exactly like the kind of things a young fan of Jacques Cousteau might invent for his own imaginary voyages. (Anderson apparently enjoyed working with Selick so much that the two are reportedly teaming for an animated version of Roald Dahl's book *The Fantastic Mr. Fox*.)

The movie concludes back at the same festival the next year, with Steve's new film getting rapturous applause. But Steve is not inside to hear it. He sits meditatively on the red carpet outside, where he is joined by a small boy (introduced earlier as Klaus's nephew). The boy perhaps represents to Steve things that he has lost—his son, and his own youth—but losses he has learned to live with. Turning to the boy, he says, "This is an adventure," and hoists him onto his shoulders as the crowd begins to pour out of the theater behind them. For Zissou, and maybe for Anderson as well, the moral seems to be that simply living every day is adventure enough.

Anderson made his first four films before he turned 35, and they feel like young-man's movies. Even though several of them are concerned with men of middle age or older (Herman Blume, Royal Tenenbaum, Steve Zissou), the characters are all in varying stages of arrested development—in contrast to the more fully adult figures in the films, who tend to be women (the major exception being Henry Sherman in *The Royal Tenenbaums*, whose dignified reserve sets him far apart from Royal). Anderson's stories return again and again to overgrown man-boys, whose rashness and irresponsibility make them both lovable and infuriating. In different ways, the movies all trace character arcs of maturity. As Anderson himself grows older, it will be interesting to see if this struggle with adulthood continues to dominate his stories.

It will also be interesting to see whether he continues to refine his visual approach along ever more baroque and hermetic lines, or if he will outgrow the stagy storybook contraptions. The mixed reaction to *The Life Aquatic* suggests that he may have pushed his insular style as far as audiences are willing to go (not to mention studios; it is unlikely he'll get another budget the size of that film). In any case, he has already proved himself a distinct, quirky talent: an eccentric aesthete with a garage-rock heart.

7

CHARLIE KAUFMAN, SPIKE JONZE, AND MICHEL GONDRY

The relationship between writers and directors in Hollywood is famously one-sided. Although there have been plenty of notable screenwriters who never directed a film, they rarely rise to the level of public or critical acclaim granted to directors. Think of *The Big Sleep* and *Rio Bravo*, for example, and the first name that comes to mind is Howard Hawks, who directed them, rather than Jules Furthman, who wrote them. From the earliest days of movies, filmmakers who wanted maximum control of their work, and recognition for it, have been writer/directors. Even the highest-paid writers in Hollywood are often treated more like skilled technicians, brought in to buff up a script, than stand-alone artists.

So the emergence of Charlie Kaufman has been singular and close to unprecedented. He has written movies so identifiably his own—in one case even inserting himself as the main character—that it is possible, and has become common, to talk about "a Charlie Kaufman film" in the auteurist manner usually reserved for directors. This distinction is especially remarkable considering how enthusiastically weird his scripts tend to be, and therefore how dependent they are on a sympathetic director to bring them to fruition. Surrealist farces and romances full of fantasy sequences, philosophical conundrums, and meta-commentary on the nature and process of cinema, they seem unlikely vehicles to attract stars and studio funding. The script for what became his first film, *Being John Malkovich*, circulated through Hollywood for years, acquiring admirers and a double-edged reputation as a great movie that would never get made. As Sharon Waxman put it in *Rebels on the Backlot*, "People read it, marveled at it, and put it on the pile of Things To Do As Soon As I Get Some Money."[1]

Kaufman's screenplays are not written with much regard for the conventions of storytelling as Hollywood understands it. One of them, *Adaptation*, is partly a jeremiad against the creative bankruptcy of story-arc formulas and market-driven studio timidity. Kaufman wants movies to *say things* and *do things*, to surprise their audiences and grapple with big questions. But, crucially, he also wants to entertain. His scripts are filled with absurdist humor and odd moments of old-fashioned slapstick. He is not above a device as hoary as the hard-of-hearing receptionist in *Being John Malkovich*, who misunderstands everything everybody says to her. He knows it's a hoary device, of course; his tacit acknowledgment of that is part of what makes it funny. This self-awareness is central to Kaufman's approach, and also of course an obstacle that he wrestles with (most explicitly in *Adaptation*). He wants his movies to work as movies, but without falling into the rote patterns and mechanics that "movies" are generally understood to comprise.

It seems fitting that the two directors who have so far been most successful in making cinematic sense of his writing were themselves strangers to Hollywood convention. Spike Jonze and Michel Gondry both got their starts as self-taught videographers, cobbling together inexpensive clips that made a virtue of their lack of resources. Although their styles are different—Jonze is cooler and grittier, Gondry is warmer and dreamier—they both practice what could be called kitchen-sink surrealism, using low-key and often low-tech effects to introduce fantastical elements into deceptively humdrum settings. Both of them came to filmmaking via music videos and advertising, although with distinct routes.

Jonze was a suburban skateboarder and BMX biker who started out writing and taking photographs for niche sports magazines, and graduated to making self-produced skater videos that deliberately blurred the line between documentary and drama. (His real name is Adam Spiegel; as a teenager, he took on the name Spike Jones—presumably after the legendary comic musician—which eventually became Jonze.)[2] His early music videos, for songs like the Beastie Boys' "Sabotage" and the Breeders' "Cannonball" (which he codirected with Kim Gordon of Sonic Youth) show his preference for grainy over- and underexposure and a knack for conceptual goofery. "Cannonball," a more or less normal rock-video performance clip, is punctuated by scenes of a black cannonball rolling down city streets and sidewalks with great velocity and possibly ominous intent. "Sabotage" is a send-up of 1970s cop shows, with the three Beasties wearing bad mustaches and cheap suits, enacting a series of cliché chases, fights, and showdowns.

Jonze went to work for Satellite Films, a division of the music video and commercial production house Propaganda, which had been founded in the early 1980s by a group of filmmakers including David Fincher. A lot of the videos that followed had relatively simple ideas executed with obsessive virtuosity (a man on fire running down the street, in lyrical slow motion, for Wax's "California"; Christopher Walken dancing, and eventually flying, around an empty hotel lobby for Fatboy Slim's "Weapon of Choice"). Maybe the purest example is the video for "Drop" by the rap group the Pharcyde, which is a series of long tracking shots, run in reverse. Jonze helped the rappers learn to mouth the lyrics backward so the lip-synching would at least come close to matching. They dance and leap around the frame, and everything about their motions and their relationship to gravity is just slightly off. Jonze's videos also show a skater's particular awareness of urban settings, a sense of adventure awaiting down city streets and alleys.

Gondry, the only non-American director in the group considered here, grew up in Versailles, outside Paris, and started teaching himself photography when he was 12.[3] He began to make short films in his early twenties, while he was also playing drums in a French band called Oui Oui. The interests naturally collided, and he produced several animated videos for the band. But his breakthrough came in working with the Icelandic singer Bjork, who recruited him for "Human Behavior," the first single of her solo career. (She had been the lead singer in the Sugarcubes.)

Several other Bjork videos followed, all of them playful and disturbing, and Gondry also began to pick up commercial work and other music video assignments. For the Rolling Stones' concert recording of Bob Dylan's "Like a Rolling Stone," he pioneered a method of shooting the same scene from multiple angles and then digitally morphing the images to give the illusion of a frozen three-dimensional image. A higher-budget version of this technique was popularized in the first *Matrix* film (it came to be called "bullet time," after the suspended projectiles that Keanu Reeves dodges). But it was just one of Gondry's ways of manipulating images, which range from the simplistic (images projected on objects) to the staggeringly ornate (the painstaking stop-motion animation of the video for the White Stripes' "Fell in Love With a Girl," which Gondry spent two months filming with Lego blocks).

Gondry also had an affiliation with Propaganda Films, and it was inevitable that he and Jonze would cross paths. (They even worked with some of the same artists, each directing videos for Bjork and Daft Punk.) In the booklet accompanying a DVD collection of Jonze's video work, Jonze recounts meeting Gondry. "We ended up talking for five hours, about everything we wanted to do," Jonze says. "I was asking him how he did this or how he did that. He was telling me about this thing I couldn't even understand—how he wanted to build a camera that could somehow change the cogs in the gears so instead of it rolling at 24 frames a second, half the camera would roll at 24, and half the time it would roll at 25. I don't remember exactly what the idea was because I had no idea what he was talking about. He was thinking on a whole other level." As that suggests, Gondry is the more mechanically adept of the two. He is also the more educated in film history. Many of his videos mimic specific visual styles and eras, from silent films to movie musicals. Jonze is more of a gut-instinct artist, with only the vaguest historical or technical grounding. (Sharon Waxman quotes John Malkovich as being stunned to discover that Jonze has never heard of *A Streetcar Named Desire*.)[4] But Gondry envies those instincts: On a section of the DVD of his own video collection, he recalls a dream in which he watched Jonze making a video and was madly jealous of Jonze's ideas.

In any case, they got along well, and it was through Jonze that Gondry eventually met Charlie Kaufman. Kaufman, invariably described in print as introverted and slight (the Internet Movie Database lists his height as 5′ 4$^1/_2$″), spent the mid-1990s taking whatever TV writing jobs he could find and trying to sell his screenplays. (Among other things, he worked with his friend Chris Elliott, the comedian, on short films for David Letterman's talk show.) Jonze was one of the dozens who had read and fallen in love with the script for *Malkovich*. When he was given a chance to direct a movie (by R.E.M. singer Michael Stipe, who had started a production company), *Malkovich* was his first choice. The convoluted tale of its production is recorded in Waxman's book; suffice to say it faced skepticism at every step of the way (including from Malkovich himself). But after screenings at the Venice and New York film festivals in 1999, it became one of the most talked-about films of the year. In *The New York Times*, Janet Maslin called it "endearingly nutty" and "irresistible," and singled out the "terrific original screenplay by Charlie Kaufman."[5] Although only a modest hit, the film earned Oscar nominations for both Jonze and Kaufman, and made them hot properties in Hollywood. Or at least on the artier fringes of Hollywood, to the extent that such fringes exist. (It didn't hurt that Jonze had also earned notice as an actor the year before in David O. Russell's *Three Kings*. He and Russell had become friends a few years earlier while working on an adaptation of the children's book *Harold and the Purple Crayon*, which was never produced.)

Gondry's first film with Kaufman, *Human Nature*, which Jonze produced, was not as critically or commercially successful. But his second, 2004's *Eternal Sunshine of the Spotless Mind*, was widely lauded and a medium-sized hit to boot. (Its international box office actually exceeded what it made in the United States, giving it a respectable global take of $72 million.) It also won a screenwriting Oscar for Kaufman, Gondry, and their partner Pierre Bismuth.

With both Jonze and Gondry, Kaufman found complementary spirits, free-spirited filmmakers with the seeming ability to channel images from the subconscious directly onto the screen. Like Kaufman, both of them casually mingle the surreal with the naturalistic, and the conceptually naive with the technically sophisticated. Their almost childlike playfulness matches up well with the more intellectual absurdity of Kaufman's writing, leavening and humanizing the abstractions of his stories. Metaphysical comedy requires a careful balance of balloon and ballast, and collectively the work of Jonze, Gondry, and Kaufman manages to float more than sink (but without simply floating away). By comparison, the only other director to take a crack at Kaufman so far—George Clooney, in his directorial debut with *The Most Dangerous Man in the World*—is well intentioned but flat-footed.

Kaufman's concerns as a writer are primarily existential, but with a socio-biological bent; his questions about who we are and how we got that way are underscored by an appreciation of evolutionary biology, as well as a roman-tic's skepticism of the limitations of science. His stories are all about quests for transcendence of one kind or another—via love in *Eternal Sunshine*, art in *Adaptation*, science in *Human Nature* and, well, John Malkovich in *Being John Malkovich*—and the ways that those quests are invariably flawed and frustrated. None of them have completely happy endings, but neither are they despairing. Kaufman tends to populate his narratives with cynics, including one named "Charlie Kaufman" in *Adaptation*, only to show up their bitterness as reflexive insecurity. In his stories, the search for some kind of connection is cast as an almost unavoidably sordid affair, full of selfishness, deception, and compromise. But it is also, potentially, sometimes, worth the effort.

Being John Malkovich (1999)
WRITTEN BY: CHARLIE KAUFMAN
WITH: JOHN CUSACK (CRAIG SCHWARTZ), CAMERON DIAZ
(LOTTE SCHWARTZ), CATHERINE KEENER (MAXINE), JOHN
MALKOVICH (JOHN MALKOVICH)

The buzz about *Being John Malkovich* started well before the film was released, although early reports got the film's focus somewhat wrong. Plot summaries tended to emphasize the last two words of the title more than the first one. The prospect of John Malkovich, or any well-known actor, playing himself in a movie about people crawling inside his head made good fodder for a celebrity-obsessed age. But while Malkovich both as a persona and a cast member is essential to the film—with any other performer, it would be a different movie in all kinds of ways—he is also a red herring, or at least a MacGuffin. The movie is not really about being John Malkovich, or about being a celebrity (the Malkovich in the movie, at least, is a very peripheral celebrity anyway; a lot of people haven't heard of him, and the ones who have keep getting his movies mixed up with other people's). It is mostly about the chance to be someone else, *anyone* else. It is a not altogether uplifting contemplation of identity, art, and the search for transcendence. It's also, fortunately, very funny.

The main character, more or less, is Craig Schwartz, a frustrated slacker-artist type. His art, improbably, is puppetry—a form that, even more improbably, has a significant public following in the world of *Being John Malkovich*. Craig watches grumpily as a rival puppeteer stages spectacular televised events, like suspending a 60-foot puppet of Emily Dickinson from a bridge for a performance of *The Belle of Amherst*. Craig is kind of a morose jerk, and is brusque with his neurotic wife, Lotte, who works to support both of them. But his puppetry is actually very good, full of balletic effects and achingly romantic themes. (Its suggestive sexuality tends to get Craig assaulted by angry parents on the street, after children stop to watch.) Craig's work establishes the theme of the film; as he explains at one point, the appeal of puppetry is "perhaps the idea of becoming someone else for a little while, being inside another skin, thinking differently, moving differently, feeling differently."

That is the experience offered by the portal into Malkovich's brain that the film revolves around. Craig finds the portal after taking a filing job in a records firm on the $7\frac{1}{2}$ floor of a Manhattan office building. (The origin of the low-ceilinged half-floor is explained in an orientation video that is a spot-on parody of corporate training films. As he demonstrated in his music-video send-ups of TV shows and musicals, Jonze is a gifted mimic.) Moving a filing cabinet, Craig happens on a small door that leads into a dirt-floored tunnel. Crawling in out of curiosity, he suddenly finds himself sucked deep into darkness, and then into what turns out to be John Malkovich's head. He spends about 15 minutes there, watching through Malkovich's eyes as he reads *The Wall Street Journal* and eats breakfast, before being dumped out onto a scrubby slope alongside the New Jersey Turnpike.

Jonze uses deliberately primitive effects to convey all of this. The experience of being inside Malkovich is conveyed by simply painting a black oval on the lens (to suggest the restricted vision of someone sitting a little distance behind Malkovich's eyes) and muffling the sound slightly. And, crucially, most of what people who enter Malkovich experience is mundane: Malkovich taking a shower, Malkovich ordering a rug from a catalog, Malkovich having dinner. Because it is someone else's mundane life rather than their own, the people who pay Craig and his business partner Maxine for the privilege of entering the portal find it exhilarating. When Lotte enters the portal, the exciting experience of being a man convinces her that she is a repressed transsexual. Significantly, Maxine, the movie's most confident, self-possessed character, does not enter the portal (at least, not until near the end, when Lotte chases her into it). She isn't curious about being someone else, although she gets turned on by the idea of *controlling* other people. Her manipulation of Lotte and Craig when they're inside Malkovich is just an extension of the way she manipulates people in her daily life.

And that's the dark side of the movie's fantasy, the way the relatively innocent impulse to merely escape one's self changes easily into the impulse to subjugate others. What starts out as a search for transcendence becomes a search for control. Malkovich is hijacked and exploited, first by Craig and Maxine and then by the group of people (assembled by Craig's employer Dr. Lester) who move into Malkovich to escape their own mortality. In a further twist on the transcendental urge, Craig ends up trapped inside the head of Maxine and Lotte's daughter, as a passive observer unable to exert any influence over her. (His lack of control is conveyed by an even smaller visual portal, as if he is looking out her eyes at the end of a long tunnel.) In contrast, the only lasting interpersonal connection in the movie is made between Lotte and Maxine, who realize finally that they can be happy with each other as they are. It is a fairly straightforward moral for such a convoluted fable, but that is true of most of Kaufman's stories.

The cast gives admirably unlovable performances. The characters are by turns needy (Craig and Lotte), narcissistic (Maxine) and egomaniacal (Dr. Lester). Cusack—a fan of the script who told his agent to let him know if anyone ever got around to making it—gamely buries his casual good-guy charm under Craig's scruffy insecurity. Cameron Diaz, who was fresh off her sparkling role in *There's Something About Mary*, is nearly unrecognizable in Lotte's frizzy hair and frumpy wardrobe, her effervescence channeled into anxiety. And Catherine Keener is flinty, sexy, and sadistically inaccessible as Maxine, an openly contemptuous object of desire. She softens somewhat by the end, of course, but Maxine's happy ending is still notable: Not many male writers or directors have ever conceived such a brashly emasculating *femme fatale* without feeling the need to punish her. (Keener received an Oscar nomination for supporting actress—and, one imagines, a lot of masochistic fan mail.)

The most important performance, and the most complex, comes from Malkovich. Not only does he have to play Kaufman's version of himself, but he also has to play himself as inhabited by, first, Craig, and then by Dr. Lester. Just being willing to make the movie at all marked Malkovich as a more than good sport, especially considering that the script calls for a scene of ungraceful, half-naked dancing; but he is also, of course, a terrific actor. His natural inclination toward understatement works with the material the same way Jonze's flattened visual style does; a more frenzied approach might have made the movie merely ridiculous rather than compellingly strange. He makes the moments when he is fighting for control of his body with Craig simultaneously funny and frightening. (They recall Steve Martin's similar loss of physical command in *All of Me*.) Charlie Sheen also provides a likable cameo, parodying his own image as a womanizing party animal (in the movie's epilogue, which takes place seven years after the main story, he shows up bald and paunchy in a Hawaiian shirt).

Of course, in addition to being a riff on the human state in general, Kaufman's story is a parable about writing, acting, and filmmaking. A story-teller creates, inhabits, and controls characters, as does an actor. A director manipulates both actors and their characters, like a puppeteer. An actor is in a perpetual state of trying to inhabit another body. Part of the joke in the idea of being John Malkovich is that John Malkovich himself isn't John Malkovich, at least as far as the general public is concerned. He is an amalgamation of all the roles he's played (and even roles he hasn't played, as people in the film continually mistake him for other actors). Other people in the movie strive to be him, just as he, in movies, strives to be other people.

And the film suggests there is always something compromised in the attempt—that no matter how artful the illusion (and Craig's puppet shows are very artful, as is Malkovich's acting), there are barriers that even the imagination can't leap. Nobody ever really escapes themselves, at least not in life. (Kaufman's worldview is pointedly secular, so the possibility of post-life transcendence doesn't concern him much.) His movies are full of people trying and failing to circumvent their own limitations, but making discoveries along the way.

Being John Malkovich also wrestles with quasi-scientific questions, as many of Kaufman's stories do. Although the science-fiction part of it is left cheerfully unexplained (as if there could be a rational explanation for the brain portals), the movie's central conundrum—what makes us *us*?—reflects ongoing scientific inquiry into the nature of consciousness. In the movie, the self is clearly located in the consciousness; the body is a puppet of the mind. So when the mind becomes subject to manipulation (via the portals here, or via memory erasure in *Eternal Sunshine of the Spotless Mind*), so does the entire sense of self-identity. And our awareness of what drives us is shaky at best, as Jonze and Kaufman illustrate in one of the movie's set pieces: Lotte chasing Maxine through Malkovich's subconscious, tumbling from one traumatic or exciting memory into another. (Gondry and Kaufman staged an even more elaborate variation on the same scenario in *Eternal Sunshine*.)

Kaufman's ideas update the Surrealist fascination with the subconscious, which was heavily Freudian, to incorporate more recent neurological insights about the role of brain chemistry and the way different areas of the brain take charge of different functions. In Kaufman's view, who we are is a fluid thing, the product of a constant struggle for authority in our own minds between competing impulses and influences. How much control we can consciously assert over those impulses was the subject of the next of Kaufman's scripts to reach the screen.

Human Nature (2002)
WRITTEN BY: MICHEL GONDRY
WITH: TIM ROBBINS (DR. NATHAN BRONFMAN), PATRICIA
    ARQUETTE (LILA JUTE), RHYS IFANS (PUFF BRONFMAN),
    MIRANDA OTTO (GABRIELLE)

One of Michel Gondry's first videos to gain international attention was for Bjork's song "Human Behavior," which begins with the lines, "If you ever get close to a human/And human behavior/You'd better be ready to get confused." For the video, Gondry used a combination of charmingly ragged effects—rear-screen projection, stop-motion animation, people dressed in animal suits—to create a whimsical but unnerving fairy-tale setting. At some points, Bjork and a slow-moving hedgehog are menaced by a zooming car while trying to cross a highway. At another point, a giant, lumbering teddy bear tracks a hunter (who is tracking the bear), and beats him to death. The bear later eats Bjork, and Gondry shows her singing from inside the bear's stomach. But then we see Bjork back in her forest cottage, with the bear's head superimposed inside her own: She's in the bear, and the bear's in her.

The video suggests Gondry's affinity for the material in *Human Nature*, which is essentially a nature-vs.-nurture story turned on its head. Rather than asking whether genes matter more than environment, Kaufman's daffy but somewhat melancholy script asks whether we can ever be free of either. The answer, as one might expect, is no. We're pretty well stuck. Lila Jute, one of the film's three main characters, tells detectives in a jailhouse where she's being held on murder charges, "I've been in jail my whole life anyway: a jail of blood and tissue and coursing hormones. A jail called the human body." The dialogue is delivered in deadpan melodramatic fashion, but it is also the movie's thesis statement: We can contain and condition ourselves in any number of ways, but we still run into the limits and demands of our own biological functions.

Despite the involvement of Kaufman and Jonze (who coproduced and also helped with second-unit work), *Human Nature* arrived too late to catch any real post-*Malkovich* buzz. It is also, frankly, a lesser film, entertaining and inventive in its own right but not as deeply imagined in the script or richly realized on the screen. It opened to middling reviews and sank with barely a trace at the box office, registering a domestic U.S. take of just over $700,000. But for a minor work, it engages with some major themes. And as Gondry's feature debut, it affirmed his ability to harness his visual and narrative playfulness in the service of a full-fledged story.

Via flashbacks, the film introduces its three principals as children: Lila, as a 12-year-old, discovering to her horror that she is beginning to grow hair all over her body; Nathan Bronfman, the adopted son of neurotic, etiquette-obsessed parents, who send him to his room without supper if he uses the wrong fork for his salad; and Puff, who as a young child is kidnapped by his deranged father and taken to live as apes in the forest. (The flashbacks have the grainy, washed-out look of old Super-8 movies, one of several small signs of Gondry's expansive visual vocabulary.)

In her adulthood, Lila, covered in light brown fur and tired of working in freak shows, also runs off to the woods. Gondry stages an out-of-left-field musical number, in which Lila cavorts with woodland creatures while singing lines like "I once thought God a creature diabolical/ He gave the nod to each one of my follicles." It's a live-action spoof of Disney cartoons—just as a later scene, in which Lila pursues Puff from branch to branch, swinging on tree vines, is a well-staged homage to Tarzan. Lila writes a series of best-selling nature books, including one called *Fuck*

Humanity! But she is lonely, and, more to the point, horny; her reproductive instincts ultimately drive her out of the forest and back to the city to seek a mate.

The two men she ends up involved with represent two extremes: Nathan, the uptight and oppressive scientist determined to tame nature (he is using electric shock to teach mice table manners); and Puff, the naked, feral tree-dweller, raised to believe he is an ape. Nathan's repression manifests itself physically, in a very small penis. But even a shrunken organ can't keep natural impulses in check, as Nathan discovers somewhat to his disgust. As his relationship with Lila progresses, he realizes that "love is nothing more than a messy conglomeration of need, desperation, fear of death and insecurity about penis size." Meanwhile, Puff, who has been captured by Nathan for study, starts to take his behavioral training seriously after he sees Nathan and his assistant Gabrielle having sex on the floor of the laboratory. "To use the vernacular," Puff says, "I wanted me some of that. And I think I understood from that moment that in order to get some, I'd have to play their game." So his incentive to civilize comes not from eliminating animal urges, but from seeking to realize them.

But if Nathan's hubris about civilization is deluded, so is Lila's idealization of the "natural" world. Convinced that Puff has been broken and corrupted by modern human life, she kidnaps him and takes him back to the woods, where they live for a while in a sort of Edenic bliss. (Gondry cannily makes the natural world seem more dreamy than "natural," using soundstages and artificial lighting to evoke Lila's utopian illusions.) Lila is even willing to go to jail to protect Puff after he shoots and kills Nathan, because she believes she is sacrificing herself so that he can continue to live in the wild. At her request, Puff testifies to Congress about his experience, concluding, "There is indeed a paradise lost. Humans have become so enamored of their intellectual prowess that they have forgotten to look to the earth as a teacher." Lila, watching on TV in prison, smiles triumphantly.

But in the movie's final scene, Puff turns out to be lying. A crowd of cameramen and admirers follows him on his trek back into the woods—he sheds his clothes along the way—but after the onlookers leave, Puff reemerges to be picked up in a car by Gabrielle. "Do you have some clothes?" he asks her. "I'm freezing my ass off." Kaufman's point seems to be that human nature *is* animalistic, that we can layer learned behavior on top of biological drives, but the biological drives still hold a lot of sway. Humans don't need to live like some other kind of animal in order to be in touch with our animal selves; our animal selves are always there, whether we're in the jungle or a traffic jam. The falsehood is in imagining ourselves cut off from nature, when we are always inextricably part of it.

And the story doesn't hold out much hope for any kind of nature beyond the physical. Nathan narrates his parts of the story from the afterworld, but the afterworld isn't anything much. He sits alone in a small white room, at a small white table. When he tries to leave via one door he just reenters through the opposite one. There is no redemption, reward, or punishment, just an absence of being alive.

The performances are not bad: Patricia Arquette actually fights through the absurdities of her character to make Lila sympathetic, and Rhys Ifans plays Puff's inappropriate social outbursts for the film's best laughs—he musters a range of expressions that suggests both his chagrin at his lack of control and his glee in giving rein to his libido. But the characters are so laden with quirks, most of them intended to make overly obvious metaphorical points, that the whole enterprise feels a little forced. Gondry does what he can to keep the tone light; there is a breezy momentum to his camerawork and comic pacing, and he juggles the three narrative points of view deftly. But for all of its meditations on science and nature, it never quite matches the combination of whimsy and dark creeping desires Gondry captured in the Bjork video. "If you ever get close to a human," Bjork sang, but the problem is that *close* is all Gondry and Kaufman get. The film remains outside its core subject, looking in.

Adaptation (2002)
DIRECTED BY: SPIKE JONZE
WRITTEN BY: CHARLIE KAUFMAN (AND DONALD KAUFMAN)
WITH: NICOLAS CAGE (CHARLIE KAUFMAN/DONALD KAUF-
    MAN), MERYL STREEP (SUSAN ORLEAN), CHRIS COOPER
    (JOHN LAROCHE)

"Do I have an original thought in my head?"

That's the first line of *Adaptation*, spoken over a black screen just before the opening credits. The voice is Nicolas Cage's, in the person of Charlie Kaufman. The movie proceeds to answer the question in a variety of ways. The most obvious answer is, "Yes," Charlie Kaufman has *lots* of original thoughts; *Adaptation* is one of the most cheerfully experimental American films of its era. But Kaufman, being Kaufman, is not satisfied with obvious answers. He wants to know what an "original thought" *is*, where thoughts come from, where he comes from. *Adaptation* is a dizzy meditation ("dizzy

Adaptation: Donald Kaufman (Nicolas Cage) and Charlie Kaufman (Nicolas Cage) debate screenwriting, in Spike Jonze's film of a script by ... Charlie Kaufman. (Courtesy of Photofest)

meditation" is no oxymoron when it comes to Kaufman) on art, evolution, Hollywood, and the pursuit of happiness.

Never mind that it was supposed to be something else entirely; as the credits note prominently if not altogether candidly, it is "Based on the book *The Orchid Thief* by Susan Orlean." But of course, *The Orchid Thief* by Susan Orlean, a work of nonfiction by a writer for *The New Yorker*, does not actually include a self-loathing screenwriter named Charlie Kaufman. *Adaptation* is not a movie of Orlean's book, it is a movie about a screenwriter named Charlie Kaufman trying to figure out how to write a screenplay based on Orlean's book. It not only includes Kaufman himself as the protagonist, it includes Orlean as a central character, sometimes in scenes drawn from her book, but just as often (and, as the film goes along, with increasing absurdity) in scenes completely invented by Kaufman.

As the opening voice-over continues, Cage-as-Kaufman muses, "Maybe if I were happier my hair wouldn't be falling out." He wonders why he is so filled with doubt. "Maybe it's my brain chemistry," he says. "Maybe that's what's wrong with me. Bad chemistry. All my problems and anxiety can be reduced to a chemical imbalance or some kind of misfiring synapses. I need to get help for that. But I'll still be ugly though. Nothing's going to solve that." And so immediately, effortlessly, the film rejoins the continuing saga of Charlie Kaufman, already in progress: the existential angst, the sense of confinement in a body, the biological determinism, the urge to break free.

What *Adaptation* is really about—and, the movie suggests, what *The Orchid Thief* is really about too—is the struggle for honest, heartfelt expression of human experience. Charlie wants to be true to Susan's book. Susan, in turn, wants her book to be true to its subject, an eccentric Florida horticulturist named John Laroche. Susan envies Laroche's fierce dedication to the orchids he harvests (illegally) in the Everglades. In a voice-over taken from her book, she says, "I want to know what it feels like to care about something passionately."

Susan's obstacles to connecting with Laroche are intellectual and cultural, not to mention professional. She is a journalist, with a default setting of dispassionate observation; her urban, urbane cultural circle is full of smart people talking smartly, full of intelligence and irony but not necessarily passion. In one scene at a Manhattan dinner party, she catches herself telling stories about Laroche for comic effect: his missing front teeth, his rattletrap van. When a friend says to her, "He sounds like a gold mine," she smiles and says, "He could be." But her own detachment, her willingness to exploit Laroche, bothers her; she looks at herself in the bathroom mirror with dismay.

In adapting Susan's book, Charlie also has both personal and professional difficulties. He is supposed to be writing scripts for movies that people might actually want to see. The studio executive who recruits him for *The Orchid Thief* adaptation suggests that in the movie, the characters of Susan and Laroche could possibly become romantically involved. But Charlie resists the formula. "I just don't want to ruin it by making it a Hollywood thing," he tells the executive, played by Tilda Swinton, "like an orchid heist movie or something, or changing the orchids into poppies and turning it into a movie about drug running, you know?" The executive nods, unconvincingly. (Swinton gives the role a calculated warmth; when she smiles, you can hear cash registers ringing.)

Even more problematic for Charlie, he is lumpish and lonely, with thinning hair and a thickened middle. Around other people, he is both arrogant and insecure—qualities that especially come out in regard to his shallow twin brother Donald, who is staying in Charlie's house while he tries to start a screenwriting career of his own. Charlie's obsessive self-centeredness makes it hard for him to connect to the characters of Susan and Laroche. "I have no understanding of anything outside my own panic and self-loathing and pathetic little existence," he says, in a crucial realization. "It's like the only thing I'm actually qualified to write about is myself."

And so he does, turning his script into a hall of mirrors. The most vertiginous scenes show Charlie writing scenes about Charlie writing scenes about himself. These are funny, disorienting moments, temporarily suspending the distance between the viewer and the film; by identifying with Charlie, we are sucked into the creation of the very thing we are watching. But all of these self-referential tricks could get tiresome if Kaufman didn't have a larger purpose in mind.

In fact, the Charlie storyline is just as fictional as everything else in the film. The character is not based on the real Kaufman, any more than Kaufman's Malkovich is based on the real John Malkovich. At the time he wrote the script, Kaufman was not a chubby, balding, middle-aged loner, but a small, slim, happily married man. The set of *Being John Malkovich* that Charlie visits is not the real *Malkovich* set but a re-creation (staged, of course, by Jonze). Charlie also does not have a twin brother named Donald, no matter what the writing credits on *Adaptation* say. Kaufman invents Donald as Charlie's inverse doppelganger, blithely self-confident and unreflective. Donald takes screenwriting seminars, despite Charlie's derision of them, and constructs a script according to narrative formulas. The story he writes, an absurd multiple-personality serial-killer thriller called *The 3*, is a send-up of the kind of films *Adaptation* had to contend with for space at the multiplex. But Kaufman ultimately turns this skewer on himself.

As the film progresses, it becomes clear that its title is operating on multiple levels, the biological as well as the literary. An early clue comes with a montage that condenses 4.5 billion years of the history of Southern California into less than a minute, showing magma, the formation of the earth's crust, the emergence of life, the evolution of man, and finally the birth of Charlie Kaufman: all processes of adaptation, of one kind or another. In scenes drawn from Orlean's book, Laroche gives mini-scientific lectures about the astonishing variety of orchids, the way each of them has evolved in conjunction with specific environments and insects. "Adaptation's a profound process," Laroche says. "It means you figure out how to thrive in the world." "Yeah," Susan counters, "but it's easier for plants, I mean, they have no memory. They just move on to whatever's next. But for a person, adapting's almost shameful. It's like running away." This is a point the movie turns on: the morality of adaptation. Is there something objectionable about simply evolving to fit changing circumstances?

Laroche and Donald are fearless adapters; they accept the demands of their environments and thrive in them. (Late in the movie, Donald sells his screenplay for hundreds of thousands of dollars; Laroche discovers the Internet and promptly launches a successful online porn venture.) Susan and Charlie worry about ethics and integrity and the implications and consequences of their actions, in a way that flowers and insects presumably never do. How much of that concern is moral sensitivity and how much is egomania and arrogance? Charlie faces that question directly when, at his wits' end, he attends a writing seminar recommended by Donald. The seminar is taught by a story guru named Robert McKee, and it shakes all of Charlie's assumptions about his craft. (Robert McKee is an actual story guru, and the lecture is drawn from his actual writings, but he is played by Brian Cox with the bravado of an Irish beat cop. McKee had to approve his depiction, and selected Cox for the part.[6]) When Charlie raises his hand and asks what McKee would do with a story where nothing really happens—"more a reflection of the real world," as he puts it—McKee explodes at him. "Nothing happens in the world?" McKee roars. "Are you out of your fucking mind? People are murdered every day. There's genocide, war, corruption. Every fucking day, somewhere in the world somebody sacrifices his life to save someone else." Building to a righteous outrage, he shouts, "If you can't find that stuff in life, then you my friend don't know crap about life. And why the fuck are you wasting my two precious hours with your movie?"

Later, Charlie takes McKee out for a drink and explains his specific problem in adapting Orlean's book. McKee listens and says, "That's not a movie. You've gotta go back, put in the drama." And so Charlie does. He calls Donald to help him finish his script, and then the final act of the film suddenly *becomes* the kind of movie McKee is talking about, the kind that Charlie had said he didn't want to write, with sex, violence, drugs, and car chases. The Kaufman brothers start spying on Susan Orlean and discover that she is carrying on a relationship with Laroche. They trail her down to Florida, where they find Laroche running a narcotics ring based around powder extracted from the elusive ghost orchid. It all culminates in a breathless and ultimately tragic chase through the Everglades, which leaves both Laroche and Donald dead. It is ludicrous. It is also entertaining. Kaufman's underlying joke is, This is what "adaptation" means. Orlean's book was successful *as* a book—it made the nonfiction best-seller list—but transplanted to the alien environment of Hollywood, it lacks the attributes necessary for survival. In order to thrive, it has to mutate and find ways to meet the needs of an entirely different audience.

But does that have to mean sex, drugs, and shoot-outs? In the hands of a lesser screenwriter, maybe. In Kaufman's hands, though, it becomes something else again—neither a literal rendition of the book, which would be all but unfilmable, nor a rote Hollywood dumbing down. Instead, it is an imaginative recasting of some of the essential questions posed by Orlean's book, managing to incorporate entire passages of her writing and a complex, colorful performance by Chris Cooper as Laroche (Cooper won an Oscar).

The movie's success as a movie is of course also the work of Jonze, whose inventiveness is more restrained than in *Malkovich*, but no less assured. The most obvious feat is the convincing illusion of having two Kaufmans (two Nicolas Cages) on screen together, using a combination of stand-ins and digital effects. It is a nearly seamless trick, with little of the reverse-shot awkwardness that tended to accompany such stunt casting in the past. Jonze also shows traces of music-video razzmatazz in the quick-cut montages and time-lapse photography that accompany some of Charlie's brainstorms. More impressive is the way Jonze shifts cinematic gears in the last section of the film, moving into Hollywood thriller mode so smoothly that at first it's easy to miss what he's doing. Ominous music builds on the soundtrack, the camera holds sustained reaction shots to build tension, and suddenly the film's goofy metaphysical comedy has given way to genre noir. It confirms Jonze's almost effortless command of cinematic language, and his ability to scramble conventions and clichés in new and quietly dazzling ways.

The performances have to make similar shifts. Cage does the most impressive work, playing Charlie and Donald as different people who happen to have identical bodies. Their postures, body language, and facial expressions differ in subtle but careful ways so that each is always identifiable, Charlie always a little bit slumped, Donald always with wide eyes and a slightly dazed smile. They are unflattering roles—Cage had to gain weight and make himself look schleppy—and without any of the tragic payoff that actors often seem drawn to in taking such parts (like Robert De Niro in *Raging Bull* or Cage himself in *Leaving Las Vegas*). Meryl Streep as Susan Orlean is practically typecast; Streep has exactly the kind of pale, inquisitive seriousness one would imagine in a New Yorker writer. But she also has to do the most complete overhaul in the final section, letting Susan Orlean's hair down and reimagining her as a woman liberated by drugs and raw passion. In a scene where she tries the orchid drug for the first time, she softens her face—you can watch the tension lift from her cheeks and eyes—and loosens Susan's entire bearing without losing a basic sense of the character. Cooper, meanwhile, lights up Laroche with a tragicomic spark that might have been hard to imagine from his previous, mostly taciturn performances. Laroche's patter about orchids, science, and life in general is equal parts brilliant and bullshit, and he knows it. His generosity and love of nature are matched by deep-seated resentment and pain. Cooper manages to make him seem both dangerous and decent, a guy with good instincts who occasionally fails to heed them.

If there was one big question left dangling about Kaufman by *Adaptation*, it was whether he *could* actually write the kind of story McKee urges him to: one with everyday characters, conventional drama, love and loss, sacrifice and redemption, and so on and so forth. As it happened, at the time the movie came out, he was already well along on something kind of like that.

Eternal Sunshine of the Spotless Mind (2004)
DIRECTED BY: MICHEL GONDRY
WRITTEN BY: CHARLIE KAUFMAN (STORY BY CHARLIE KAUF-
MAN, MICHEL GONDRY AND PIERRE BISMUTH)
WITH: JIM CARREY (JOEL BARISH), KATE WINSLET (CLE-
MENTINE KRUCZYNSKI), KIRSTEN DUNST (MARY SVEVO),
MARK RUFFALO (STAN), ELIJAH WOOD (PATRICK), TOM
WILKINSON (DR. HOWARD MIERZWIAK)

The title of *Eternal Sunshine of the Spotless Mind* comes from the poem "Eloisa to Abelard" by Alexander Pope, which Kirsten Dunst (as the doctor's assistant Mary Svevo) recites at one point in the film: "How happy is the blameless vestal's lot!/ The world forgetting, by the world forgot/Eternal sunshine of the spotless mind!/Each pray'r accepted, and each wish resign'd." It is more than a passing literary reference. The tale of Heloise and Abelard, medieval lovers forced apart by Heloise's family, obviously resonates with Kaufman; it is the inspiration for one of the puppet shows Craig Schwartz performs in *Being John Malkovich*. And in some ways it provides the foundation for *Eternal Sunshine*.

Heloise and Abelard, a student and her teacher in twelfth-century France who secretly married against her family's wishes, are archetypes of romantic longing and despair. Their lovelorn letters, discovered some years later, inspired centuries of poetry, drama, and art. (Although the letters' authenticity is unverifiable and has been frequently challenged, many historians accept the manuscripts as genuine.) Writing to each other from their respective confinements—Abelard in a monastery and Heloise in a convent—they by turns entreat each other to forget their past passions and lament their inability to do so. "How happy should I be could I wash out with my tears the memory of those pleasures which I yet think of with delight," Heloise writes. Abelard is of a similar mind: "[T]hose prosperous days which had seduced us were now past," he writes, "and there remained nothing but to erase from our minds, by painful endeavours, all marks and remembrances of them. I

Clementine (Kate Winslet) and Joel (Jim Carrey) scramble through Michel Gondry's surreal landscapes in *Eternal Sunshine of the Spotless Mind*. (Courtesy of Photofest)

had wished to find in philosophy and religion a remedy for my disgrace; I searched out an asylum to secure me from love. I was come to the sad experiment."[7]

The suffering lovers in Kaufman's script, Joel and Clementine, also undergo an experiment—more literal than the one envisioned by Abelard, but no less sad. Although the film has many funny moments and is, overall, generous in spirit, it is also Kaufman's most bittersweet story to date. The entire movie is colored by a candid awareness of the difficulties and disappointments of romantic love. And much more than *Human Nature*, it provides a vivid platform for Gondry's cinematic imagination. A significant part of the film takes place inside Joel's mind, and Gondry achieves remarkable effects with relatively minimalist technology: lots of handheld lights and cameras, plus some stop-motion and time-lapse filming. (Compare it, for example, to the gaudy, baroque sets and digital effects used to illustrate the subconscious of a serial killer in the 2000 thriller *The Cell*, directed by another music-video veteran, Tarsem Singh.)

The science-fiction trappings and effortless surrealism somewhat mask the movie's most audacious stroke, which is its narrative structure. With a lot of diversions along the way, it essentially tells the story of its central romance backward, from break-up to first-sight. It is full of details that accumulate meaning as the film goes on, and that become even more significant on a second viewing. (On the commentary track accompanying the DVD release, Kaufman says, "We always wanted it to be a movie that you would watch more than once and have differing reactions to.")

The film opens at what later turns out to be its denouement. Joel, a middle-class professional of some kind (his job is never made clear) wakes up groggy on Valentine's Day in his Long Island apartment. Wandering out to his car, he finds a dent in the driver's-side door that he doesn't recognize. Waiting for his commuter train into the city, he suddenly decides to take the day off from work and catches a train in the other direction, out to Montauk. The only other person on the cold, windy beach is a woman in an orange sweatshirt, whom he later sees around town and on the platform waiting for the return train. On the ride home, they end up talking. Her name is Clementine, and her hair is half-dyed a vivid blue. He is friendly but quiet; she is talkative but abrasive. When he tells her she seems nice, she replies offhandedly, "I'm a vindictive little bitch, truth be told."

He gives her a ride home from the train station, and accepts when she asks him in for a drink. The next night, they drive together up to the frozen Charles River and lie down on the ice. Joel is afraid it might break; Clementine says, "It's not gonna crack, or break. It's so thick." But an overhead shot shows a large crack webbing through the ice right next to them. They drive back into town, and Clementine asks if she can come sleep at his place. He agrees.

It is only at this point (about 20 minutes into the movie) that the credits roll. The scene shifts to Joel, in his car at night, sobbing. Clearly we are in a different part of the story. What emerges over the next hour and a half is that Joel and Clementine have broken up after two years together, and Clementine has gone through a medical procedure at a clinic called Lacuna to have all memories of Joel wiped from her mind. Joel is so hurt by this that he decides to do the same, after meeting with the doctor who runs the clinic, Howard Mierzwiak. Joel goes home and goes to bed, and while he sleeps two assistants from the clinic, Stan and Patrick, come into his apartment and hook him up to Mierzwiak's software, which has been programmed to find and remove all traces of Clementine. They are joined by Stan's girlfriend Mary, the office assistant.

Mierzwiak and his three assistants give the film its secondary story lines, and Dunst, Tom Wilkinson, Mark Ruffalo, and Elijah Wood give nicely shaded supporting performances. Maybe most notable is Wood. He filmed his part as Patrick after wrapping up the *Lord of the Rings* trilogy, but because of the staggered release of the Tolkien films, *Eternal Sunshine* arrived in multiplexes just as the last of them was finishing its run. It was interesting if a little disconcerting to see him shift so suddenly from heroic mode—as Frodo, Tolkien's wide-eyed world-saving protagonist—to a nervous, creepy loser who pesters Clementine into dating him. If Wood was looking to avoid being typecast, he picked a good role.

The central performances by Jim Carrey and Kate Winslet are also somewhat against type. As Joel, who saves most of his self-expression for his journal, Carrey considerably ratchets down his usually hyperactive screen persona. Winslet, on the other hand, maintains the sparky intelligence she always brings to her roles, but toughens it up; where her best known previous roles were somewhat reserved and sophisticated, Clementine is brash, foulmouthed and impulsive. She and Carrey play off each other well, and they make Joel and Clementine seem like the kind of people who would be attracted to each other. The film furls backward through their relationship, as each successive memory is erased from Joel's mind, and Carrey and Winslet hit a convincing array of domestic and romantic notes, from the bickering that undoes them all the way back to the tentative excitement of their first meeting. The reverse chronology builds a sort of repentant momentum: as Joel delves further back into the relationship, he is increasingly reminded of how much he loved Clementine, and why. He clings desperately to any scrap of memory he can, until they are finally all removed.

Gondry has a field day with the visual depiction of Joel's disappearing recollections. In scene after scene, landscapes blanch or darken, buildings crumble and faces blur. The effects are disconcerting and nightmarish, but brightened here and there with funny moments—Joel tries to hide Clementine in his childhood memories, giving Carrey a chance to indulge briefly (and amusingly) in little-boy antics. Gondry keeps Joel and Clementine in the foreground, never letting the shifting settings overwhelm the characters; the world inside Joel's head literally revolves around them. By the time the final memory is wiped away (an achingly sad scene in which a massive oceanside home falls around their ears), their relationship has been deftly sketched in a series of small, poignant moments. And the stage is set for it to begin again.

As in his earlier scripts, Kaufman seems to suggest that we are stuck with who we are and what we've done. People might be able to learn and change, but what they can't do is escape themselves. Like *Malkovich* and *Human Nature*, the movie registers skepticism about the wisdom of scientific tinkering with the organism. Even with their memories gone, Joel and Clementine promptly gravitate back toward each other. Eloise's fantasy of a "spotless mind" is revealed as a false hope. If there's any *real* hope in the story's moral, it comes only through knowledge and experience and the willingness to put up with disappointment and complication. At the end, after they've rediscovered their history together and Clementine wants to walk away, Joel protests. "I can't see anything that I don't like about you, right now," he says. "But you will," she says. "And I'll get bored with you and then I'll feel trapped, because that's what happens with me." Joel looks at her for a moment and then says, "OK." Clementine looks puzzled. "OK?" she asks. They grin at each other, and she repeats, "OK!" It is a conditional affirmation, one that accepts that they may well break up again. But it feels hard-won, and honest.

Eternal Sunshine of the Spotless Mind marked the full maturation of Kaufman as a writer (and Gondry as a director). It is the first of his scripts to connect emotionally as much as intellectually, and the textured, detailed construction of its characters sets it apart from his previous work. (Even the character of Charlie Kaufman in *Adaptation* is less fully formed than Joel and Clementine.) And it achieves all of that without sacrificing either originality or Kaufman's particular brand of outlandishness. Like Richard Linklater's *Before Sunset*, which came out the same year, *Eternal Sunshine* is a romantic drama with its eyes wide open; both films take apart the conventions of boy-meets-girl storytelling, but not to mock or degrade them. What they seek to do is recapture from formula and cliché the central wonder of the romantic experience: the connection, against all obstacles and improbabilities, of two people. Because that, more than the ache or the loss, is the real story of Heloise and Abelard.

As an American absurdist, Kaufman faces a sort of double bind. The convictions of his philosophy stand apart and run counter to the myths of his society. Kaufman's stories suggest that we can never get fully away from ourselves, that we're better off living with ourselves honestly than seeking some kind of external redemption or regeneration. But he is working in the United States, a country built on the idea of self-invention and reinvention, where Ralph Waldo Emerson exulted, "So shall we come to look at the world with new eyes."[8] Kaufman respects the transcendentalist impulse—most of his characters are driven by it—but he is dubious about its prospects. He is not only doubtful of the ability to get beyond the limitations of the self, he is deeply aware of the complications inherent in the idea of "self" to begin with. Is a self just a body? A consciousness? A collection of biological functions? A data bank of stored experiences? Kaufman's stories explore all of those possibilities, without coming to any firm position. All he's really sure of is that, whatever we are, we have to live with it.

As for his collaborators, after two films each with Kaufman, movies that established them as major directors and gave them freedom to pursue other projects, both Jonze and Gondry headed off in their own directions. Gondry's first feature as a writer-director, *The Science of Sleep*, was released in September 2006, to generally warm reviews. After *Adaptation*, meanwhile, Jonze turned to an adaptation of his own (working with the writers Dave Eggers and Michael Goldenberg): a full-length animated version of Maurice Sendak's children's classic, *Where the Wild Things Are*. It is scheduled for a 2008 release. Kaufman also has another project in the works, a story about a playwright tentatively called *Synecdohe, New York* and starring Philip Seymour Hoffman. The director attached to the film is somebody named Charlie Kaufman.

Kaufman's move into the director's chair was probably inevitable, and its results are impossible to prejudge. But he will be lucky if he turns out to be as skilled an adaptor of his own work as either Jonze or Gondry—just as they will be lucky to find scripts as keenly suited to their talents as Kaufman's.

8

FELLOW TRAVELERS: DAVID FINCHER, SOFIA COPPOLA, AND RICHARD KELLY

T he three directors grouped here for reasons of convenience do not have much in common with each other, beyond a general sense of alienation. In the cases of Coppola and Kelly, they have not produced enough work to warrant their own chapter; in the case of Fincher, his inclusion is on the basis of just one of his films, the adaptation of Chuck Palahniuk's novel *Fight Club*.

But *Fight Club*, which is about male anxiety in late-capitalist Western culture, does make an interesting counterpoint to Coppola's films, which are about female anxiety in the same (the Versailles of *Marie Antoinette* serving as an obvious forerunner/analog to decadent capitalism). The men of *Fight Club* have lost their standing in a society they used to control; the women and girls of Coppola's films are still trying to find theirs. Meanwhile, the tragic title hero of Kelly's striking debut, *Donnie Darko*, is consumed by a similar sense of meaninglessness in his deceptively mundane suburban adolescence. All three directors present characters in search of something larger than themselves to live for, or die for.

Fincher, born in 1962, followed a career path similar to those of Spike Jonze and Michel Gondry (and, as a founder of Propaganda Films, hired both of them at different points). A son of a magazine writer and a nurse, Fincher grew up in Marin County, California, and in Ashland, Oregon. He was interested in photography and filmmaking from a young age, and rather than going to college he hustled his way into a job at George Lucas's Industrial Light and Magic. By the mid-1980s, he was working on his own as a commercial and video director, and in 1987 he formed Propaganda with a small group of friends.[1] He made videos for Madonna ("Vogue"), Paula Abdul ("Straight Up"), Sting ("An Englishman in New York"), and many others. But his ambition was always to make feature films. His first chance came with 1992's poorly received *Alien,*[3] which put Fincher's stylishly dark sensibility at the service of a relentlessly glum story. His breakthrough came three years later with the violent serial-killer tale *Se7en,* which also introduced him to Brad Pitt.

Fincher is not a writer, but there are consistent themes of paranoia, isolation and disruption running through his films. The self-righteous fervor of the monks in *Alien*[3] presages the perverse moralizing of the killer in *Se7en,* and the neo-fascist cultists of *Fight Club.* The intrusion of the unexpected on predictable, affluent American life—a major subject of *Fight Club*—is prominent in *The Game* and *Panic Room* as well. Fincher works almost exclusively in the realm of the thriller, and his films have mostly been medium- to high-quality examples of Hollywood nail-biters, written by a parade of middle- and top-shelf screenplay specialists. Many of them are clever films, without quite being smart. They are more flashy than illuminating. *Fight Club* stands apart in his work to date, thanks to the nervy intelligence of its source material and Fincher's unflinching fidelity to its spirit.

Sofia Coppola, of course, was infamous before she was famous. Of all Hollywood progeny who have entered the industry, it is possible that none had a rougher introduction and reception. Although her father, Francis Ford Coppola, had given her cameos as far back as the early *Godfather* films, when she was an infant, she only really came to public notice in the belated third installment in that series. Janet Maslin in *The New York Times* called it a "flat, uneasy performance,"[2] and *The Washington Post* called her "hopelessly amateurish."[3] Although she has had minor roles in a handful of films since, Coppola, maybe understandably, did not pursue a serious acting career. Instead, she studied photography and helped start a clothing company.[4] And then, after making a short in 1998 called *Lick the Star,* she made her feature debut as a director in 1999: an adaptation, written by her, of Jeffrey Eugenides's novel *The Virgin Suicides.* The film was dreamy and odd, and it earned largely positive reviews without entirely shaking Coppola's image as a well-bred dilettante.

In fact, even after the critical and commercial success of her next movie, *Lost in Translation*—which earned Coppola an Oscar for its screenplay and grossed more than $100 million internationally—her chorus of detractors remained strong. They resurfaced with the release of *Marie Antoinette* in 2006, with some critics knocking the film and Coppola herself for a basic lack of seriousness. The case against Coppola usually revolves around such complaints: that she is frivolous, that her movies lack heft, that they look good but communicate little. There is some basis for these criticisms in all of Coppola's films—her style is ethereal, sometimes to the point of insubstantiality—but it is hard to miss the archly condescending tone with which some critics dismiss her, and hard not to wonder why exactly the most prominent female American director of her generation elicits it.

Richard Kelly, who is a few years younger than Coppola, knows a thing or two about condescending dismissiveness. At Cannes 2006, where *Marie Antoinette* earned some boos from the crowds, Kelly's second feature, *Southland Tales*, was lambasted by audiences and critics alike. There were exceptions—J. Hoberman in the *Village Voice* called it "a visionary film about the end of times"[5]—but the overall reaction was so negative that for a while it appeared uncertain that the film would even find an American distributor. (It did, eventually, but too late for contemplation in this book.) Even with a cast full of marketable names (Justin Timberlake, Sarah Michelle Gellar, and The Rock), Kelly was a hard sell.

Not that that should surprise anyone who saw his first film, the remarkable *Donnie Darko*. A darkly comic fable about the Reagan era, it likewise generated puzzlement on its initial go-round before establishing a midnight-movie cult following that led to a second, "director's cut" release 3 years later. Kelly, born in 1975, is young enough to cite David Fincher as an influence; he has said that Fincher's 1989 video for the Aerosmith song "Janie's Got a Gun" showed him "how you could tell a story with a camera."[6] *Donnie Darko* shows the influence of music videos, but also of Steven Spielberg and David Lynch. Whatever Kelly watched growing up, he clearly watched it closely. His script for the 2005 Tony Scott thriller *Domino* showed that he understands genre well enough to work his way into the Hollywood system. But his work as a director suggests that the system is going to have a hard time digesting him.

Fight Club (1999)

DIRECTED BY: DAVID FINCHER
WRITTEN BY: JIM UHLS, BASED ON THE NOVEL BY CHUCK
  PALAHNIUK
WITH: EDWARD NORTON (THE NARRATOR), BRAD PITT
  (TYLER DURDEN), HELENA BONHAM CARTER (MARLA
  SINGER), MEAT LOAF (ROBERT PAULSON), JARED LETO
  (ANGEL FACE)

In some ways, David Fincher's very violent, very funny adaptation of Chuck Palahniuk's very violent, very funny novel never had a chance. Its release date was set for the summer of 1999, by Fox studio marketers who had not anticipated that in the spring of 1999 two students would commit mass murder at Columbine High School in Colorado. Suddenly, entertainment companies were very concerned about violence, particularly violence presented without a clear moral or message. *Fight Club* was pushed back four months, to October.

Even then, the critical reactions to the film were reminiscent of the gasps of outrage that had greeted Arthur Penn's similarly sly, brutal, and morally complicated *Bonnie and Clyde* in 1967. That film had Bosley Crowther of *The New York Times* blustering, "This blending of farce with brutal killings is as pointless as it is lacking in taste" and decrying "blotches of violence of the most grisly sort."[7] More than 30 years later, Kenneth Turan in *The Los Angeles Times* called Fincher's film a "witless mishmash of whiny, infantile philosophizing and bone-crunching violence,"[8] while David Denby in *The New Yorker* somewhat more kindly found it "ridiculous and even boring."[9] What *Fight Club* has in common with Penn's high-spirited bloodbath, and what set the voices of decency against both of them, is that they both suggest violent revolt as a viable path to self-realization. Tyler Durden in *Fight Club* is not motivated by ideology any more than Warren Beatty's Clyde Barrows; what they both want is to find a way to somehow make their lives matter. They both collect followers, and cut out press clippings of their exploits. And, most infuriating to their critics, even though neither Tyler nor Clyde comes to a good end, they both make outlaw life look immensely more appealing than its alternatives.

Fight Club begins where, arguably, much of the film takes place: inside the head of its unnamed Narrator. But literally inside. Like David O. Russell's animated tour of the torso in *Three Kings*, Fincher's digitally enhanced tracking shot starts at the level of dendrites deep in the brain and then pulls back and back through layers of tissue and bone until it emerges from a pore in the Narrator's forehead. (Because of the script's riffs on medical books about a character named Jack, the Narrator is often referred to as Jack in discussions of the film. But his actual name is not provided in either the book or the movie.) That opening shot is followed moments later by one that drops vertiginously out the window of the building, down into an underground parking garage and into a van loaded with explosives. These whirling zooms from micro- to macro-level and back again are more than deft bits of state-of-the-art cinematography; they signal the story's almost Nietzschean obsession with individual power, the potential of an idea or an ideology to transform

Fight Club: Tyler Durden (Brad Pitt) watches the carnage in David Fincher's adaptation of the novel by Chuck Palahniuk. (Courtesy of Photofest)

the world. What begins as vague notions inside the Narrator's mind leads eventually to the explosives in the van.

One of the things that makes *Fight Club* disturbing is its failure to explicitly condemn the actions of its antiheroes. Although it is essentially a cautionary tale, it also exults in the mayhem it depicts. And it suggests that the violence perpetrated by its characters—from bloody, bare-knuckles brawling to outright urban terrorism—is rooted in deep social disconnects. The Fight Club members are not just sociopaths, a la Travis Bickle; they are the undervalued, overlooked, disrespected drones of a callous service economy. Their actions are extreme, but their grievances are real. Tyler Durden's version of will-to-power appeals to them because of their powerlessness within a system that depends on them but barely acknowledges them. As Tyler says to the police commissioner, who has been taken hostage by a group of Fight Club members, "We cook your meals, we haul your trash, we connect your calls, we drive your ambulances. We guard you while you sleep. Do not fuck with us."

In a previous generation that would have sounded Marxist, but *Fight Club* doesn't suggest anything so dialectical. Its fundamental conflicts are not economic or political but spiritual. The alienation of the Narrator, and of those who become his followers, is not so much from means of production as from means of expression and connection. In particular, the film is concerned with the plight of the service-sector American male, who has been reduced to monotonous labor (white- or blue-collar) for faceless institutions, where conformity is prized and self-assertion discouraged. The trade-off for this is the comfort of the consumer culture, what the Narrator calls the "Ikea nesting instinct," where personality is defined by preferences in thread counts and sofa styles. This critique is not new, obviously; it is the basis of every alienated company-man riff from "Bartleby the Scrivener" to "Dilbert." But *Fight Club* ties the loss of self explicitly to a loss of masculinity.

The story is driven by fears and fantasies of emasculation. Early in the movie, the Narrator joins a series of support groups for people with chronic or terminal illnesses; he is not sick himself, he is just looking for some kind of sympathy. The one that has the most effect on him is a group of survivors of testicular cancer, many of whom have had their testes removed. (The most notable of these is a large man named Bob, whose hormone therapy has caused him to grow breasts.) Later, after the Narrator's apartment is destroyed in an explosion, his new acquaintance Tyler Durden says (in a reference to the case of Lorena Bobbit and her husband), "It could be worse. A woman could cut off your penis while you're sleeping and throw it out the window of a moving car." And when the Fight Club eventually evolves into Tyler's anarchic Project Mayhem, there are repeated references to cutting off the balls of anyone who stands in the way or betrays the organization.

The corporate-consumer world is understood to be fundamentally demasculinized. "Why do guys like you and I know what a duvet is?," Tyler asks the Narrator. He then goads the Narrator into hand-to-hand combat: "How much can you know about yourself if you've never been in a fight?" They trade blows in the parking lot of a bar, swinging harder and harder until they're both bloody. Afterward, they relax with a beer and a cigarette in a quasi-postcoital moment. "We should do this again sometime," the Narrator says. And the idea of Fight Club is born. The film's latent homoeroticism was much commented on, and Fincher, Pitt, and Norton have a good time playing up the flirtations and jealousies between Tyler and the Narrator. But the relationship is complicated, of course, by the revelation that they are actually the same person—that Tyler is the product of the Narrator's traumatized mind. He represents the Narrator's own sublimated masculinity, bubbling uncontrollably to the surface.

Fight Club came at the tail end of a decade that had been marked by the emergence of what the mass media took to calling the Angry White Male. These were men, so the story went, unsettled by shocks in the economy (the mass layoffs of the early 1990s, the rise of globalized manufacturing) and the culture (the growing presence and power of minorities in the workplace, and of women both at work and at home). The traditional prerogatives of their race and gender were suddenly not anything they could take for granted. Their vague but deeply felt resentment helped drive the insurgent presidential campaign of Ross Perot in 1992, and they also became the base audience for the rise of right-wing talk radio, which validated their anger and gave it a political context. The first Angry White Male film was Joel Schumacher's 1993 *Falling Down*, in which a put-upon everyman played by Michael Douglas rebels against everything from traffic jams to poor service at fast-food restaurants. *Fight Club* is darker and smarter; where *Falling Down* externalized all of its character's rage, Palahniuk and Fincher are primarily concerned with an internal malaise. In their story, everyone is complicit in their own oppression, and liberation comes from within. *Fight Club* marries the Angry White Male to his touchy-feely men's-movement counterpart, Iron John. One of Palahniuk's sharpest insights is that combat is itself a particularly male form of intimacy; the Fight Club is really just another support group.

There is a lot of humor in the movie—it is basically a comedy, albeit an uneasy one—but the jokes allow it to fudge its morals a little. When Tyler and the Narrator steal extracted fat from liposuction clinics and use it to make boutique soap, the gag is obvious: "We were selling rich women their own fat asses back to them." But when the Fight Club metastasizes into a multicity underground movement centered on acts of anticorporate vandalism, it is harder to know just who or what is being satirized: The corporations? The sad sacks who sign up for Tyler's quasi-fascist militia? Tyler's reductive ideas about masculinity? The answer seems to be all of the above, to some degree.

Still, the film seems at the conclusion to settle on banishing Tyler back into the recesses of the Narrator's subconscious. When the Narrator blows a hole out the side of his head, it is an act of ego reasserting control over the id. Tyler represents a certain kind of liberation, and he may be right about a lot of things, but he is also by definition dangerous. He is an embrace of danger. And in the end all he has to offer is destruction. Like the heroes in many of the movies discussed in previous chapters, the Narrator is really struggling to grow up, to find a mature basis for dealing with the world around him. It is not a struggle that a corporate-consumer society encourages, of course, because a lot of things about corporate consumer culture—with its combination of authoritarianism and wanton self-indulgence—are at odds with the idea of maturity. But Tyler's rebellions are just as juvenile. The Fight Club is ultimately a dead end. As Norton says on one of the DVDs commentary tracks, "What gets explored in this film is that nihilism is a very sexy idea when you're young and feel frustrated, but that becoming mature means recognizing the practical limits and in some ways the hypocrisies that nihilism lends itself to."

Most of the negative press for the film revolved around its violence. The fight scenes are brutal, and painful to watch in ways that movie fights are usually not. Some of the revulsion and anger they produced were undoubtedly the result of breaking the simple, unspoken compact that violence in Hollywood films is there to entertain, not discomfit. Even more unnerving than the fights are the physical manifestations of their aftermath. People have split lips, black eyes, cuts, and bruises. The Narrator shows up at his white-collar insurance job battered and bloodied, daring his coworkers to say anything. Violence has visible, ugly effects on the human body, and *Fight Club* revels in them. It has to. The idea of violence as a liberating force can't get any traction if it doesn't cause disruption at the most basic, corporeal level.

The film's deceptively reductive title, and the controversy over its content, led some people to miss its points entirely. Sharon Waxman quotes a Fox marketing executive as lamenting after the fact that "the general public wasn't ready for a gritty take on the world of semiorganized bare knuckles street fighting"[10]—making you wonder if he had actually seen his own studio's product.

There is one glaring narrative problem the film never really overcomes. The central conceit that Tyler is imaginary, someone seen only by the Narrator, is more problematic on film than on the page. And this is because of the simple but inescapable difference between Brad Pitt and Edward Norton. They are both very good in the film, but they are also very different. Norton is appropriately belligerent in his own fight scenes—he's no milquetoast— but he is allowed to play the more reserved, skeptical, intellectual half of the persona. Pitt has the firecracker part, and he makes sparks with it. The film is structured cleverly; on repeat viewings, there are plenty of early clues that Tyler does not really exist. But the clever structure cannot quite compensate for the idea that there is no Brad Pitt, that the Fight Club and Project Mayhem are actually cooked up by Edward Norton's Narrator. The movie needs Pitt's cocky cool, and it is hard not to think that the Fight Club would need it too.

Still, it is an interesting and inventive film. Fincher has a lot of fun playing with the frame; both the Narrator and Tyler address the camera directly at different points, and Fincher also uses Tyler's night job as a movie theater projectionist to set up the film's final joke. In an early scene, the Narrator describes how Tyler likes to insert one or two frames from pornographic films into family films, which flash by so quickly that people aren't sure what they saw. One of the images is a nude male torso with an erect penis. That image resurfaces, briefly but distinctly, inserted into the closing moments of the film. Likewise, close viewing on DVD reveals a number of inserted pictures of Tyler early in the movie, before the Narrator has "met" him. He flickers briefly in the background of at least three (and probably more) scenes. Fincher also at various points shakes and blurs the picture as if the film were caught in a rickety projector. More than just cute tricks, these are all ways of unnerving the audience, persistently and gleefully disrupting the suspension of disbelief, constantly asserting the untrustworthiness of what is being presented. (Just as Tyler challenges his disciples to disrupt the numbing conventions of their culture.)

At the time of the film's release, Amy Taubin in the *Village Voice* suggested that it could be a "vertiginous, libidinous preview" of the twenty-first century.[11] In some ways, it was a prescient statement. It is now impossible to watch the final scene of exploding skyscrapers and not think of September 11. But because of that, *Fight Club* also seems already dated, locked in its particular time, in a 1990s America defined by self-contemplation and bland corporate homogeny. The stagnating era it captures was bound for a shake-up, but not one that even Tyler could have contemplated.

The Virgin Suicides (1999)

DIRECTED BY: SOFIA COPPOLA
WRITTEN BY: SOFIA COPPOLA, FROM THE NOVEL BY JEFFREY
    EUGENIDES
WITH: KIRSTEN DUNST (LUX LISBON), JAMES WOODS (MR.
    LISBON), KATHLEEN TURNER (MRS. LISBON), JOSH HART-
    NETT (TRIP FONTAINE), HANNA HALL (CECELIA LIS-
    BON), LESLIE HAYMAN (THERESE LISBON), CHELSE SWAIN
    (BONNIE LISBON), DANNY DeVITO (DR. HORNIKER)

It was a coincidence that *The Virgin Suicides* came out the same year as *Fight Club*, but in some ways Sofia Coppola's ethereal suburban fable is the feminine inverse of Fincher's grimy urban one.

Sofia Coppola consults with Kirsten Dunst on the set of Coppola's ethereal first film, *The Virgin Suicides*. (Courtesy of Photofest)

It is a quiet and mysterious movie, but it was startling in its announcement of Coppola's talent. She emerged from the very long shadow of her father and family name (and the shorter but not inconsiderable shadow of her then-husband, Spike Jonze) as a seemingly fully formed filmmaker. In adapting Jeffrey Eugenides' novel, Coppola placed herself in the interesting position of being a female director translating a story written by a male novelist, a story about girls told from a boy's perspective.

The five Lisbon sisters are ciphers in Eugenides's book, beautiful, unknowable, and unattainable. Coppola accepts the unsolvable puzzles of their family and, eventually, their deaths. But, probably for the obvious reason that she was a teenage girl herself, she gets inside the girls' world more than Eugenides did. Their glances and giggles feel like a conspiracy that the movie is in on, in a way the book was not. In contrast, the neighborhood boys who observe and document the girls' story are barely characterized beyond the needs of narrative function.

Not that "narrative" per se is the movie's strength, or Coppola's. She specializes in atmosphere, conveying ideas through a combination of beguiling images, gliding camerawork and artfully deployed music. Her films feel designed as much as directed, which is not intended as a slur. She has a fashion photographer's eye for composition and suggestion (not a surprise, given her background as both an occasional model and a clothing designer), and a striking sense of the use of light. She is in many ways an experimental filmmaker, but because she draws partly on the effects and vocabulary of commercial photography and music video, it is easy to confuse her means with her ends. As a director, she shows some obvious debt to Wong Kar-wai, particularly the longing romanticism of movies like *Happy Together* and *In the Mood for Love*. The deceptive narrative neutrality of *Virgin Suicides* and *Marie Antoinette* also has something in common with the recent films of Gus van Sant, *Elephant* and *Last Days*, which observe their characters' troubling actions with a blank stare. But Coppola's style, for all its coolness, is less clinical than van Sant's, and not as lush as Wong's. Her movies have a kinetic buzz that sets them apart, even in their missteps.

The Virgin Suicides is a strange little movie. It begins with the attempted suicide of one of the five Lisbon sisters, and ends with the self-annihilation of the other four. In between, it depicts the hormonal thrum of early adolescence in a 1970s suburb, looping back and forth between the sisters and the boys who become obsessed with them. The actual causes of the Lisbon family's pathology are never explored, but are hinted at in the nervous authoritarianism of their mother and the mumbly insecurity of their father. Kathleen Turner and James Woods give tense but understated performances; Mr. and Mrs. Lisbon clearly have some problems, but they're not monsters. An early scene shows city workers tagging blighted trees for removal, establishing a sense of creeping malignancy in the heart of the apparently safe, friendly neighborhood. (The Lisbon sisters' final public act is an unsuccessful attempt to save the tree in their yard.) Fortunately, Coppola doesn't push this theme too far; the story is not just another exposé of suburban decay. It is about fear and alienation—the mother's phobia of the world, the daughters' isolation from it—and also about the age-old conflict between the idealization of the feminine and the urge to dominate and degrade it. The neighbor boys worship the Lisbons like demigods, watching their rituals and seeking any secrets that might come from them. On the other hand, when one boy, the dreamy jock Trip Fontaine, manages to seduce Lux, he leaves her sleeping on a football field and never calls her again.

The teenagers are all well cast. For one thing, they all seem like actual adolescents: the boys are still more boys than men, with the exception of the blooming Trip Fontaine (Josh Hartnett, radiating cocksure sensuality), and the girls are mischievously girlish. The roles do not require too much of them—the boys have to look confused and horny, the girls mostly have to smile or frown—but Coppola films them all with great sympathy. Kirsten Dunst stands out as first among equals; she is Coppola's muse in the film, and maybe her stand-in (each of her movies has revolved around young, privileged women who seem to reflect Coppola to one degree or another). The movie was important in Dunst's evolution from child star (she was 12 when *Interview with the Vampire* was released in 1994) to mature actor. It catches her in-between, at 17, her secretive cat-eyed smile poised between impulsive and knowing. Dunst's subsequent performances, in the *Spider-Man* franchise and elsewhere, have demonstrated only medium depth but abundant charm. That works fine for Coppola's purposes, both here and in *Marie Antoinette*, because the depths of her movies come more in their overall visual and narrative composition than from specific characters or performances.

What is most striking about the movie is its spectral gauziness; the whole thing seems a little airy, it floats. This is achieved partly through abundant use of natural light—Coppola has a great eye for skies and the hues of sunshine—and also through the excellent, hazy electronic soundtrack by the French duo Air. Of the directors discussed in this book, only Todd Haynes and Wes Anderson can match Coppola's cinematic awareness of music as a primary storytelling element. In possibly the movie's best scene, the boys and the Lisbon sisters play songs to each other from their bedrooms, by holding the telephone to the speakers of their stereo systems. The songs, 1970s swoon-rock classics like "The Air That I Breathe" and "I'm Not in Love," articulate the breathless flirtation of teenage crushes. Like Haynes, in his depiction of glam rock as a doorway to self-discovery, Coppola shows the intimacy between the song and the listener, how pop culture is appropriated and made personal by its audience. And her use of two sexually charged Heart songs as Trip Fontaine's theme music ("Magic Man" and "Crazy on You") amplifies his power as an object of female desire.

There is also mastery in the climactic scene, in which the boys discover the four dead girls. Coppola heightens the horror by showing only glimpses of their bodies: legs dangling in the air or sprawled across the floor, Lux's hand and head leaning out a car window in the carbon monoxide-filled garage. It is a dark, dreamlike sequence that offers no explanation, just a sense of inevitability. A subsequent montage of simple-minded TV news reports perfectly captures the shocked, sanctimonious tone with which our institutions tend to respond to local tragedies. The superficiality of the reporters' questions and the shallowness of their feigned concern suggest how little they know or want to know about anything. In contrast, the neighbor boys continue to watch the house, searching for any sign of something that will help them make sense of the events. Years later, the narrator tells us, they're still trying. But the movie suggests that they will never really have an answer—that the girls could not be understood, just observed.

Lost in Translation (2003)

DIRECTED BY: SOFIA COPPOLA
WRITTEN BY: SOFIA COPPOLA
WITH: SCARLETT JOHANSSON (CHARLOTTE), BILL MURRAY
  (BOB HARRIS), GIOVANNI RIBISI (JOHN)

Lost in Translation was an unlikely hit. It is full of long shots and careful silences. The movie is as much about what doesn't happen as what does, and the hows and whys of it. It's also about being in an unfamiliar place (in this case, Tokyo), and the excitement and isolation of unfamiliarity. We see the city through strangers' eyes, as a blur of flashing lights and chanting monks and karaoke bars and a persistent sense of unreality. It's not a comedy, but it is often funny. It's a drama where nothing very dramatic happens. It grossed nearly $120 million worldwide (*Virgin Suicides* made $10 million), more than 60 percent of it overseas. It was nominated for four Oscars, including best picture and best director, making Coppola the first American woman nominated for the directing award. She didn't win that—it went to Peter Jackson, for the final installment of *Lord of the Rings*—but she did win for best original screenplay.

Her father's first Oscar was also for screenwriting, for *Patton*. (Francis Ford Coppola won the award on April 15, 1971. Sofia was born the next month.) It is hard to imagine a movie more different from that grinding, blustering battlefield epic than *Lost in Translation*. The conflict in the latter film is entirely inter- and intrapersonal, as its two principal characters grapple with their own feelings about their respective relationships. And even those struggles are muted; there is barely a raised voice in the film.

The movie's two American protagonists have their own reasons for being in Tokyo. Bob Harris, a Hollywood star on the downside of his career, is making commercials for a brand of Japanese whiskey. Charlotte, a young married philosophy graduate, has tagged along with her hotshot photographer husband, who's taking pictures of a rock band. But they're also both adrift. Bob is losing his sense of dignity; even though he's being paid $2 million for the endorsement, he knows there's something pathetic about the job. (The scenes of him filming the commercials while getting koan-like instruction from a Japanese director are among the funniest in the movie.) Charlotte is fresh out of school with no particular plans, married to a successful and driven man whom she's beginning to suspect she doesn't know very well.

Both Charlotte and Bob suffer from jet lag and insomnia. It's no surprise that they meet in the hotel bar. What *is* surprising is what happens next. Coppola isn't interested in anything as obvious as a May-September romance. There is erotic tension between Charlotte and Bob throughout the movie, but it's kept at a simmer. What they really want from each other is a less physical kind of intimacy. They want to be understood. (Hence the title.)

The delicate balance of a new friendship might seem like a slight thing to hang a movie on. A less talented and self-assured filmmaker would have been tempted to liven it up with subplots, action, or intrigue. But Coppola trusts her story to unwind at its own gentle pace, only nudging it here and there with occasional bursts of humor, mostly courtesy of Murray. Some of these are misguided, and indulge in lazy Asian stereotyping: there is a shot of Murray in an elevator towering over short Japanese passengers, and a completely unnecessary bit of silliness with a prostitute dispatched to his room by the company paying for the commercial. (She can't pronounce her Rs, and keeps telling him to "Lip my stockings!") What is strangest about these throwback racial routines is that Coppola has a good feel for the pop commercial currents of modern Tokyo; she films the city like someone who knows it. It is, through American eyes, an alien enough place on its own that it hardly needs funny-Japanese jokes to make the point. On the other hand, a scene of Bob losing control of a treadmill in the hotel gymnasium is an effective, affectionate piece of slapstick, a nod to Murray's classic clown skills.

Lost in Translation has something of the lightness Coppola displayed in *The Virgin Suicides*; it glides and buzzes even when (as is often the case) nothing much is happening. But it is grounded in the solid ache of daily life. Coppola observes her characters in the in-between places that movies rarely pay much attention to: riding elevators, taking baths, lying around half-dressed and indecisive.

She also made perfect casting calls. She wrote the part of Bob Harris with Murray in mind, and he rewards her with a tender and thoughtful performance. He is not cast against type, exactly; he retains his smirky charisma, and we can see that the same qualities that made Murray a star are present in Bob. But by this point, those are surface reflexes for Murray, and that's how he plays them here; they're mostly a shield against a world that he's too tired to keep fighting. He's worn out, but he pulls up short of self-pity. He's too aware of his own bullshit, both personal and professional, to simply feel sorry for himself. The character is a melancholy step from the midlife maunderer he played in *Rushmore*, less impulsive and more listless. Murray has continued to refine this character in *The Life Aquatic* and Jim Jarmusch's *Broken Flowers*, almost to the point of catatonia. In the part of Bob Harris, he at least retains enough playfulness to wear a tie-dyed T-shirt for a night out on the town.

Likewise, Johansson makes Charlotte considerably more than a convenient pretty girl. She isn't the first movie character identified as an Ivy League philosophy major, but she's one of the few who actually *seems* like one. She's unabashedly smart and confident, but she also understands the limits of theory in the face of experience. Johansson is a potentially interesting actress who, like Charlotte, doesn't feel fully formed. In her most notable performances before this, she had been a foil, to Thora Birch in *Ghost World* and to Billy Bob Thornton in *The Man Who Wasn't There*. In *Lost in Translation*, she has more room, and she fills it easily. There are lovely, wistful scenes of her exploring the rainy city, alternately puzzled and amused by what she finds.

Coppola manages to make busy, high-tech Tokyo seem both dreamy and a little sad, in a way that movies have traditionally reserved for Paris and other Old Europe capitals. But the setting is not really crucial. The film as a whole is sympathetically global in outlook. It could just as easily be set in New York or, for that matter, Omaha, anywhere that strangers from other places meet. Its not-so-subtle subtext is that cultural divides are nothing compared to the chasms between individuals, and that few things in life are more valuable than bridging those chasms—even temporarily, with a stranger, in another city.

The film is Coppola's most personal to date, the only one not adapted from another source, and it is not hard to read autobiography into it. Charlotte's hipster husband has obvious parallels with Spike Jonze, and the portrayal is unsympathetic enough to have angered some of Jonze's friends. Michel Gondry said in an interview in *The New York Times Magazine* that he reprimanded Coppola for it. "It was not nice," he said. "I don't believe in being mean-spirited or mocking, and I told her that."[12] Another character, the ditsy and annoying American actress whom Charlotte and her husband encounter in their hotel, seems clearly modeled on Cameron Diaz (who starred in Jonze's *Being John Malkovich*). It was hardly surprising that the release of *Lost in Translation* was followed shortly by news of Coppola and Jonze's divorce.

But if the film leaves Charlotte's own marriage looking doomed, it is more optimistic about Bob's. Although his phone conversations with his wife are full of obvious strains and silences, his one-night stand with a lounge singer leaves him feeling embarrassed and regretful. By the end of the movie, he seems actually to be looking forward to returning to his family. His doubts and difficulties provide an odd kind of reassurance to Charlotte: that no relationship is ever easy, but also that they can be maintained.

The low-key climax to the film is in a scene where Bob and Charlotte, exhausted from nights of insomnia, collapse into bed together. The inevitable sexual tension that has been kept at a low simmer through the film heats up a notch, but Bob (and Coppola) wisely defuses it with a gentle, platonic hand on her ankle. In the final scene, after saying goodbye to Charlotte, Bob chases after her on a busy city street and whispers something in her ear. The camera watches from a respectful distance. The intimacy that has been established between them is something secret even from the movie itself.

Marie Antoinette (2006)
DIRECTED BY: SOFIA COPPOLA
WRITTEN BY: SOFIA COPPOLA
WITH: KIRSTEN DUNST (MARIE ANTOINETTE), JASON
    SCHWARTZMAN (LOUIS XVI), JUDY DAVIS (COMTESSE DE
    NOAILLES), STEVE COOGAN (AMBASSADOR MERCY), RIP
    TORN (LOUIS XV), JAMIE DORNAN (COUNT FERSEN)

When Coppola's third film premiered at Cannes in the spring of 2006, the reception accorded to it was so confused that there were even conflicting reports about exactly how loud the boos were. Some accounts had it being practically hooted off the screen, while others had the detractors being balanced if not drowned out by admiring applause. The uncertainty seems appropriate. *Marie Antoinette* is a hard-to-figure film. Neither a serious period piece (as the rock 'n' roll over the opening credits makes clear) nor a send-up of them, it is a teen-dream history scrapbook, with overtones and undertones that are darker and smarter than it at first lets on. The less kind critics called it frivolous, but that is wide of the mark. There is plenty of frivolity on display, but it has both context and consequences.

In a way, the key to the film is its title sequence. It opens with the blaring guitars of the Gang of Four anthem "Natural's Not in It," as punkish pink credits spray the screen. The song is practically a thesis statement for the movie. Originally released on Gang of Four's 1979 debut—*Entertainment!*—the lyrics cast a sardonic eye on affluence and consumerism. The credits are interspersed with shots of assorted fineries, and one langorous look at the film's title character, embodied by Kirsten Dunst, sprawled on a chaise longue. She smiles knowingly into the camera and shakes her head, as if refusing to answer a question. The shot recalls Dunst's teasing wink during the opening of *The Virgin Suicides*, and it is hard to miss the parallels. Like Lux Lisbon and her sisters, Antoinette is alluring, elusive, and—of course—doomed. From the very beginning, Coppola plays against the audience's knowledge of Antoinette's fate (as she did with the foretold deaths of *Suicides*). As Antoinette finds her way through the absurdities of court life, chatters with her friends, dotes on her children, and fusses over her gardens, the coming revolution looms over all of it, giving an inevitably dark tint to the movie's Champagne shimmer.

The film was derided by some critics as an apologia, and by others as lacking any point of view at all. But while there is undeniable sympathy in Coppola's script, and in Dunst's performance, the depiction of Antoinette hardly amounts to a defense of either her or her court. Coppola's Versailles is a world of privilege, vanity, and waste, where power is both elaborately deferred to and endlessly sought. It is insulated and isolated from the concerns of the broader world—although not, of course, as insulated as it seems. There is a lot to gawk at in this hothouse jewel box, but not much to admire. Coppola lavishes attention on the resplendent table settings, wardrobes, and wallpaper, but always with a queasy eye; these things are all beautiful, because they are meant to be beautiful, but it is a kind of wanton and ostentatious beauty that suggests an underlying rot. The mountains of fruits and fishes that pile up uneaten between Antoinette and her almost autistically unresponsive husband, Louis, are monuments of choreographed decay.

Still, it would be a mistake to see the movie as primarily a representation of or commentary on prerevolutionary France. Although Coppola has clearly done her homework on some of the details, it is not a historical drama. The repeated interjections of rock 'n' roll, combined with the casual banter of Antoinette and her friends, signal the lack of concern with any kind of period authenticity. (There's a brief glimpse of Converse sneakers in one scene, just to hammer the point home.) The movie is really a series of riffs on the idea of Marie Antoinette, refracted through various prisms: fairy-tale princess clichés, feminist historicism, Hollywood celebrity gossip, post-9/11 tension. Like *The Virgin Suicides*, *Marie Antoinette* is not exactly a narrative. It does have a story, but it doesn't bother to fill in a lot of the background, nor does it detail the ultimate fates of Antoinette and Louis; it assumes that all of that is well enough known. The movie is largely interested in the atmosphere of Versailles, the way the abundance and indulgence mask the insularity and oppression of the place.

It plays at first like a contemporary teen drama, with Antoinette as the new kid in court, suffering the disdain and pomp of Versailles (which she describes, in exasperation, as "ridiculous"). But her guilelessness gives way eventually to a sense of propriety and proprietorship. This is most clear in Antoinette's treatment of Mme. Du Barry, the social-climbing consort of the dying monarch, Louis XV. In the kind of teen-princess movie that *Marie Antoinette* deliberately echoes, Antoinette's natural giddiness and empathy would cause her to reach out to an ostracized taboo-breaker like Du Barry and teach everyone a lesson about tolerance. But this is a different teen-princess movie, about an actual princess whose ideas were shaped by the aristocracy in which she was raised. She is repulsed by Du Barry. When she finally deigns to speak with her, for political reasons, the gesture is brief and not repeated.

Likewise, what initially seems like refreshing disregard for custom on Antoinette's part—as when she stands and applauds at the opera, violating the rules for royal performances—is over time revealed as a willful self-centeredness. Antoinette's greatest indulgence is the miniature country village she builds on the grounds of Versailles, to which she retreats with her young daughter in a fantasy of pastoral simplicity. She lies on the grass and reads Rousseau, exulting in the earthy pleasures of the "natural" world. She even creates a light opera for herself, in which she plays a simple country girl, sweeping out her cottage. This sequence has historical basis—Antoinette built just such a village, which were popular with the aristocracy of the time—but it also works as a sort of low-key send-up of contemporary affluent spirituality. Antoinette playing at shepherdess and going back to nature on the well-tended grounds of her palace is not so different from Hollywood stars dedicating themselves to trendy Kabbalah or ad hoc Sufism. The distance between Antoinette and actual country girls of her era does not need to be shown to be understood. She is indulging in a privileged fantasy of the simple life (like the reality-TV adventures of Paris Hilton, whose name was almost universally invoked in reviews of the film). For Antoinette, anything outside the palace is essentially fantasy. Apart from a few interludes in Paris and Austria, there are no scenes outside Versailles at all.

The analogy to Hollywood also plays out in the popular gossip that surrounds Antoinette, and in her casual dismissal of it. Told of widespread reports of her alleged "Let them eat cake" comment, she says with irritation, "I would never say that." (She says it with a conviction that rewards Coppola's decision not to have the actors attempt any kind of accent. It frees up Dunst, who is best at her most exuberant, to react without the inhibition of a stilted cadence.) She and her ladies-in-waiting regard the popular discontent with amusement and exasperation, but not much concern.

As Antoinette and her clique indulge themselves in shopping sprees and masked balls and gambling, the detritus of their consumption piles up around them: plates stacked with gooey half-eaten cakes, empty hat and shoe boxes, the morning-after ruins of late-night parties. Antoinette's worrywart adviser, Ambassador Mercy, entreats her again and again to rein in her expenditures, to consider her duties to the kingdom and her reputation among its citizens. She mostly ignores him, not out of malice or even selfishness so much as a complete incomprehension of his words. They don't relate to anything in her limited knowledge and experience.

But, crucially, Coppola and Dunst do not approach Antoinette primarily as a symbol, of excess or anything else. They see her first of all as a girl and a woman. This is perhaps where the film attracted its loudest detractors, its insistence on humanizing and, to some degree, empathizing with Antoinette. Even as it documents her aristocratic prejudices and follies, it recognizes the regimentation and reductiveness of her assigned role. Antoinette is a piece of political chattel, exchanged between kingdoms to secure political ends. Early in the movie, she is transported to the French-Austrian border, stripped of her clothes and examined for virginal purity, and then reclothed in new, French garb and taken by carriage to her designated husband. For all the fineries and fripperies of her life at Versailles, she remains as much property as person. She has no privacy; she is dressed in the morning by a coterie of attendants, and her marriage bed is inspected eagerly for signs of sexual activity. Her principal function, as Mercy repeatedly reminds her, is biological: she is to produce an heir.

The failure of Louis to successfully consummate the marriage for several years places increasing pressure on Antoinette. She tries, again and again, to seduce her unwilling or unable husband, but the blame for the difficulty reverts to her. The fault is presumed to be always on the side of the woman. Ambassador Mercy hints darkly that if she cannot produce, she may well be thrown aside. Antoinette's life is cast in stark terms: she is a vessel. The womb has primacy over the woman. It is hard to imagine a male director conveying the creeping dread of that realization as effectively as Coppola does. (And when Antoinette finally takes a lover—the handsome horseman Count Fersen—her discovery of sexual pleasure is portrayed with pure delight rather than lasciviousness.)

All of this is conveyed with Coppola's now familiar, cool detachment. She shoots some scenes from a static distance, isolating characters in luminescent landscapes. Even when she uses handheld cameras to come in close to Antoinette and her entourage, it feels more intrusive than intimate. The camera's

studied neutrality creates an interesting tension with Dunst's appealing open-
ness, and with the giddy luxury of the palace. Some of Coppola's smartest
moves are on the soundtrack, which mixes light classical airs and minuets
with an iPod playlist of postpunk bomp and electronic ambience (including
songs by Siouxsie and the Banshees, Aphex Twin, Bow Wow Wow, and her
old friends Air). The music can be coy (like "I Want Candy" in a scene rife
with pastries, and a sexy song by the Strokes for a scene that teasingly suggests
masturbation), but for the most part it avoids self-consciousness; the film is
never in danger of turning into "Rock Me Amadeus."

The performances are fine, if somewhat constrained by Coppola's obser-
vational remove. Dunst is in many ways the key to the story, and she hits
a balance of girlish playfulness and, as Antoinette ages, savvy and sadness at
her situation. She doesn't work overhard to make Antoinette lovable, but she
makes her many lapses seem more foolish than venal. Coppola's cousin Jason
Schwartzman makes Louis an almost comical eccentric, while also suggesting
an easy sense of entitlement. (His obsession with keys and locks—although
based on historical accounts—seems like one of the film's few clumsy tropes,
a too-obvious metaphor for his sexual difficulties.) Because of Coppola's mix-
and-match approach, the actors are free of many of the burdens of conventional period films. Most notably, they are not forced into awkward or florid
conversational styles. The dialogue is deliberately modern and casual.

Looming somewhere behind and over all of this is a sense of impending
catastrophe. When it comes, Coppola maintains her close focus, watching
Antoinette and Louis at supper while an angry crowd thunders outside.
Antoinette eventually emerges onto a balcony to face the mob—seen only in
a few silhouetted fists and pitchforks—and silences it by bowing her head low.
It is a gesture of imperious surrender, grandeur in defeat, suggesting both her
too-late understanding of her situation, and her difficulty in accepting it. It
also, of course, foreshadows the guillotine. The film ends with the royal family
fleeing. The final shot is a silent view of their bedchamber, after the mob has
rampaged through and trashed the place. The choice to end there, rather than
with the iconic beheadings, which came four years later, is telling. Coppola's
interest is not in Antoinette, but Antoinette *at Versailles*. The film begins with
her arrival there and ends with her departure, the palace in shambles.

Coppola has protested that she wasn't making a political film, and she
is right, in the sense that it is not an ideological movie. But the film is
certainly politically aware, as the Gang of Four song signals from the start.
The song is about Western consumer capitalism, and so in its own way is the
movie. Coppola may or may not have intended Versailles as an analogy to

modern Western affluence, but that is how it reads. The destruction glimpsed in the final shot can't help recalling the destruction of September 11. The point is not that there is any direct correlation between the French mobs and the Islamic terrorists—in their grievances or their aims—but that the obliviousness of Antoinette and her entire social caste has disquieting echoes in the comfortable quiescence of American society at the turn of the twenty-first century. What is lost at the end of the film is not Antoinette herself, but the illusions of safety and privilege promised by Versailles.

Donnie Darko (2001)

Directed by: Richard Kelly
Written by: Richard Kelly
With: Jake Gyllenhaal (Donnie Darko), Jena Malone (Gretchen Ross), Maggie Gyllenhaal (Elizabeth Darko), Patrick Swayze (Jim Cunningham), Mary McDonnell (Rose Darko), Holmes Osborne (Eddie Darko), James Duval (Frank), Drew Barrymore (Karen Pomeroy), Noah Wyle (Prof. Kenneth Monnitoff), Beth Grant (Kitty Farmer)

Donnie Darko is a secret history of the 1980s. Its mysteries are rooted in the experience of growing up during the Reagan era, with its odd mixture of Cold War dread and MTV exuberance. The movie explicitly nods to a number of films central to 1980s adolescence (the *Back to the Future* series, *E.T.*, *Risky Business*, John Hughes's high school dramas), but it bundles its references up in an ominous puzzle of a story that never quite gives up its code. Richard Kelly's style is a sort of dreamy naturalism punctuated by jags of nightmare. Everything in the movie seems a little unsteady, not quite awake. The mood is sustained to a large degree by the heavy-lidded, slightly sinister performance of Jake Gyllenhaal, whom the film helped turn into a star.

Set during the month of October 1988, the movie is several things at once: a spooky piece of *Twilight Zone*-ish science-fiction; an affecting teen drama; a philosophical treatise; and a scrapbook of an era. Its tone is distinct and strange, melancholy, sometimes scary, but also funny (lines like "Sometimes I doubt your commitment to Sparkle Motion" are part of what made it a cult favorite). It marked Kelly as a significant new talent, although it also left plenty of critics and audiences scratching their heads. It really only came into its own when it was adopted by midnight-movie crowds, whose devotion prompted the theatrical release three years later of a longer "Director's Cut" version. That recirculation was somewhat more successful than the initial,

Donnie (Jake Gyllenhaal) tries to go through the looking glass in Richard Kelly's gloom-ridden fantasy, *Donnie Darko*. (Courtesy of Photofest)

little-seen run, but even so the film has a combined total gross of just $1.3 million. (Its budget was a reported $6 million.)

The story, to the extent that it can be coherently patched together, is about an emotionally disturbed high school student, Donnie Darko, who begins to experience unsettling visions of a man in a large, ugly rabbit costume. The visions are accompanied by bouts of sleepwalking from which Donnie awakes far from his plush suburban home. While he is away on one of these night wanderings, a jet engine falls from the sky through the roof of his family's house and into his bedroom. It would have killed him if he had been there. At first Donnie thinks the rabbit man—whose name, he learns, is Frank—has saved his life. But he eventually comes to believe that both he and Frank are caught in a time vortex and that Frank has been sent back from the dead to recruit him in an effort to close a space-time portal before it turns into a world-destroying black hole. Or something like that. Over the course of the next few weeks, Donnie meets and falls in love with a new girl at school, Gretchen, whose fate ends up entwined with his. When she is killed during a climactic fight, in which Donnie in turn kills Frank, Donnie realizes that the only way he can make things right is to sacrifice himself. He waits for the portal to reopen and propels himself into it, back through time, landing in his own bed just before the jet engine falls. When it does, Donnie is killed, but both Gretchen and Frank are saved.

That synopsis, muddled as it is, hardly does justice to the film's convolutions or its haunting, haunted manner. It is full of strange, striking images: the statue of a dog-headed man that serves as the mascot at Donnie's school; the translucent, wormlike appendages that Donnie sees snaking out of people's torsos, foretelling their movements; Donnie carrying Gretchen's body down the middle of a quiet suburban street. Kelly uses a grab bag of effects, making abundant use of both slow-motion and sped-up film to echo the story's notions of fluid time. After Donnie's physics teacher gives him a book called *The Philosophy of Time Travel*, the film begins to incorporate bits of the text as chapter headings in the story. (These bits are rarely shown for long enough to read them in their entirety, making DVD viewing an advantage. Predictably, the film's fans have transcribed all of the snippets on numerous Web sites.) There are also a couple of semi-satirical subplots, one involving a fatuous motivational speaker (played with oily enthusiasm by Patrick Swayze) and the other detailing the efforts of a teen dance team—Sparkle Motion—whose members include Donnie's younger sister Samantha.

But all of this is mostly grist for Kelly's free-associating evocation of the era, and particularly of its movies. In some ways, *Donnie Darko* seems like a portrait of the 1980s by someone who experienced the decade primarily through its films. The teen-drama aspects—particularly Donnie's romance with Gretchen and his affectionate sparring with his sister, Elizabeth (played by Gyllenhaal's real sister, Maggie)—are drawn straight from the John Hughes template. (It is easy to forget how influential Hughes was in his canny presentation of the minutia of adolescent life and the ways tiny events assume melodramatic proportions.) The time travel plot refers directly to *Back to the Future*; Donnie even discusses the movie with his physics teacher, asking if a car could really serve as a time machine. In the end, Donnie uses the family Taurus as his vehicle into the portal. A nighttime scene of Donnie, Gretchen, and their friends riding their bicycles with headlamps turned on nods to *E.T.*, although the bicycles never leave the ground. Repeated close-ups of static-ridden TV sets seem like a gesture toward *Poltergeist*. Donnie also has a spooky conversation with Frank at a movie theater showing an improbable but apt 1980s double bill: *The Evil Dead* and *The Last Temptation of Christ*, films that both in their own way prefigure Donnie's self-sacrifice. And a party that Donnie and Elizabeth throw while their parents are out of town recalls the climax of *Risky Business*.

The presence of *Dirty Dancing* icon Swayze is a nice bit of period stunt casting, as is Drew Barrymore's supporting role as an opinionated English teacher. Barrymore, who launched her career as the kid sister in *E.T.*, was one of the film's producers. Kelly also sets the whole film to a well-selected soundtrack of moody electropop, with special devotion to the duo Tears for Fears, whose lyrics ("Funny how time flies," "The dreams in which I'm dying are the best I've ever had") suit the film well.

In an interview at the time of the movie's original release, Kelly acknowledged that *Donnie Darko* was an attempt to encapsulate his own high school years. "Everybody has one nostalgia movie to make and this is mine," he said.[13] But as nostalgia, it is not exactly fond. The gloom that surrounds Donnie seems to emanate partly from the society itself. (Kelly heightens the sense of foreboding with the subtle use of unenhanced natural lighting, which gives a darkened cast even to sunny days.)—The film has as its backdrop the 1988 presidential campaign; bits of debates between Michael Dukakis and George H.W. Bush are glimpsed on the Darko family TV set, and Elizabeth banters with her Republican parents about her intention to vote Democratic. Donnie is disgusted with all of it; his general view, confirmed in his dealings with small-minded teachers and school administrators, is that authority figures in general are dim-witted hypocrites. It is a view Kelly seems sympathetic to, and one that someone who became politically aware during the Reagan-Bush years has probably come by honestly.

For all of those multireferential layers, the characters are well written and rounded. All five members of the Darko family emerge as likable and distinct, and Kelly gives some substance even to stereotypes like the class bully and the picked-on fat girl. He pays attention to details like the ways tensions between teenagers (or between a boyfriend and girlfriend) can play out in classroom discussions of assigned reading. Even Frank, the undead rabbit man, is eventually granted a bit of a backstory. (The origin of the rabbit suit is revealed in a montage near the end.) The result is a film that is emotionally affecting even while remaining an intellectual jigsaw puzzle. The final shot of Gretchen waving hesitantly to Donnie's mother as Donnie's body is loaded into an ambulance is sad and elegiac—a farewell, maybe as much as anything, to Kelly's own adolescence.

Kelly and Coppola, at least, seem like serious talents who are likely to continue making interesting films for some time to come. With *Southland Tales*, Kelly has already broadened his scope to include other media; a cryptic Web site for the movie began operation more than a year before the film's release, and Kelly also released three graphic novels that he wrote as prequels to the movie.

The condescending reaction Coppola received for *Marie Antoinette* in some quarters suggests that it will take a while for some people to think of her as something other than her father's spoiled daughter. But to whatever extent that notion of her upbringing is rooted in reality, it seems to have given her a strong sense of self-confidence that will withstand a fair amount of skepticism.

Fincher, meanwhile, is an original director, but since *Fight Club* he has not found a project that allows him so much creative range. Unlike most of the directors in this book, he has opted to work largely within the strictures of big-budget, commercial Hollywood. But he is currently reported to be working on an adaptation of F. Scott Fitzgerald's fantasy story "The Curious Case of Benjamin Button," using a new, expensive digital motion-capture system. It could be a hard sell in its own way, but at least studio executives are unlikely to mistake it for a bare-knuckles boxing movie.

9
CONCLUSION:
AFTER THE ORGY

The period of American history spanned by the films discussed here—roughly from 1990 to 2006—has been a hell of a ride. It starts with the end of the Cold War and ends in what may be the middle of a hotter one, including along the way two recessions, one impeachment, a manic technology boom and the mass murders of September 11. It has also been a time of rapidly expanding cultural and economic globalization, which has had the paradoxical effect of both extending the reach of American influence and diffusing its power.

For this generation of filmmakers, these years have been their entry into adulthood, and their movies reflect all of the uncertainties and anxieties of the era, combined with its sense of proliferating possibilities. As technicians, they have embraced the possibilities afforded by digital media. As storytellers, they have experimented freely with form and genre, displaying an easy familiarity with cinematic conventions and a nonchalance about disassembling and re-combining them for effect. But far from rote irony, their stylistic maneuvers are in the service of Big Questions: about themselves, their culture, and their times.

Most of the directors reflect the sensibilities of American affluence—they lack the working-class orientation of contemporaries like Victor Nuñez (*Ruby in Paradise*) or David Gordon Green (*George Washington*). Even the blue collar-by-birth Max Fischer in *Rushmore* is aristocratic by inclination. But the affluence is provisional and often poisoned: by disease and deception (in Todd Haynes's films), emotional or physical abuse (in Wes Anderson, Paul Thomas Anderson, and David O. Russell), materialism (*Fight Club*, *Marie Antoinette*).

Cumulatively, they very much feel like the work of artists in a wealthy society in decay.

And also of a society in transition. The complexities of modern gender roles, for example, play out again and again—in *Flirting with Disaster, Before Sunrise/Before Sunset, Punch-Drunk Love, Lost in Translation, Velvet Goldmine, Being John Malkovich, Eternal Sunshine of the Spotless Mind*. These are all movies in which traditional ideas of romance and relationships contend with postfeminist ideas of equality, individual achievement, mutual respect, and commitment without coercion. Relationships in these movies tend to be messy. They are rife with divorces, remarriages, fights, misunderstandings, breakups, and reconciliations. They reflect the difficult realities of a culture that has, on the one hand, made romantic detachment and reattachment the norm, and on the other hand produced ever more elevated ideas and ideals about what a relationship is supposed to be. Still, the films are for the most part hopeful about the potential for navigating those currents. There are happy endings of one kind or another more often than not. For all the candor of their doubts, they largely serve the affirmative role of conventional romances.

Their political outlook is more jaundiced. From the cynicism of *Three Kings* to the ranters and would-be terrorists of Richard Linklater's films to the fatalism of *Velvet Goldmine*, there is a persistent sense of corruption and creeping fascism. The films are mostly not ideological in any obvious way, concerning themselves more with interpersonal affairs than international ones.

They could be accused of an ethnocentric solipsism, itself characteristic of American society at the millennium, but globalization peeks in around the edges: in the wired world of *Three Kings*, connected by television and cell phones but divided by mutual incomprehension; in the close-knit Latino immigrant community of *Bottle Rocket*; in the endless verbal volleying of Jesse and Celine in *Before Sunrise* and *Before Sunset*; and in the alienation and allure of Tokyo in *Lost in Translation*. The larger world lurks just outside the comfort zone of these films, not often seen but murmuring like the gathering mobs outside Versailles.

One thing many of the directors have in common is a focus on adolescence and early adulthood: the process of growing up, the traumas and travails of school and family and figuring out what to do with your life. These seem like natural subjects for young filmmakers, and particularly filmmakers of a generation that was defined early on by its uncertainty about the future and inability to commit to relationships, jobs, and career paths. But by now, these directors are only nominally "young." The oldest, David O. Russell, is in his late forties; the youngest, Richard Kelly, is already entering his mid-thirties. It will be interesting to see how they handle issues of aging, parenthood, midlife crises—or whether they continue to be drawn to the problems of maturity that have tended to define them to date.

Forthcoming projects from the group suggest a broadening scope of interests. At least two of the directors seem to be reaching still farther back into their childhoods. Wes Anderson's on-again off-again plans to adapt the Roald Dahl book, *The Fantastic Mr. Fox,* as a feature-length animated film are apparently on again. (He has been reported to be working with the animator Henry Selick, who designed the imaginary fish in *The Life Aquatic.*) Similarly, Spike Jonze is working on an adaptation of Maurice Sendak's classic book, *Where the Wild Things Are*, with a screenplay by the writer Dave Eggers. Paul Thomas Anderson, on the other hand, is bringing forth an ambitious adaptation of the Upton Sinclair novel *Oil!*—based on the scandals of the Harding administration. (Anderson's film has the more evocative if less succinct title *There Will Be Blood*.) David O. Russell is making a movie about an obnoxious talk radio host, and Charlie Kaufman is directing a film about a playwright tentatively titled *Synecdoche, New York*. A *Los Angeles Times* writer who got hold of an early version of the script described it as "a wrenching, searching, metaphysical epic."[1] Todd Haynes, meanwhile, is due to release his experimental biography of Bob Dylan, *I'm Not There*, in 2007.

The range of material also indicates a continued willingness and eagerness to play with new technologies and experiment with the forms and rules of filmmaking. For a group of directors who have become more daring and more idiosyncratic as they have gone along, the possibilities of the digital media explosion seem boundless. They will undoubtedly have misfires, as they have already, but they seem likely to remain an unconventional and unpredictable force in American cinema. And in one way or another—whether through romances, cartoons, tragedies, musicals, or whatever other forms might occur to them—they seem likely to return again and again to the central questions about identity, morality, and purpose that have shaped their work to date. To answer Baudrillard's tongue-in-cheek question, what they're doing after the orgy is figuring out what to do after the orgy.

NOTES

Chapter 1: Introduction

1. David Foster Wallace, *Infinite Jest* (Back Bay Books, New York, 1997), p. 694.

2. David Foster Wallace, "E Unibus Pluram," in *A Supposedly Fun Thing I'll Never Do Again* (Back Bay Books, New York, 1997), pp. 67–68.

3. Jean Baudrillard, "Beyond the Vanishing Point of Art," in *Post-Pop Art*, ed. Paul Taylor (The MIT Press, Cambridge, MA, 1989), p. 182.

4. Francis Fukuyama, "The End of History?" *The National Interest*, Summer 1989.

5. Baudrillard, "Beyond the Vanishing Point of Art," p. 182.

6. Ibid., p. 188.

7. Wallace, "E Unibus Pluram," p. 81.

8. Armond White, "American Soul, Aisle Five," *New York Press*, 17(39).

9. Rex Reed, "It's Anarchy! Film's New Hacks," *New York Observer*, October 4, 2004.

10. Jasia Reinhardt, "Pop Art and After," in *Pop Art: A Critical History*, ed. Steven Henry Madoff (University of California Press, Berkeley, CA, 1997), p. 18.

11. Lynn Hirschberg, "Being Charlie Kaufman," *The New York Times Magazine*, March 19, 2000, p. 80.

Chapter 2: Richard Linklater

1. Tim Rhys, "Hanging Out With Richard Linklater," *MovieMaker*, February 1997.

2. David M. Gross and Sophronia Scott, "Proceeding with Caution," *Time*, July 16, 1990.

3. Jessica Winter, "Days of Being Riled," Village Voice, December 28, 2004.

4. Mike Russell, "The Richard Linklater Interview," CulturePulp No. 54, www.culturepulp.com.

Chapter 3: Todd Haynes

1. Oren Moverman, "Human Haynes," *Interview*, February 1997.
2. Ibid.
3. Collier Schorr, "Diary of a Sad Housewife," *ArtForum*, Summer 1995.
4. Caryn James, "Politics Nurtures 'Poison,'" *New York Times*, April 14, 1991.
5. Larry Gross, "Antibodies," *Filmmaker*, Summer 1995.
6. Roger Ebert, "Safe," *Chicago Sun-Times*, July 28, 1995.
7. Steven Schaeffer, "Gold Miner," *The Advocate*, September 15, 1998.
8. David Michael, "Todd Haynes: Far From Heaven," www.bbc.co.uk/films/2003/02/13/todd_haynes_far_from_heaven_interview.shtml.
9. James, "Politics Nurtures 'Poison'."

Chapter 4: Paul Thomas Anderson

1. Margy Rochlin, "The Innocent Approach to an Adult Opus," *The New York Times*, October 12, 1997.
2. "Boogie Nights," *Exotic Magazine*, November 1997.
3. Lynn Hirschberg, "His Way," *New York Times Magazine*, December 19, 1999.
4. Sharon Waxman, *Rebels on the Backlot* (HarperCollins, New York, 2005), p. 191.

Chapter 5: David O. Russell

1. Ellen Pall, "A Boy and His Mom Are Soon Partners," *New York Times*, July 10, 1994.
2. Sharon Waxman, *Rebels on the Backlot* (HarperCollins, New York, 2005), p. 52.
3. Peter Biskind, *Down and Dirty Pictures* (Simon & Schuster, New York, 2004), p. 161.
4. Waxman, *Rebels on the Backlot*, p. 50.
5. Dan Markowitz, "Director Examines Ways of the Suburbs," *The New York Times*, October 16, 1994.
6. David Denby, "I Heart Huckabees," *The New Yorker*, October 11, 2004.
7. David Edelstein, "I Hate Huckabees," *Slate.com*, October 1, 2004.
8. Andrew Sarris, "Guess What, I Heart I Heart Huckabees," *New York Observer*, October 18, 2004.
9. Manohla Dargis, "On a Stroll in Angstville, With Dots Disconnected," *The New York Times*, October 1, 2004.

Chapter 6: Wes Anderson

1. Marshall Sella, "Boyish Wonder," *The New York Times Magazine*, December 2, 2001.

2. "Futura and Wes Anderson," November 23, 2004, http://www.kottke.org/04/11/futura-and-wes-anderson.

3. Wes Anderson, "My Private Screening with Pauline Kael," *The New York Times*, January 31, 1999, Section 2, p. 20.

4. Alisa Pomeroy, "Wes Anderson: The Royal Tenenbaums," BBC, February 27, 2002, http://www.bbc.co.uk/films/2002/02/27/wes_anderson_the_royal_tenebaums_interview.shtml.

5. Jay Sweet, "Going Deep with Wes Anderson," *Paste*, No. 13, December 2004, http://www.pastemagazine.com/action/article?article_id=1301.

CHAPTER 7: Charlie Kaufman, Spike Jonze, and Michel Gondry

1. Sharon Waxman, *Rebels on the Backlot* (HarperCollins, New York, 2005), p. 155.

2. Ibid., pp. 158–162.

3. Lynn Hirschberg, "Le Romantique," *The New York Times Magazine*, September 16, 2006, pp. 54–59.

4. Waxman, *Rebels on the Backlot*, p. 154.

5. Janet Maslin, "A Portal Leading to Self-Parody," *The New York Times*, October 1, 1999.

6. Ian Parker, "The Real McKee," *The New Yorker*, October 20, 2003.

7. *The Love Letters of Abelard and Heloise*, http://www.sacred-texts.com/chr/aah/index.htm, November 7, 2006.

8. Ralph Waldo Emerson, *Nature*, Chapter VIII, 1836, http://www.vcu.edu/engweb/transcendentalism/authors/emerson/nature.html.

CHAPTER 8: Fellow Travelers: David Fincher, Sofia Coppola, and Richard Kelly

1. Sharon Waxman, *Rebels on the Backlot* (HarperCollins, New York, 2005), pp. 142–147.

2. Janet Maslin, "The Corleones Try to Go Straight in 'The Godfather Part III,'" *The New York Times*, December 25, 1990.

3. Hal Hinson, "The Godfather Part III," *The Washington Post*, December 25, 1990.

4. Lynn Hirschberg, "The Coppola Smart Mob," *The New York Times Magazine*, August 31, 2003.

5. J. Hoberman, "Code Unkown," *Village Voice*, May 23, 2006.

6. Amy Taubin, "Brought Up on Spielberg and Other Old Masters," *The New York Times*, October 28, 2001.

7. Bosley Crowther, "Bonnie and Clyde," *The New York Times*, April 14, 1967.

8. Kenneth Turan, "The Roundhouse Miss," *The Los Angeles Times*, October 15, 1999.

9. David Denby, "Fight Club," *The New Yorker*, November 1, 1999.

10. Waxman, *Rebels on the Backlot*, p. 264.

11. Amy Taubin, "21st-Century Boys," *Village Voice*, October 13, 1999.

12. Lynn Hirschberg, "Le Romantique," *The New York Times Magazine*, September 16, 2006, pp. 54–59.

13. Amy Taubin, "Brought Up on Spielberg and Other Old Masters."

CHAPTER 9:   Conclusion: After the Orgy

1. Jay A. Fernandez, "Reading Charlie Kaufman's Next Project," *The Los Angeles Times*, September 13, 2006.

INDEX

About the Author

JESSE FOX MAYSHARK is a staff editor for the *New York Times News Service*, a contributing editor to *No Depression* magazine, and a journalist with 13 years of experience working for daily and weekly newspapers, covering subjects from pop music to welfare reform.